Living Life Inside Out

Daily Meditations for Life, Love, Recovery, and Hope

D0838709

By Barb Kampbell

ISBN: 978-0-615-30005-4
First printing: June 2009

For more information visit
www.barbkampbell.com or
www.livinglifeinsideout.com or send e-mail to
beaglebrd@sbcglobal.net.

Published by:

Beagle Bird Press

3815 W Capitol Ave.
Little Rock, AR 72205
501-412-7710

Printed in the USA
By Morris Publishing
3212 East Highway 30
Kearney, NE 68847
800-650-7888

Dedicated to Buddy the beagle who taught me about unconditional love and was my companion for almost twelve years. He crossed the Rainbow Bridge not long after our photo was taken for the cover of this book.

Special thanks to David Quinn and Jackie Kampbell for hands-on help with making this book a reality. And thanks to all the loyal readers of my blog who continually gave me feedback and kudos which always helped me to continue writing.

January 1
Happiness Comes from Within
"Who you are is okay, you always have been."
—Unknown

How many times do we look at someone else and think they have it all? They may have more beauty than us or be more handsome than the next guy. Or they may seemingly have everything available in the physical world; the best house, the finest automobiles; boats; "perfect" children; etc.

But do we know that those things equate to happiness? I've had things before that I thought would make me happy only to find out that while I enjoyed those things; I wasn't truly happy.

True happiness comes from within. It comes from knowing who you are and what you want out of life. It happens when we live honest lives and are true to ourselves.

If getting those "things" means additional stress because we can't truly afford them, what's gained in that? We get ulcers, alcoholism, drug addiction, abusive relationships, or bankruptcy, to name a few.

Think about who you are and what you really want from life. Begin to work from the inside out. When happiness on the inside is there, the outsides will follow and they will matter less too.

It's not what is on the outside that matters. Happiness is on the inside.

❧

January 2
Time Heals if We Let It
"Time cools, time clarifies; no mood can be maintained quite unaltered through the course of hours."
—Mark Twain

Hours, days, weeks, months, time goes on. We may feel as if time stands still when we are in pain, but it doesn't.

One day while in a lot of pain I was reading from my daily meditation books, praying, and journaling, doing anything to feel better.

Suddenly I realized something. I had been there before. Maybe not in the same exact pain, but nonetheless hurting and having the feeling of being stuck. That's when I realized and wrote:

"If I allow time to pass while working/thinking through problems or issues, they will be resolved. I cannot hurry the process; it takes whatever time it takes, but it will work: it has worked."

And it does. That's not to say we sit and wait or crawl into bed until sufficient time has passed, it means we put one foot in front of the other and do the best we can until the lesson is learned and we can move on.

Time truly does heal all. It may not take all the pain quickly; but things will get easier.

∽

January 3
We Are Unique Like Snowflakes
"No one like you was ever born or ever will be."
Constance Foster

One of a kind we each are, yet we so want to fit in that we often twist ourselves like a pretzel to try to be liked or loved. And it doesn't work.

It doesn't work because we can only be who we are. That's not to say that we can't grow and evolve, but it does mean that even when we grow and evolve we are the unique person who was born and there will never be anyone exactly like us

Once we learn to love ourselves in all of our imperfection, we begin to see that uniqueness and self-love grows even more. While we try to be someone else we only fall short because we cannot be someone else.

Observe as you go through the day how you react to certain people. If you act differently around some people than others, most likely you are trying to fit into the mold you think fits you into that person's mindset.

We are each and every one of us unique and special in our own way and we should not try to be someone else.

∽

January 4
Expectations Create Turmoil
"The best things in life are unexpected — because there were no expectations." —Eli Khamarov

Disappointment always follows unfulfilled expectations. Sometimes our expectations aren't even realistic so we set ourselves up. And it's difficult not to expect and want certain things to happen.

What we have to do is try to not expect anything to happen in a particular way, especially things we have absolutely no control over.

We can drive ourselves crazy trying to will something to happen the way we want it. So much so that we don't enjoy the moment because we are worried about the next hour, or week or year.

Life tends to happen in its own way and its own time. This doesn't mean we don't take responsibility for the things we do have control over, it means we let go of that which we cannot control.

Grant me the serenity to accept the things I cannot change, courage to change the things I can, and wisdom to know the difference. —Serenity Prayer

✆

January 5
Take Care of You First

"Should the cabin lose pressure, oxygen masks will fall from the ceiling. If you are traveling with small children, place the mask on yourself first, then place a mask on the child."
—Airline passenger instructions

Flight after flight millions of people are instructed every day to take care of themselves first, because if they don't, they cannot help those who cannot help themselves. It makes perfect sense when we hear it from a flight attendant. But we don't often carry that into our lives once we leave the airplane.

But isn't it just as important in every aspect of our lives? If we have nothing to give we can give nothing. And while the flight instructor specifically mentions small children, we all have others who need us besides those who are parents.

We are bosses, employees, friends, parents, children, partners, lovers, etc. We, as people, are in relationships unless we are hermits, and therefore we give and take. It's not selfish to take care of your self, it's healthy, and it's necessary.

Self-care includes our physical, mental and spiritual well being. Never think of self care as selfish. Think of it as putting the oxygen mask on yourself so you can then put it on a child or some other person who otherwise could not do for themselves.

You can't pump water out of an empty well.

✆

January 6
The Work is on the Journey
"Wisdom is nothing more than healed pain."
—Robert Gary Lee

It really isn't too comforting to know that it takes pain to gain wisdom; although knowledge of that may make the pain more tolerable.

We don't grow emotionally and spiritually during the easy times of life, we grow and evolve when we are in the midst of pain and we usually only see that when we are on the other side of it waiting on the next lesson.

It certainly doesn't feel that way in the middle of our agony; when we are hurt and angry; sad, lonely and fearful, full of angst. It is difficult in itself to put one foot in front of the other and to do the next right thing, let alone see that we are going to come out of the lesson with some new tools and wisdom.

We only have to look to our past to see that this is true, that we did grow tremendously when we passed through the fire, but that lesson isn't learned just by getting on the other side, the work is on the journey where we feel our feelings and think our thoughts, where we live in the pain as we move through it.

We won't learn it drugged or drunk, by abusing our bodies, or by running from it. We must live through it and feel it.

It's calm after the storm too, not just before.

∾

January 7
Time Moves at Its Own Pace
"Time sometimes flies like a bird, sometimes crawls like a snail; but a man is happiest when he does not even notice whether it passes swiftly or slowly." —Ivan Turgenev

One day I was in a huge hurry to get to the gym and get my workout finished so that I could move on to the next thing in my day. I was on an elliptical machine which I had set for a particular amount of time and I found myself pushing faster as if that would make the time go faster.

The time on any clock is not changed by my will or anyone else's will. Time is a set number as were those 40 minutes I had set on the elliptical. In order to finish my program I had to stay on there for 40 minutes no matter how fast or slow I peddled.

I realized at that moment on the elliptical that I have wished for time to hurry and wished for time to slow down in my life, mostly to hurry. And no amount of wishing or pushing harder has ever changed time.

We all do the time thing, especially at work. Is it 5 yet? Is it Friday yet? Lunchtime? And while we really have no effect on the time in our lives we can waste it by wishing it to pass.

This doesn't mean we have to be busy "doing" every moment of our lives. We can just be sometimes. We can have fun, work hard, play hard, sleep, rest, whatever we need to do at the moment. But being aware of how we wish time to pass may help us to enjoy the moment more.

As we grow older time becomes more and more cherished and we are less apt to hurry it along, lest it be our last hour.

Time is not effected by the will to hurry it along, only wasted.

✎

January 8
You Get What You Need

"I can stand what I know. It's what I don't know that frightens me."
—Frances Newton

The unknown is scary, yet we really never do know what's going to happen today, tomorrow, or next year. We can't feel what we don't know and so we are in limbo wondering what if.

When I'm in a place of wanting to know something about an outcome my stomach gets tied up in knots and I cannot eat. My mind takes me to all kinds of places, usually negative so as not to be disappointed if the outcome is not what I want it to be. By the time I get the answer to whatever it is that has me upset, it is usually anti climactic because I've worn myself out with worry.

What is the best thing to do during these times? We can try to stay in the moment and occupy our time with things we need to do. We can feel our fear, because really that's what the knots are about, fear that we aren't going to get what we want, but sometimes getting what we want may not even be the best thing for us.

During these anxious moments we can pray, meditate, relax, exercise, whatever helps us to get through it.

Also we can realize that with or without the particular outcome we are looking for, we will be okay. We will survive with or without the person, job, situation or whatever it is we are fretting about.

Sometimes the outcomes aren't what we want, but what we need.

✎

January 9
Secrets Make Us Sick
"You're only as sick as your secrets."
—Unknown

Keeping something locked inside can be like poison to us. Just think back on a time when you had a secret. Maybe it consumed your thoughts, maybe it caused you to act out. Perhaps you ate too much or too little, drank too much, used drugs, abused yourself or someone else. Maybe you still have that secret and have never experienced the freedom that comes with letting it out.

You don't have to tell everyone your secret. The Twelve Steps used by Alcoholics Anonymous and other recovery groups, teach those in recovery to tell God and at least one other person anything that they have done that is troubling to them. This includes things that may not be wrong, maybe they are just secret and the person has shame issues around that situation.

I've personally experienced the freedom that comes with letting things out. I've experienced it through practicing the Twelve Steps, in therapy and just with friends. I can honestly say that I've never regretted having opened up, at least not after the initial fear of it wore off. And I've often been surprised that what I told was not a big deal to those I told it to, it was only a big deal because I'd made it that in my head.

Letting go of secrets offers us freedom.

January 10
Being Alone Not Worst Fate
"It's better to be alone than to wish you were."
—Unknown

So often we feel the need to be in a love relationship whether or not the right person is available for us or not. We try too hard to make something happen with someone who is emotionally unavailable, addicted, abusive, or sick otherwise.

For many of us, it's not until we've lived through the horrors of being with someone unhealthy that we realize that being alone isn't the worst fate in life.

It takes a great deal of strength to end bad relationships and depending on the behaviors of the other person, it can be almost impossible to leave. Sometimes it takes calling in law enforcement to get away from certain circumstances.

On the other hand, being alone affords us the opportunities to make new friends, learn more about ourselves, do what we want to do, and sometimes just the opportunity to heal from past relationships.

Being alone forever may be a scary thought. Being alone now does not mean we are alone forever though. Enjoy it while you have it and don't let it go just because you don't want to be by yourself.

Use alone time to learn and grow; you may find the answers you need to ensure not getting into another abusive relationship.

∽

January 11
Letting Go is a Process
"Some people think it's holding on that makes one strong —
sometimes it's letting go."
—Unknown

Let go, take it back, let go, take it back. Sometimes letting go can go on forever it seems. We let go and take the thing back so many times that it seems never ending. Some things are easier to let go of than others, there's no huge lesson in that, but the things that are so difficult are the ones where we let go and learn and grow in the process.

I can know 100 percent in my mind that a person, place or thing is not good for me; that it's not good for my future and even for the present, but I will hang on as if I cannot live without it. Looking back on those things I have let go of, I realize that I'm still here, perhaps grateful that I let go of whatever it was, I may be sad, but nonetheless, still alive and past it.

Of course, no matter how many times I've experienced the lesson of letting go, I still have to learn it again when a new situation is at hand. It's a process. Sometimes, usually in fact, it's an ugly process to let go of that which we need to let loose but don't really want to. Sometimes when we let go and stop clinging so much we find out we still have what we let go of anyway.

If you love something let it go, if it comes back to you it was meant to be.

∽

January 12
Listen, You May Just Hear Something
"I believe the greatest gift I can conceive of having from anyone is to be seen by them, heard by them, to be understood and touched by them." —Virginia Satir

In this hustle and bustle world too seldom do we let others know they are important to us. Nor do we truly listen and understand others. Sometimes because we don't really want to and often because we are too busy and much too wrapped up in our own world.

Many of us may feel that nobody has ever truly been there for us since we may have been raised in dysfunctional families that were that way for one reason or another. Each of us has our own unique needs and if they are not met we are not whole.

Having someone "get" us can be one of the greatest feelings in the world. It has not happened to me very many times in my life and some of those who understood me are no longer in my life, but having had the experience I can say that it honestly gave me more pleasure and gratitude than any monetary gift or pay I have ever received. To not only be understood, but for someone to stop long enough to listen and also hear, it's something that does not have a price tag or pay check.

How do we get that, though? I'm not sure we can go after it and actually find it, but we can give that gift to someone else. We can stop long enough to see, hear and understand another person. We may find that we receive the gift back from the person we gave our time to, or it may come to us later from another source.

Give the gift of listening and truly hearing to another; it's one of the greatest gifts we can give and receive.

∽

January 13
I Think I Can
"Whether you think that you can, or that you can't, you are usually right."
—Henry Ford

The above is such a simple yet profound statement. What we think does impact what we do and especially our confidence. The old story: The Little Engine That Could where the saying "I think I can, I think I can," came from is a powerful lesson for children, but also one that we need to be reminded of even as adults.

Sometimes we tend to not think positively about certain situations for fear of being disappointed. And maybe that's okay in situations that are completely out of our control. But when we think positively about the outcomes of those things that our actions have impact on, it can only be a good thing. We clearly won't get positive results if we don't think we will succeed because that will affect our actions.

In all reality we are all we've got. We may have support from a spouse or partner. We may be surrounded by friends. But what we believe about our self is our truth. If we want positive outcomes we must think positive thoughts.

It takes real intestinal fortitude to face change whether that be starting or ending relationships, setting new boundaries, changing jobs or careers, returning to school, overcoming an addiction, or anything that requires a dedication and commitment when the outcome is unknown. And we won't succeed in anything that difficult or even the easy stuff if we don't think we can.

Believe in yourself and everything is possible.

∽

January 14
Courage to Change the Things I Can
"Time spent attempting to change others affords little time for personal change." —Georgette Vickstrom

As if we don't have enough on our plates taking care of our own side of the street, we often try to change others. Anyone who has ever been in a dysfunctional relationship whether it is with our family of origin, in a friendship, love relationship, or with a new family, knows that if we could change them we would. We know this because we have tried.

However, as most of us have discovered, we cannot change "them." We can only do our work on us. Sometimes when we do the work to change us for the better, it means more distance from and sometimes an end to those other relationships.

And that's sad to think of, losing those we care about. Sometimes it is the only way to not only survive, but to also grow. While often we have to leave others behind to grow, occasionally those we moved on from will catch up and we have the opportunity to reunite with them on a new level at a new time.

What we must decide is if it is worth staying stuck or if we are better off growing and moving on. That is something we have to weigh relationship by relationship. And each of us is the only one who can answer that for our self.

Focus on changing only what is yours to change.

∽

January 15
The Truth Shall Set You Free
"You never find yourself until you face the truth"
—Pearl Bailey

Many of us were taught not to show the outside world what we were like on the inside; what our family was like behind the walls of our home. We carried that into our adult lives where we pushed our feelings down and locked them away for nobody to see.

Each of us has our own truth. That less than perfect thing or things we don't want anyone to see or know about. We keep it locked away in shame and/or guilt. We hide it lest anyone find out that we aren't as perfect as we appear or for fear that they might not like us anymore.

Holding emotions and feelings inside can often turn into physical pain. Some of us have headaches, for others it is a stomach problem, or maybe a backache. If you are in touch with your body you may know when your particular pain area feels the emotional side of your life more than others. This is a sign that we need to bring something to the surface and face it.

Some of who we are occurred by nature, some by nurture. Parts of us cannot be changed and we simply must face that truth and embrace it.

The truth really can set you free.

∽

January 16
Credit Comes with the Effort

"It is not the critic who counts, not the man who points out how the
strong man stumbled, or where the doer of deeds could have done
better. The credit belongs to the man who is actually in the arena;
whose face is marred by the dust and sweat and blood; who strives
valiantly; who errs and comes up short again and again; who knows the
great enthusiasms, the great devotions and spends himself in a worthy
course; who at the best, knows in the end the triumph of high
achievement, and who, at worst, if he fails, at least fails while daring
greatly; so that his place shall never be with those cold and timid souls
who know neither victory or defeat."
—Theodore Roosevelt

How often we want to do certain things only to step back and think better of it. And when we do step forward, putting ourselves out there for some lofty goal or dream we realize just how alive we feel. Blood, sweat and tears feel better than sitting on our hands wishing we had done something.

Many times in my quest to grow and move forward in life I have fallen short, failed even. And many times I have been successful in the things I've challenged myself to do. We don't have to do anything perfectly. Most things do not have a rule book either.

I have let go of things that I should have hung onto and fought harder for, and I have held on to things too long that I should have let go of sooner. I have not attempted things because of fear, usually centered on money, sometimes around the fear of failure.

The greatest moments were when I realized an achievement and felt the joy of having done that thing I didn't think I could do. In that moment the joy is all that is felt and the pain, agony, sweat and tears are momentarily a thing of the past, only to be remembered later, perhaps in the next challenge or in continuing on the journey with the current achievement.

Strength comes out of attempting to do what seems to be out of reach. True living comes out of trying whether we see victory or defeat in our efforts.

Doing that which seems impossible is well worth the blood, sweat and tears.

∽

January 17
Consequences May Not Be Enough
"Too often going after what feels good means letting go of what you know is right."
—Meredith, a television character on Grey's Anatomy.

Giving up on what we know is right to have the momentary pleasure of what feels good is too often the case in our lives. The consequences usually give us plenty of punishment although often not enough to fully teach us the lesson the first time, tenth time, or maybe indefinitely, especially if we want the thing that feels good so badly that we are willing to forego what's right.

The thing that we want so badly, that which we are not willing to give up over what is right, could be one of a number of things. Maybe we eat more than we should because one more piece of cake is what we want even though the first piece wasn't even on our diet. Or maybe it's having sexual relations with someone who has either hurt us previously or is involved with someone else which makes it inappropriate for us to be with this person. Other issues may involve using drugs or drinking when it's not an appropriate time or if we are an addict or alcoholic.

The problem is that many times what feels good at the moment isn't what we need in the long run and we end up miserable after having done it. For me it's beating myself up with self talk that is destructive way beyond what the consequences of the action were.

Why we are willing to do this to ourselves is not some great mystery. It reminds me of the old 70's saying, "If it feels good, do it." What I want to do is find a way to see past feeling good at the moment to a place where I know that I'll feel good later, yet still have fun in my life. It is called self-control.

We must weigh short-term pleasure against long-term peace.

January 18
Stay in the Moment
"One Day at a Time."
—Alcoholics Anonymous slogan

One Day at a Time. I've heard that slogan and read it in many daily meditation books. I usually only equate it with addictions or problems.

One day the musician Sting was interviewed on a television talk show. When asked how he had stayed married so long he answered, "One Day at a Time."

It was like I heard it for the first time. Yes, we can use it in all parts of our lives. We don't have to know when we begin a relationship the exact outcome. And we don't know if we'll be successful at our job; in school, starting a new career or business. We don't know how our children will turn out. We don't know anything about the future. Try as we might to guess outcomes; we'll always fail because we cannot know how things turn out until we get there.

Staying in the moment, living one day at a time in all areas of our lives will keep away some of the fear, help us to stay grounded, make things less overwhelming and overall make our lives easier.

It's not a new concept; it's just something that is easy to forget.

Living "One Day at a Time" works.

January 19
Stop and Think Before Reacting
"Regret is unnecessary. Think before you act."
—William Shockley

We live in a fast paced world with almost instant contact with people who may be in the next office, down the street or thousands of miles away. With text messaging on our phones, e-mails, and the old standby, regular phone calls, it's easy to get caught up in responding quickly to things and be so accustomed to it that we forget to stop and think about what we are saying and doing.

Anytime we are uncertain about what to do, the best policy is to stop and think things through before taking any action. And if we are sending a text message or e-mail, especially, we should consider how that is going to be taken by the other party. Tone is very difficult to convey in e-mails and text messaging is even more problematic.

Slow down and take a deep breath before shooting off an e-mail or text that could hurt someone. Then you won't feel regret or have to apologize or perhaps lose the friend or business acquaintance forever.

This isn't just a concern when using new technology; it can also happen in face-to-face contact at work, home or other places. Emotions can get the best of us. We may interpret something incorrectly and rather than sorting things out, we react. Stop, take a breath, ask questions, and make sure that when you respond to the other person, you are knowledgeable about the situation so that you don't put your foot in your mouth.

Action rather than reaction is often best.

∽

January 20
With Life there is Joy and Pain

"To spare oneself from grief at all cost can be achieved only at the price of total detachment, which excludes the ability to experience happiness." —Erich Fromm

On many occasions I have found myself grieving the loss of someone who I have grown close to. Whether it is a friend or romantic relationship, sometimes things do come to an end. And sometimes it feels as if the endings are all that happen.

Life is not all full of endings; it is just that endings are painful and are etched into memory because usually the pain is felt more deeply even than the joy, at least it seems to last a lot longer.

When confronted with the pain of grieving another loss we can do one of two things: vow never to get involved again and shut ourselves off; or take the chance again with additional wisdom and knowledge from past relationships. Shutting down and shutting off from future relationships is like death — we would exist without the pain, but also without true joy.

While in the midst of heartache it is never a good time to make decisions about our future relationships; at least not anything too binding. We will pull out of the grief when we have felt our feelings and when the time is right. And when our minds are clear and free of the pain that is when we can start to think about shutting down or opening up again. Hopefully we choose to take another chance when we are finished with the old business.

Sometimes it is good to be detached. We may need that time to heal and lick our wounds. Later, we move on and see that life goes on with or without any particular person.

Shutting off from love is not the solution to grief.

∽

January 21
Acceptance Helps Us Find Serenity

"And acceptance is the answer to all my problems today. When I am disturbed, it is because I find some person, place, thing or situation — some fact of my life — unacceptable to me, and I can find no serenity until I accept that person, place, thing or situation as being exactly the way it is supposed to be at this moment."

—Alcoholics Anonymous Big Book

Acceptance is such a comforting thing when we remember this wonderful quote. How often in our lives are things just the way we want them? Rarely, I'd say, and since nothing stays the same for long even IF things are just the way we want them to be at any given moment they won't stay that way forever.

No matter how many scenarios we play out in our minds about how we think something should be that something is what it is, and will be what it will be. We have no magical powers to make it into something else.

There are only certain things we can control. The sooner we are able to accept a person, place, thing or situation as being what it's supposed to be at any particular moment, the sooner we can move on and find some semblance of serenity.

To do this we may need to read the above quote over and over again. And we may only find peace over the situation or thing briefly, but if we keep at it, eventually we will fully find acceptance.

Serenity comes with acceptance.

∽

January 22
Crack the Walls, See What Lies Beyond

"Letting someone in means abandoning the walls you spent a lifetime building." —Unknown

Most of us have certain things we don't wish to experience, especially in relationships, so we put up walls to protect ourselves from getting hurt. We could have built these walls in childhood and have had them for decades in order to protect our feelings, our self. Or we could have put them up while in a recent relationship that was dysfunctional.

Sometimes these walls are necessary and, yet, often there comes a time when we feel safe enough to knock them down, or at least begin to chip at them.

It has been my experience that on occasion I have begun to dismantle a wall as if to take a brick off one at a time, only to hurry back and fill up the hole because it got too scary or someone unhealthy came along. And at other times I've knocked the walls down quickly as with a wrecking ball never to put them back up.

We do what we need to do when the time is right and we feel safe. And like a lot of things in life, it's often one step forward and two steps back. As long as we are aware of the walls we use to shut us off and protect ourselves we are on our way to tearing them down.

We can remove our walls brick by brick at our own pace.

January 23
We Can Each Make a Difference

"I am only one, but still I am one.
I cannot do everything, but still I can do something;
And because I cannot do everything
I will not refuse to do the something that I can do."
—Edward Everett Hale

If we were to look back in history at some of the people who made a difference, we'd find many who were not rich, not highly educated, and often would have gone unrecognized for anything publicly had they not done something so powerful. There are people like the Little Rock Nine who boldly entered a public school which had barred blacks from doing so. Or look at someone like Rosa Parks who refused to give up her seat on a bus simply because she was black; her simple act of protest galvanized America's civil rights revolution.

We may think we cannot do much because we cannot do everything, but one simple act can affect many. It takes small acts to create big change.

We can look at this as a personal issue, at what we need to do for ourselves, and we can also look at this as a global issue, what we can do for the world.

If you don't like something in your life or the world, do something, start where you are and affect change. You can make a difference whether you have a Ph.D. or a GED. But that unique thing that you bring to the universe cannot be given by any other. It has to come from you.

I will not refuse to do the something I can do.

❦

January 24
Trust is an Option We Must Use

"Trust no one, tell your secrets to nobody and no one will ever betray you." —Bigvai Volcy

People often hurt us and let us down, but if we never trust anyone we will lead quite a lonely life. Sometimes we just have to take that risk that the other person is going to do what they say and be who they say they are.

Many times people will portray themselves in a way that is not true. Sometimes this comes out of mental illness or personality disorders. It can come out of their fears. All we can do is trust those we choose to trust, at least until they prove untrustworthy.

Hopefully along the way they will give us plenty of reasons to trust them. We must remember that no person is perfect and we will suffer disappointments with anyone, after all we disappoint others and ourselves. But those who go around knocking others down with lies and deception should not be given second and third chances. Move on, let them go, tell yourself you trusted wrongly, but you can get away from the destruction of their lies.

I have difficulty trusting others, but I want to try to be better at that and if I get hurt in the meantime then I get hurt. The only other option is to never get to know anyone. I choose to take the risk.

We will get hurt sometimes, but trusting others is imperative to our lives.

❦

January 25
The Answers Do Come

"We don't receive wisdom; we must discover it for ourselves after a journey that no one can take for us or spare us."
—Marcel Proust

Sometimes when life is going well we expect others to be as happy as we are; happy for our successes, achievements, new love relationship, job, whatever the "thing" is. This does not always happen. Sometimes people in our lives have their own issues that may currently be causing them pain and they just aren't looking outside themselves.

And unfortunately some people cannot be happy for others because of their own insecurities or jealousy.

It could even be that the person sees something that we don't see; some danger or past behavior that we've shown which makes them doubt that whatever success we're currently having is going to last.

What we have to do is look within for our happiness and satisfaction. Only we know our own truth. If we feel disappointment at how someone reacts to our sharing we can look at it and process what we feel. Then we will know if we truly are on the right track and they just don't get it for whatever reason.

Or we find that we need to work on the situation because they do see something, a danger or obstacle that we missed. Whatever the situation, if we take time to sit with our self and think, pray, meditate, be still, the answers will come, maybe not at that moment but it will happen. We may get the answer we want and we may not.

Trust yourself. Only you know your truth.

᠅

January 26
The End Result is Worth Drudgery

"The victory of success is half won when one gains the habit of setting goals and achieving them. Even the most tedious chore will become endurable as you parade through each day convinced that every task, no matter how menial or boring, brings you closer to fulfilling your dreams." —Og Mandino

It's enlightening to know that even the most hated chores are not only part of our existence in this world, they ensure successes. I think my most hated chore is doing laundry, but it's so easy to see that if I don't do laundry I won't have anything clean to wear and then what would I do? When we use this analogy in other areas of our lives we see that to be successful we have to endure and achieve all of what goes into success.

If we are a business owner, we have to do the paperwork that goes along with keeping up with finances. If we love to have a pretty yard, we have to pull weeds from the flower beds, or rake leaves when they are shed in the fall. If we are raising children, we must discipline them and give them consequences when they don't behave properly.

Any given achievement has underlying issues and problems that those who see the final goal may never think about. It's easy to get bogged down in those things when we are staying the course, trying to complete our actions for the final goal. But all parts of something are necessary to succeed.

Keeping that in mind when we must endure the portion we don't want to do can keep us focused and moving forward. It doesn't make it more fun, it just makes us more aware.

Set your sights on your goal and then do whatever it takes to reach it.

∽

January 27
Blame Will Get Us Nowhere but Stuck
"When you blame others, you give up your power to change."
—Dr. Robert Anthony

Every one of us can find things in our lives that aren't quite how we want them to be and we can always find someone to blame. We can blame our parents, siblings, boss, friends, lovers, the government, and anyone else around that we can put our problems on.

A popular saying, and one that's also the title of a book is, "If it's not one thing, it's your mother." It's always something; life is full of problems and solutions. And while blaming others takes a load off of us temporarily it also keeps us stuck in the problem and not looking for a solution.

Recognizing the origin of our issues and problems is a good start at healing. We can resolve some of our issues by accepting that things were done to us that were not always in our best interest or healthy for us. Sometimes we find that we blame ourselves for something someone else did.

For instance, we may have never felt loved by a parent and turned that blame around on us, only to figure out that we could not have caused them not to love us. That was their issue; ours is to move on and love ourselves. This blame of ourselves for things that we didn't do is not healthy either.

We can move past blaming ourselves and others when we are ready to face our issues. This is when we can change and grow past blaming and into freedom and healing. We take responsibility for what we do, right or wrong or somewhere in between, but we move past blame into solutions.

Blame only keeps us stuck in the problem.

∽

January 28
Gratitude Brightens Our Lives
"Gratitude unlocks the fullness of life. It turns what we have into enough, and more. It turns denial into acceptance, chaos to order,

confusion to clarity. It can turn a meal into a feast, a house into a home, a stranger into a friend. Gratitude makes sense of our past, brings peace for today, and creates a vision for tomorrow."
—Melody Beattie

An attitude of gratitude can brighten any of our worst days.

Saying thank you for what we have takes our focus off of what we don't have. Most of us, most of the time, want something that we don't have. And while we are desirous of that something we may totally overlook what we do have. It's the old "a bird in the hand is worth two in the bush" thing.

We may have a decent job, home, automobile, friend, or partner. But we are too busy trying to have more that we overlook the wonderful things that we already have for that better thing.

Gratitude really does work. It doesn't mean we get all that stuff we are trying to get, it simply means we stop for one minute and thank God and the universe for giving us the blessings of our lives. One good friend is better than a dozen so called friends. A car that runs and is paid for can be much more of a pleasure than one with a high payment every month. The partner that we have, who we were once madly in love with, is still that person we fell for despite the fact that the relationship is not a new thing anymore.

Sometimes we don't even know that not getting what we want is something we should be grateful for at the moment. Often we can see in hindsight that what we wanted so badly and were angry we didn't get was really not a good thing and then we are grateful. Learning to be grateful while we aren't getting what we want can help us get through that time in our lives. We'll still be thankful in hindsight.

Be grateful for the gifts already received.

January 29
Sensitivity is a Gift
"I would rather feel things in extreme than not at all."
—Bonnie Raitt

Those of us who allow ourselves to feel deeply, who are sensitive, know that it is the only way we can be. No matter how much we try to be different, we were born to be this way and we have to live with it, both its good and bad aspects.

Others will often put us down because they just don't understand. They may call us crazy, emotional, psycho, any number of names. And those labels do fit some people. But feeling things means we are alive. It means we live our lives inside out. Surface, what is on the outside of us and others, just doesn't matter to some of us as much as what is on the inside.

Living this kind of life is not easy. But as M. Scott Peck said, "life is difficult." The option is to go through life like a zombie never feeling much pain but therefore never feeling any joy either. We who have this desire to feel things more deeply than others have a gift. At least that's how I choose to look at it. I no longer curse my sensitivity, I accept it.

It means we cry more, but it means we laugh more too. If we allow ourselves to accept who we are and also accept that by feeling pain we find joy, then it is all worth it in the end. We must stay aware not to internalize the feelings of others. And we must always take care of ourselves and nurture ourselves because we tend to wear our feelings on our sleeves.

I will use my sensitivity to help others, but I will take care of myself in the process.

∽

January 30
Lies Perpetrate More Lies

"Every act of dishonesty has at least two victims: the one we think of as the victim and the perpetrator as well. Each little dishonesty makes another little rotten spot somewhere in the perpetrator's psyche."
—Lesley Conger

Every one of us has told a lie at one time or another. Sometimes people lie to keep from hurting someone or to keep something hidden. Sometimes lies are to cover up something and then there are the malicious lies that could never be justified no matter what.

Once a lie is told more untruths must be spoken in order to keep the lie secret. It makes life more complicated than it already is. If we simply tell the truth when faced with a choice we will find that things will work out okay. We will have more peace and we will be free from the added stress that will burden us to keep the lie hidden.

Think of a lie you once told. It could be a life lie, as in living the life of addiction and always trying to hide it. Or maybe you took something that was not yours and live with the knowledge that you were dishonest. Perhaps you had an extramarital affair. Or it could have just been a lie about nothing important, but having told the lie you had to keep lying to cover it up.

Now think about all of the energy you had to use to keep that lie from being discovered. It takes a lot of energy to lie. It might be difficult to be honest in the moment, but the moment will be over soon. A lie and all of the lies that go with it could last a lifetime.

And in the process of telling all of those lies you not only hurt yourself you hurt those you lied to.

It's easier to just tell the truth; it takes a lot less energy in the long run.

∽

January 31
Habits Can Be Replaced

"Habits ... the only reason they persist is that they are offering some satisfaction. You allow them to persist by not seeking any other, better form of satisfying the same needs. Every habit, good or bad, is acquired and learned in the same way — by finding that it is a means of satisfaction." —Juliene Berk

We are creatures of habit which is visible in all areas of our lives, both in the things that are healthy for us and those that are not healthy.

Routine is not a bad thing as long as we aren't stuck in a rut. Some things we do routinely are actually very healthy. For example, reading our daily meditation books is a healthy activity. Praying every day is good. Having a workout routine and sticking to it is healthy. All of these done in a routine manner will become habit and we will miss doing them when we get too busy.

Getting bogged down in the mire and muck of life's everyday activities, however, can get us stuck before we even realize it. And with that "stuckness" we'll suffer depression, anxiety, and laziness. It can happen before we realize it; then we may find it almost impossible to pull ourselves up by our bootstraps and make that change that's got to be made in our lives.

When we do make the changes necessary to rid ourselves of our bad habits we can replace then with healthy habits. We can replace smoking with trips the gym; we can replace negative thinking with positive thinking; whatever our bad habit is, we can find something healthy to put in its place.

Take a look at your habits and see which ones need to be replaced.

∽

February 1
If at First You Don't Succeed; Try a Different Way

"Insanity: doing the same thing over and over again and expecting
different results." —Albert Einstein

Sometimes in life we find that we cannot seem to overcome a
particular hurdle. No matter how many times we are faced with the
same issue, the results are the same. And many times that is because
we keep doing things the same way, expecting a different outcome.

It could be that we just don't realize we are stuck in a pattern and
it's possible that we don't know a different way to handle the situation.
It is at that point that we must stop and think about what we are doing
and how we can do it in a different way. We may try another way to
succeed at clearing the hurdle and may once again fail, but at least we
are trying new ways to do something. We try again using another
method until eventually we find what works and we are on to the next
lesson.

Sometimes we have to think outside the box and use our
imaginations to find a new solution to an old problem. Once we
acknowledge that the way we are doing something is not working and
seek a new solution, we are on our way to freedom.

*You must break the patterns in your life to find freedom from
insanity.*

❧

February 2
Keep Trying Your Best, but Let Go of Perfectionism

"Aim for success, not perfection. Never give up your right to be wrong,
because then you will lose the ability to learn new things and move
forward with your life." —Dr. David M. Burns

We live in a society that teaches us to be the best. We need to make
the best grades and score highest on tests to get scholarships and
acceptance into the best schools. We are also told to be the best
athletes if that's what we do, leading many to use illegal enhancement
drugs to be stars. We think we must have perfect families, be perfect
employees, and on and on.

When we seek perfection from those we love, what we are saying is
that they must walk on eggshells lest they be human. We are all human
beings who make mistakes. We ought to not seek perfection from
ourselves either or we will spend our lives unhappy and in turmoil
because it is impossible to be perfect.

When someone we care about hurts us, it's okay to say, "You hurt
me when you ...." What isn't OK is to not let them know that they hurt

you or to hold it against them forever. If we shut out every person who is less than perfect we will find ourselves living one very lonely life.

However, we don't let people walk all over us and continually hurt us with no remorse or without attempting to treat us right. What we do though is allow them to be human, just as we are human.

Remember that no person in this world is perfect at anything. Give others and yourself a break.

֍

February 3
Direct Communication is the Best Communication
"Say what you mean and mean what you say."
—Unknown

Directness in any relationship is the best way to operate. It's not always easy to say what we mean rather than leave the other person guessing, but it's important that we are direct.

Any time we don't say what we mean the other person is left to interpret what they think we are thinking. This can lead to all kinds of problems as we all know, because it has happened to all of us. We assume the other person is thinking one thing only to find out that we are sorely mistaken. It can make for hurt feelings and arguments.

No matter how difficult we find it, being direct is the only way to be. Better to say now that we aren't in agreement on an issue, situation, or relationship, than have it come out later down the road when feelings are sure to be hurt more than in the beginning.

Directness keeps us honest and away from lies. It frees us to have healthy relationships of all kinds; personal, professional, with our children or parents. We can say what we mean and mean what we say. After all, it is our right to do just that.

Being direct with those with which we have contact is the best way to be.

It is my right to be direct.

֍

February 4
All Work and No Play ...
"Be aware of wonder. Live a balanced life — learn some and think some and draw and paint and sing and dance and play and work every day some." —Robert Fulghum

Life is a busy occupation. We have so much that fills our days, so many chores and demands at our jobs or by our families. But we don't have to spend all of our time working or doing, we can play and just be sometimes.

What we must strive for is balance. We must try to find time to have fun; to play, whatever way we each do that. We relax in the ways we know how and if we don't know how to relax, we learn how.

We balance work with play, stress with relaxation, hanging on with letting go. We try to really live life rather than simply do it by putting our heads down and charging like bulls through life making sure we get it all done and do it all right.

If we don't take time out for fun and relaxation one day we will wake up and wonder where our lives went. All of that hard work and bull-headed-get-it-done-at-all-costs attitude may have brought on its share of stress along with the physical ailments that go with that.

Stop today and think about how you spend your days and weeks. Is there time in there to relax and play? If there isn't, now is the time to find that time. Schedule it in if you have to. But do it.

Relaxing and playing are important parts of our lives too.

∽

February 5
Relationships Don't Have Road Maps

"Never idealize others. They will never live up to your expectations. Don't over-analyze your relationships. Stop playing games. A growing relationship can only be nurtured by genuineness."
—Leo F. Buscaglia

Relationships, like everything else in life, need honesty and directness. Having friends isn't something difficult to do if we have boundaries and do not expect perfection from ourselves or others.

Sometimes we expect those we know to live up to some ideal that we have set for what we think a relationship is supposed to look like. There aren't rules about how any particular relationship must be done.

We must throw out any preconceived notion of what we think a certain relationship should be. Every relationship is different. But that's not to say that there aren't things in every relationship that should be present: honesty, directness, sharing, forgiveness, love, integrity. We cannot truly have lasting relationships that are not built on good values. And those values must be present on both sides of the relationship.

We don't have a road map of how week one, month two, year one will be, we simply go about the relationship as it comes on a day-by-day basis. We understand that there will be days we will not like the other person, nor they us. We understand that we both will be hurt from time to time by the other person. We continue our friendship anyway, if it is built upon sound principles.

If, however, one person is unable to be honest, direct, forgiving, loving, or willing to share, then the relationship will not survive. We must then let go and move on in our lives. We may go through a grieving process because we care for the person, but we also must take loving care of ourselves and end something that is not healthy.

Relationships that cause more pain than joy must end.

✄

February 6
Resentments Only Hurt the One Holding Them

"When you hold resentment toward another, you are bound to that person or condition by an emotional link that is stronger than steel. Forgiveness is the only way to dissolve that link and get free."

—Catherine Ponder

Resentments can tear us apart and the other person may not even know that we are angry. They fester inside of us and come out in ways we never would intend. We may lash out at a coworker who has done absolutely nothing to deserve our wrath. Or we may come home from work or school and take the resentment out on someone in our family who is innocent.

Resentments live in us like poison and affect every part of our being; spiritual, emotional, physical, and mental. To rid ourselves of the resentment we must forgive the other person, no matter how badly they may have wronged us. In the best of circumstances we would talk it out with the person we have the resentment against, but sometimes that is just not going to be a possibility and we just have to deal with it within ourselves.

Let it go. Let them go if you have to, if that's the best situation, but let the resentment go. Pray about it and give it to your Higher Power. It won't disappear overnight since it has been there a while, but eventually it will go away and you will find freedom in the release. The other person will be free of angry energy and thoughts that you are sending their way too.

When you release resentments you free yourself.

✄

February 7
Feelings Are Better Off Felt

"Following your feelings will lead you to their source. Only through emotions can you encounter the force field of your own soul."

—Gary Zukav

When we deny our feelings and bury them deep inside without allowing ourselves to let them wash over and through us, they will fester inside and cause us much distress, even physical illness.

Relationship feelings are especially tough. Sometimes we know that we must find an end to a relationship with a friend or love interest simply because it just is not healthy. But we may find we don't want to let the person go; we hang on tightly to the good feelings and deny the not so good emotions.

Whatever our feelings are, it's okay to feel them. It's okay to feel lonely, sad, or angry, just as it's alright to feel contentment or happiness. Feelings are just that; feelings.

When we are feeling unsure of what to do, we can meditate and pray, but we need to always allow ourselves to feel. We can cry, scream, stomp our feet, whatever we need to do to feel what we feel. Talking to someone not emotionally involved in the situation may help; someone who is safe for us to share honestly with.

We may want to avoid our feelings by using drugs, drinking, exercising, overeating, or any number of ways we can come up with, but we won't get our answers by covering up the problems.

The worst thing we can do is bury the emotion and deny that it exists. We feel the feeling and wait for the answers. The answers will come if we are willing to hear them.

Feeling our feelings is the only way to move on.

February 8
If You're Okay With You, Then You're Okay

"Knowing others is intelligence; knowing yourself is true wisdom. Mastering others is strength; mastering yourself is true power. If you realize that you have enough, you are truly rich." —Tao Te Ching

In all reality there is only one person we can truly know and that person is our self. No matter how many people we share our thoughts, feelings, dreams, ideas, goals, everything that is in us with, the other person still does not know us as we know ourselves.

Life is a wonderful teacher and it is important to have people who we may use as sounding boards. There is freedom in sharing who we are with others as long as they are the type of person we feel safe sharing with.

And while sharing ourselves is good, we must still fully know ourselves as only we can. We must look ourselves in the mirror and know who we are and what we are. It is in this that we can see where we are going and what we need to work on. These are things others may help us with, but things that only we can really do.

If we can honestly live with who we are that's all that really matters.

Wherever I go there I am.

♨

February 9
Love of Self is Paramount

"My primary relationship is with myself — all others are mirrors of it. As I learn to love myself, I automatically receive the love and appreciation that I desire from others. If I am committed to myself and to living my truth, I will attract others with equal commitment. My willingness to be intimate with my own deep feelings creates the space for intimacy with another." —Shakti Gawain

When we love ourselves we don't allow other people to use or abuse us. Therefore it is imperative that we begin where we are and work on loving ourselves first, before ever trying to have a deep intimate relationship with another person.

Most of us aren't very good at self-love. We may have been taught that it is selfish. Perhaps we never thought much about loving ourselves. If we don't love our self, we cannot truly love another because we will not be able to be vulnerable enough with that person to let them see all of who we are.

When we don't love who we are it shows in our relationships because we give other people power over us. If we don't love who we are and feel good about ourselves, then we are not able to set and keep boundaries. People will control or manipulate us and keep us anxious and off track because we allow them to do that when we don't take care of us.

If we don't know how to have self love, we learn by starting where we are. We act as if.

Perhaps we start with one thing that we already know we love about ourselves and go from there. I love my independence. It was borne out of my family of origin issues and it wasn't until later in life that I realized that it was something of value no matter how it came to be. However, I have given up that independence in relationships in the past because I didn't love myself enough. Your starting point could be a value that you discovered about yourself; something that you already know you love about you. Then you find another thing about yourself that has value and you own it and love that about yourself. And it grows from there.

When we begin the process of loving who we are we discover things about ourselves that we may have not thought about before.

Love yourself. Start right this moment and begin to nurture and love you as much as you try to love and nurture others.

∾

February 10
Our Perspective Affects Everything

"Is the glass half empty, half full, or twice as large as it needs to be?"
—Unknown

It's all about perspective. We may feel hurt or wronged by someone and talk to a friend about it. They will hear a whole different side of it that we didn't because we were hurt or angry by what we heard, and they weren't emotionally involved.

Life would be simpler and easier if we always took the positive approach, but most of us aren't able to do that all of the time. If someone spits in my face I can't smile and say thank you or think of some good reason they did it; some way it benefits me.

Bad situations or encounters always having a positive aspect we can see is not reality. Yeah, there is probably some lesson to be learned when someone wrongs us, but we won't see it every time. Sometimes things just happen. It could be a rock cracks the windshield of your car, or you have a flat tire. There may not be a lesson in why it happened; the lesson is how we react to the incident. Do we keep our cool or scream about how inconvenient it is?

And if something happens involving another person, very often our perspective is not the whole truth and reality because our own issues come into play. There are two sides to every story so before blowing off someone in our lives for good because of a supposed wrong, it might be good to let someone not involved hear the story and get their perspective; although they would probably need to hear both sides to know the real truth.

Because we bring baggage and battle scars into any situation, these issues affect how we perceive things now. A person who has suffered from neglect or abandonment will react to relationship issues differently than someone who has always felt loved and nurtured. Someone who learned to get angry over spilled milk will react with anger unless they learn a new behavior. These are things to keep in mind when dealing with other people and reactions from them that we perceive as strange.

Our history plays into our present.

∾

February 11
Grow or Die
"Be not afraid of growing slowly, be afraid only of standing still."
—Chinese Proverb

That is such a fitting proverb to live by. We want to know the answers now to whatever issues we are facing. We want to be an evolved person with no struggles and always know the right reaction to every situation. But all of this is a lifelong lesson and journey. We think it's moving too slowly, but at least it's moving.

If you've ever spent time in your life where you weren't growing you will find this more fitting. I spent several years of my life stuck. I was stuck in drug abuse and drank too much and rarely if ever thought about growing or evolving. Once I hit bottom with my drug abuse and started to slowly crawl out of the hole I'd put myself in, getting out of that place just did not go nearly as quickly as I wanted.

But here I am years later and I can see where I was and how far I've come and I wouldn't trade any of it for anything in the world, now. Of course, when I was in the depths of despair struggling with financial debt and losing a lot of what I had worked for, it didn't feel like I'd get here.

And I'm not exactly where I want to be yet, especially financially, but I've come a long way. And I have hope for the future because I work on my issues every day now. It's slow but steady. It's not standing still or moving backward. It's painful and awkward sometimes, most of the time, yet healthy and rewarding too.

As long as we are moving forward the speed is not important.

⤚

February 12
Things Can Change in an Instant
"There is nothing permanent except change."
—Heraclitus

No matter how bad things seem or how low we may feel on any given day, there is always the hope that things will change. And when we least expect it that change happens and we find ourselves bewildered at how quickly our mood and disposition changes along with it.

The lesson learned is that no matter where we are in life things are going to change. Life ebbs and flows and we are rarely in control of most of it. We suit up and show up and give it our best shot, but we don't always get what we want when we want it.

Trust that things will change when you're in a spot you don't like. And trust the same when you are having a great time. Change happens.

If things are not going the way you want at any given moment, the best thing to do is step away and do something else for a while if you have that option. Go run errands, take a walk or run, take a nap, read a book, meditate, do something else and when you return to that troubling thing it is often easier to deal with and solve than it was before you walked away for a while.

Everything can change in a heartbeat.

∽

February 13
Detaching Frees All Involved
"There's an important difference between giving up and letting go."
—Jessica Hatchigan

Detaching from someone or something that is causing us stress and trauma is one of the more difficult things in life to accomplish. It takes a stick-to-it attitude and lots of back and forth progress.

There are crazy people in this world, people who have no clue how to have relationships and interact in healthy ways. There are those who are addicted and their addiction affects us. Try as we might, we cannot and will not change these people. They won't be different with us than with others, they'll be just as crazy with us and they will make us feel crazy in the process.

Detaching from these types of people takes time. It takes a conscious effort to not play into their mind games and drama. What we have to do is stand strong even when we feel weak. They may pull us in slowly, maybe they get our big toe, but we don't give them our whole foot. We pull away gradually. We stick to the things we know to do. We think of other things and find ways to distract ourselves from obsessing about them and how to solve their problems which become our problems. When we set others free, we find freedom for ourselves. When we stop trying to fix them we are detaching.

It's a long process, often, and one in which we may feel pushed and pulled with no end in sight. But once we are there, once we've let go emotionally we will know it. We will have contact and we won't feel anything anymore. No anxiety. No emotional reaction. That's when we know we've detached. What we must then do is stick to it and not put that toe back in the water with that person again.

Detaching is worth the struggle.

∽

February 14
Don't Give Up Yet
"Failure is the opportunity to begin again more intelligently."
—Henry Ford

How fragile a thing our self-esteem for those of us who suffer from lack of confidence. It seems no matter how much work we do it can take one small thing to knock us back.

Sometimes it can feel like the whole world is against us and what we want to do is give up. What looks like the easy way out is to simply walk away and leave the thing behind.

But it's not always that easy.

When things don't go as we planned we have choices. We can try again by thinking outside the box. We try approaching the situation a different way. We may get discouraged over and over again until finally we do give up, or we may find success and enough reward in our efforts that we keep trying.

Don't give up on something before you know it's the end, even when you feel like it is. Most things worth having must be worked for with much blood, sweat and tears.

You'll know when it's time to stop trying, until then, give it your all.

∽

February 15
Stay Away From Dangerous Things
"You play with fire, you get burned."
—Unknown

Again and again we stick our hand in that fire that we know is dangerous. We go to that place with someone or something where we have been burned before with some thought that the flame won't damage us this time.

But it does. Fire is fire. Whatever that danger is for you it is best to not expect the flame to be harmless the next time. It could be a person who continues to carry negative energy and affects you in a bad way; maybe it comes in a bottle or in the form of a pill; perhaps it's sexually related; or an illegal drug. Whatever burns you, stay away from it.

It matters not that the same flame may not burn everybody else; if it burns you it's dangerous for you and you are trying to take care of yourself. That is where we sometimes have to let go of thinking it's not fair that someone else can have that person, place or thing and we can't. Sometimes life is not fair. There are probably plenty of things we get that other people can't have because that thing is dangerous, it's fire for them.

Stay away from that which endangers you.

∽

February 16
Find What Works for You

"The best way of forgetting how you think you feel is to concentrate on what you know you know."

—Mary Stewart

Feeling a bit off track … restless, irritable, discontent? When we feel this way and we don't know what the cause is, or even if we do, what we need to do is stop and practice whatever recovery behavior we know works for us.

We can get quiet and think, journal, read, talk to someone about it, meditate or pray. We go back to the basics of what we know works for us. If we are in a Twelve-Step program, we can work a step, go to a meeting, or call our sponsor.

Getting centered, finding the source of our uneasiness will take us into a more serene place. We may not find serenity, but we will feel better.

Sometimes when we get into a situation where we feel out of balance and control we spin our lives into that dysfunction rather than working our way out of it. The longer we linger in it, the more it takes a hold of us. Practicing a behavior that gets us back to sanity and serenity will stop the cyclone of destruction.

It's important to find what tools work for us so that we can use them when needed. What works for some may not work for others, but we all have things we can do to settle down when our minds run crazy.

Find what tools bring serenity for you and use them when you get the crazies.

∽

February 17
True Intentions Are What Count

"Flatter me, and I may not believe you. Criticize me, and I may not like you. Ignore me, and I may not forgive you. Encourage me, and I may not forget you." —William Arthur

We truly don't forget those who honestly encourage us. Those people who come into our lives with no agenda and compliment us; bring us hope and encourage us. We believe them because they have nothing to gain by their praise or kind words.

Those who come around to criticize usually do that to gain something for themselves. Sometimes they gain self worth from putting us down. We won't like those people and we will try to defend ourselves even when we know in our hearts that we don't have to. And then there are those people who arrive full of compliments because they need us to like them or for us to do something for them. These people can sneak up on us and catch us with our guard down. And usually they are also the ones we have difficulty getting away from because we become enamored in their praise and admiration of us, even if it's more about them than us.

Occasionally we encounter the ones who ignore us. They act as if we do not exist in their presence. They won't make eye contact or talk directly to us. They do this because of their own insecurities and we are better off to not try to figure them out or let what they do bother us.

If we find that someone is less than honorable in their intentions, we can deal with that by moving on or confronting them.

Then we can look at ourselves and see which kind of person we are. Are we honest in our relations with those we encounter, or do we behave in ways to get our own needs met even if by dishonorable means?

Honest encouragement is priceless.

&

February 18
Words Are Powerful

"Sticks and stones may break my bones, but words can never hurt me."
—Unknown

Wrong. I know I've said that before on the playground when I was a little girl. We've probably all said it at least once in our lives. But words can and do hurt. A few words thrown at us can damage us very deeply, especially if we are sensitive and don't have the highest of self-esteem.

Words thrown about not only hurt our psyches; they can also incite the type of violence that can cause riots or hate crimes. Of course, that's an extreme, but we should really strive to be careful what we say to one another.

And often the wounds from words don't heal nearly as quickly as those from "sticks and stones." When possible we should always stop and think about how our words will affect another person before we speak them or write them. In the heat of an argument or any passionate exchange, things said may be taken out of context. Maybe these are times to be as quiet as we can and say the least amount that we can to move on for the moment until things can cool off.

Words can both hurt and heal; choose wisely.

∽

February 19
You Can't Please Everybody

"If you only try to please others, you're going to resent those people you're trying to please; the ones who are often closest to you. If you choose a path that you yourself want to take, then you're going to be much kinder to the people in your life."

—Sarah McLachlan

Since you can't please everybody — please yourself.

We cannot base our life and decisions on what others might think or do.

As long as we are not hurting another person by doing that person wrong then we must decide what is best for ourselves.

Sometimes doing what is best for us does hurt others, but not because we are in the wrong or are doing them harm, it just isn't what they want from us.

One day I was having one of those times where everything in my world seemed wrong. And in the middle of that I needed to make a rather large decision that would affect other people. This decision was because of something someone else had done and now I had to decide on the right thing for me, for this group.

For that day and the next I ran through every scenario of what to do and how it might affect this person, or that person, or the group. There was no way I could please every person involved, including myself.

So I decided rather than people pleasing, I'd do what my heart, gut and mind told me was best for me.

Once I made the decision to please myself, it was easier to decide what to do and it took a whole lot of the weight off of my shoulders.

We really can't please the whole world. It takes a lot of energy to figure out what everyone else thinks, especially when we really don't know what they think. And while one wants one thing from us, someone else wants another, and we can't do both.

We must do what's right for us first.

∽

February 20
Give Love a Chance

"To love at all is to be vulnerable." —C.S. Lewis

You are loveable. No matter how much it seems that people have abandoned you that does not always equate to something being wrong with you. Many of us were raised by people who could not show us love. Because of that we may have taken on the idea that we aren't loveable. At least until we find someone who really does love us and can show that love.

Many of us who were not shown love as children sabotage relationships because we expect others to abandon us, hurt us, lie to us, or otherwise not really be there for us. And often those predictions are correct, but if we allow others to care, we may just find that not everyone who loves us will abandon us.

Perhaps it's not so much that we are unlovable as it is that "they" don't know how to love or show love. In other words, it's more about them than us.

What we must do is find things about ourselves that we love. We must love ourselves when we think no one else does. What we don't do is think that we are not loveable.

We love ourselves by embracing the things about us that are our real, God given talents, characters, and values.

For me, I have spent a lifetime "suffering" from being a very sensitive person. While it has taken a lifetime for me to embrace that part of me as something of value, I still don't always like it. A life changing statement helped me to begin to love that sensitive part of me. When someone I care about said to me: "I love your sensitivity. It's one of the things I really love about you," I had to stop and think about it in a different way.

I took the sensitivity thorn out of my side and decided to love that part of who I am. And it changed how I viewed myself.

Learn to embrace all parts of yourself in love.

∽

February 21
Learn from Mistakes
"Even God cannot change the past."
—Agathon

We all do things that we come to regret either immediately or some time later. We make mistakes that cannot be erased. And sometimes we do things that we know in the very moment we are doing them that the action is wrong.

What we do with those mistakes is another matter. First of all we must insist to ourselves that we learn from our mistakes and less than honest behavior. We don't wallow in self-doubt, we move on. We make amends when possible to the person or people we wronged. If the mistake we made caused us some kind of harm, we forgive ourselves.

We try not to repeat our mistakes. If we are in the middle of something that we recognize as wrong, we stop the process and start over. Just because we're in the middle of something there's nothing to say we can't stop it right there and make a change.

We remember that no person is perfect and without error. We love ourselves even when we make a mistake. If someone tries to make amends for their mistakes, we allow that and we forgive them, in our own time and in our own way.

If God can't change the past, we certainly cannot expect to either. We can, however, learn from that past whether it was a minute ago or a year ago.

Strive to make a better future while learning from the past.

∽

February 22
Show Great Strength
"So go ahead. Fall down. The world looks different from the ground."
—Oprah Winfrey

Sometimes it is in the breakdown and through the tears that we find our answers. We often think that we shouldn't cry; that we should be stronger than that. But that is not the truth. The ability to show this vulnerability is strength.

So often I want to show great strength, but instead I cry. And yet I know that sometimes great strength means letting it all out. I'm learning that it is okay to cry. Having lived a childhood full of tears, and having been reprimanded and made fun of for crying, made it difficult for me to learn in my adult life that it is alright to cry.

Most of the time when we do get to the point of tears we can't stop them anyway. And they cleanse us. In those moments that we cry it doesn't feel like it's a good, cleansing thing, but it is.

We should forget that we were taught crying is a weakness and instead change our thinking and know that there is not only healing in tears, there is great strength.

Real men (and women) do cry.

∽

February 23
Sticking to Commitments Makes Us Honorable
"There's a difference between interest and commitment. When you're interested in doing something, you do it only when circumstances

permit. When you're committed to something, you accept no excuses, only results." —Unknown

It takes a strong person to stick to something they committed to doing when adversity strikes. Or maybe whatever it is just isn't fun anymore. Sometimes people just are not able to commit to anything for very long.

Whether it's a job, relationship, social organization, club, team, or even a personal commitment such as dieting, exercise, taking better care of our self; all of these things take a commitment to succeed. And if we give up when it's not new or fun anymore, or when we see that we may just have set our goals a wee bit too high and we become disappointed, then we lose out on everything because we didn't see it through.

We don't have to be perfect. And setting goals high and not quite reaching them does not signal failure at all. Failure comes in quitting and giving up on the whole thing because it can't be exactly the way we planned it. That's black and white thinking. It's thinking that keeps us from ever truly achieving our goals. And it gives others reason not to count on us in the future.

If you commit to something don't give up until you're finished.

∽

February 24
Love and Trust
"Love means exposing yourself to the pain of being hurt, deeply hurt by someone you trust." —Unknown

Even in the best of circumstances those we love will on occasion hurt us and cause us to lose trust. It's just part of our humanness and imperfection that we sometimes hurt others.

Being vulnerable enough to love can be difficult, but if we don't allow ourselves to love and be loved there's really not much left in life. Some of us who wear our hearts on our sleeves have many difficult days from the hurt we encounter in relationships, but then we are the same folks who will still seek out love and who give love in a big way.

It's difficult to trust again once someone we love had betrayed us or otherwise hurt us deeply. We trust as much as we can as quickly as possible. It may be a one day at a time type of progress with two steps forward and one step back. We go at it in a guarded state of mind and keep parts of us closed off to anyone who tries to peek inside.

Hopefully we don't do this for long. Little by little we allow others in. Maybe we just find one person we trust and let them in until we feel safe again. It's progress not perfection that matters in the game of life, love, trust.

No matter how closed off you may feel after being hurt, move gradually into a place where you can love and be loved again. Be kind to yourself and love yourself in the process and love will find you again.

Without love our world is truly unbearable.

February 25
Wait for the Answers

"The pendulum of the mind oscillates between sense and nonsense, not between right and wrong." —Carl Gustav Jung

Sometimes in our lives it is difficult to know what is the right or wrong thing to do. We may be stuck in a job that we dread going to every day or we're in a relationship that needs serious help. We don't know if we should leave the job or relationship; we don't know what the right thing to do is.

And we don't always have to know in the moment what to do. We wait. If we are patient, the answers will come. The way will be made clear in whatever we are seeking knowledge about. It may not happen as quickly as we would like, but it happens in its own time and way.

When we are involved in something that we know must be changed or healed if we are to remain involved, but everything about that situation is not in our control, we can say the Serenity Prayer: "Grant me the serenity to accept the things I cannot change, courage to change the things I can, and wisdom to know the difference," and let go of our worry as long as possible.

Things in life must work through a process. We cannot rush that process or make others be involved if they don't want to. We turn it over to our Higher Power and wait on the answers.

While we wait, we do what we know to do and stay alert for the answers so that when they come we get them.

Clarity and direction will come in time.

February 26
Persistent Determination

"Nothing in this world can take the place of persistence. Talent will not; nothing is more common than unsuccessful people with talent. Genius will not; unrewarded genius is almost a proverb. Education will not; the world is full of educated derelicts. Persistence and

determination alone are omnipotent. The slogan 'press on' has solved and always will solve the problems of the human race."
—Calvin Coolidge

No matter what we have going on in our lives we rarely get something we want that money cannot buy by simply saying we want it or by one single effort. We can't give up on a dream just because it isn't easy to get. It takes tenacity.

We might be trying to get clean and sober. Or we may want to start a new career. Maybe we are trying to make a sale or promote something. We could be depressed and are trying to do the simple things we have to do just to get by until it passes and we feel better. Again, it takes persistent determination and the unwillingness to give up in order to succeed.

Most of us can probably see many people in our lives that have done something that went beyond what anyone expected them to achieve. It could be someone raised in poverty who managed not only to get an education, but to go past that to achieve great things to help others who are being raised like they were.

There are people in this world who have been injured severely yet they don't let lost limbs or scars keep them from success. Where it might take us a lot of effort, for them it takes a tenacious effort to do simple things, yet they go on to succeed way beyond what any of us could see them doing.

People who have been given a particular talent and are not using it need to remember that it was given to them for a reason. Sometimes we don't know what that reason is, but it does have a purpose. It may take tenacity to find the time to use that talent to help others if we don't see how we can make a living with it, but life is not all about money. When we use the gifts we were given, we are rewarded in many ways, sometimes this may manifest as money or income, and others times it's just the joy we receive in giving.

Whatever you attempt, remember to be tenacious and you will succeed.

෴

February 27
Raw Emotions Can Blur Reality

"We are all broken and wounded in this world. Some choose to grow strong at the broken places."
—Harold J. Duarte-Bernhardt

We all experience those times in our lives where we feel so raw that we could swear that every person we encounter and every situation we are in is throwing salt in our wounds. It chafes at us constantly and it feels like it won't go away.

What we must remember is that while we are going about life with this open wound, things may not be as they seem. We must keep in mind that the world is not out to get us and that we most likely are thinking the worst when that may not be the truth.

This is a time when our issues become glaring to us. If we have trust issues, we think everyone is lying to us. Or we may think that nobody cares about us, when we know deep down they do.

We may ask how we got to that place when just a few days or weeks before we felt good and things seemed to be going well. And it could be that we can see how we got there. Maybe we are going through some growing pains. Perhaps we are dealing with grief from loss. Or it could be a series of events where we are getting hit while we're already down.

The hope is while we are feeling stuck in the pain and agony of the raw emotions that it will pass quickly, because we know it will pass. And we hope that what's on the other side is worth the pain of the growth. We trust that it is.

Eventually we pull out of it; hopefully not until we have felt what we need to feel though, because if we don't feel it now, we will have to feel it somewhere down the road. And while we feel stuck we don't allow ourselves to get stuck forever. We must do the things we know make us feel better until it passes. We take care of ourselves first and foremost and we don't let others guilt us because we aren't our usual selves.

What feels heavy now will be off your shoulders soon.

෴

February 28
Negativity Breeds Negativity

"One can overcome the forces of negative emotions, like anger and hatred, by cultivating their counterforces, like love and compassion."
—Dalai Lama

Having found myself swirling in a cesspool of negativity too many times I made the decision to avoid the undertow in the future.

Sometimes we find ourselves in the middle of something negative, usually focused around someone. We gossip with others which leads to more gossip and soon we find we're talking about another person, and on and on. We get sucked into the negativity and soon it has taken over our whole being without us being aware of it.

I can remember this happened many times at several different jobs I've had. And I've experienced it with circles of friends and at church.

It makes us feel better at times to put someone else down, but it really isn't the best way to boost self-esteem. It's better to find something good in the person we are negatively discussing or just don't gossip at all.

The more time we spend in negative thinking and acting, the more it becomes who we are until we find ourselves overwhelmed by it. It takes on a life of its own in us and produces anger and resentment over things that normally we might not even notice, and things that are certainly none of our business.

If we stop this negativity and start trying to be positive we can pull ourselves out of it. Soon we'll realize just how heavy the cloud of it was and things will start appearing more pleasant. We'll appear more pleasant.

Stopping the negative spin leads to peace.

February 29
Seasons of Life
To everything there is a season,
a time for every purpose under the sun.
A time to be born and a time to die;
a time to plant and a time to pluck up that which is planted;
a time to kill and a time to heal;
a time to weep and a time to laugh;
a time to mourn and a time to dance;
a time to embrace and a time to refrain from embracing;
a time to lose and a time to seek;
a time to rend and a time to sew;
a time to keep silent and a time to speak;
a time to love and a time to hate;
a time for war and a time for peace.
—Ecclesiastes 3:1-8

As much as we may wish it weren't so, the rules of this world mandate that we have all of the seasons of life from birth to death. Some of us live longer than we may deserve; and many go before they should.

We don't decide when life and death occur. But what we can do is live out our lives while we are here. In order to truly live we don't abuse ourselves with things that cause us harm; and we don't treat other people unkindly.

When treated with prejudice and hate we can learn to forgive and not hate back. When we are ignored or abandoned we can reach out and love someone else who may feel distraught like us. When we need to heal we allow ourselves to do what will give us peace. We speak up when we need to and keep silent when that is best.

There are many choices we make every day that affect our lives in the moment and for the future. They seem small and insignificant at the time, but may have far reaching and long-lasting outcomes. When we handle the small stuff we keep it manageable. When things get too big and out of control for us, we ask for help.

Living life in a healthy way demands that we pay attention. We are aware of our physical and emotional needs and we deal with them in healthy and appropriate ways.

To love ourselves means that we do have to put our self first and then give to others.

Wherever we are in our lives, we can know that it's the place we are meant to be at the time, and that if we are in pain, we will come out on the other side of that with new found wisdom and peace.

You are in the season chosen for you at this moment.

৵

March 1
Compassion is Available

"When we honestly ask ourselves which person in our lives means the most to us, we often find that it is those who, instead of giving much advice, solutions, or cures, have chosen rather to share our pain and touch our wounds with a gentle and tender hand. The friend who can be silent with us in a moment of despair or confusion, who can stay with us in an hour of grief and bereavement, who can tolerate not knowing, not curing, not healing and face with us the reality of our powerlessness, that is a friend who cares."
—Henri Nouwen

When we are in the midst of something difficult in our lives oftentimes the last thing we want is for someone to come in and tell us what to do. Or for someone who barely knows us to tell us that we have a particular issue as if they are our therapist. What we want is for someone to just be in our presence or even with us in spirit if physical presence is not possible.

We want to feel like they understand, even if they don't really because they have not experienced what we are going through. Or we want to know that they feel our pain if we are suffering loss and grief.

We don't expect them to fix what's broken because most likely they can't fix it anyway.

What we want is someone to listen and hear; someone who doesn't have to understand what's going on to hold our hand or give us a hug; and someone to sit with us and just let us be while knowing that we are cared about.

Sometimes just knowing someone cares is enough. It takes some of the edge off of our pain if we can feel connected to another, if we can feel their love for us.

This is something we can strive to give to others in our lives. We each have an opportunity to be there for others in their pain, difficulty, or loss. Sometimes when someone just needs to unload, let it out verbally or with tears, we can be there for them.

Learn to be there for others and someone will be there for you.

March 2
In Its Own Time
"And when the winds have blown things round and back again, what was once your pain will be your home; everything in its own time...."
—Indigo Girls

We get it when we get it and not any sooner. Whatever we are looking for, a spiritual connection, an answer for a question in our life about direction, an ending of pain or grief, whatever it is, the answer comes in its own time and its own way.

We can't make it happen any faster than it does. Our Higher Power, the Universe, brings us what we need when we need it. As difficult as that is to comprehend, it's the truth. And sometimes it just may be that the lesson in the waiting was learning to wait. Patience, or trust or faith. Sometimes we just don't know what the lesson is that we are being taught and we may miss the knowledge of having learned it, but we learn it nonetheless, or we will have to be re-taught at a later time.

It's just how things work and it is totally beyond our control to change any part of that. We still continue to use our recovery tools during any process of life even when we feel as if we cannot go on even though they don't hurry the process they help us cope while we wait.

I was experiencing a particularly difficult time where I couldn't see the lesson or the end of the pain that was occurring. While discussing with someone she said, "When my children were small they would get irritable, even feverish before a tooth came in." The analogy was that something was happening in my life, below the surface, and once "the tooth came in" everything would be better and the lesson learned. Eventually the answer does come, the change does occur.

The "tooth will come in" when it's time.

&

March 3
We Can Begin Again

"Every new beginning comes from some other beginning's end."
—Seneca

No matter what day of the year it is, we can always begin again. We can start a day over at any time during the day. We simply stop and say "this day is not going well, I choose to start over right now." It doesn't always make things better, but it can get us out of a bad spin.

Some of us set new goals on New Year's Day; some on sobriety anniversary dates or birth dates; and sometimes we set them at random days throughout the year. It matters not when we do it, what is important is that if we need to start over, we do.

We don't really start over with a clean slate. We may feel as if we begin again all the time in certain areas of our lives, and while we may have lots of new beginnings in that arena, we don't start from nowhere. What we do is start over with wisdom and knowledge of what's gone before in our lives. We may not know what works all the time, but we probably have plenty of wisdom about what doesn't work. And whatever we've found in our lives that is positive and good, we move forward with that.

Some new beginnings are huge. A new job, a recent marriage, a baby on the way; getting clean and sober; leaving a significant other when it's not a healthy relationship; these life changing beginnings can be especially stressful. Other beginnings though not as huge are important nonetheless. Starting a new diet or exercise program; deciding to look for a new job; beginning to be a non-smoker, making a decision to seek growth … there are so many ways we can begin again.

Whatever new beginning you seek today, know that you can succeed if you truly put your heart and mind into it and seek help from your Higher Power.

Each day is a chance to begin again.

&

March 4
Healing from Betrayal

"You may be deceived if you trust too much, but you will live in
torment if you do not trust enough."
—Frank Crane

Anytime we have been betrayed or hurt in some way by another
person it takes time to heal. We most likely feel that we can never trust
anyone again if the betrayal runs deep. But we will trust again, and we
may well be betrayed again, but a life of solitude is a lonely way to
spend time.

If someone has done us wrong we can walk away from them, try to
mend the relationship, or hold huge resentments against them.
Resentments mostly hurt the one holding them. And negative energy
going out of us about someone else tends to come back on us making
our life miserable.

Healing takes time and energy. It takes a willingness to feel the
anger and pain. It takes practicing healthy recovery behaviors. And it
takes self-love and nurturing.

What doesn't work is running around telling anyone who will listen
how mean the person was to us. It just keeps the negativity going on
and on. Talking it over with someone is different than spreading the
mess all over town. It's healing to talk about our "stuff" with someone
safe and caring.

*Send out the energy of love instead of negativity and see life
return to a better place.*

◈

March 5
No Longer a Victim

"The most authentic thing about us is our capacity to create, to
overcome, to endure, to transform, to love and to be greater than our
suffering." —Ben Okri

No matter what has been done to us in our lives, we are no longer
victims. We are survivors if we are still here living and breathing.
Thinking of our self as a survivor empowers us way beyond living as a
victim does.

We all know people (even ourselves) who have been through
serious trauma or have been treated badly by other people. Perhaps we
did bad things to ourselves. We have all been through so much, but we
don't have to live in that pain forever. We can move out of it and into a
better life.

Healing is available for us if we are willing to take the steps necessary to get there. We pray. We talk about what happened to us with someone safe. We learn that it wasn't our fault they did what they did to us. We find a therapist or a recovery group to attend where we can discuss our issues and learn how to deal with the past and move on. We forgive ourselves if we need to do that.

We find that we are not alone; that things have happened to others and we ask them how they became survivors instead of victims. Once we begin to heal we are able to share our experience, strength and hope with those who are just beginning to let go of their victim status.

It works. It's painful, but you can do it if you want to move into a more fulfilled life by taking that huge load of shame thrust upon you off of your shoulders.

Always remember what others do to you is not your fault.

᪥

March 6
Mind Over Matter

"The only person you are destined to become is the person you decide to be." —Ralph Waldo Emerson

We each were born with certain gifts and talents that are unique to us. And we all have things that challenge us. We are each given our fair share of pain it would seem also.

How we choose to live with these gifts and challenges is up to us. We can sit and wallow in self-pity because we aren't the most handsome; we aren't the smartest; or we don't have the most money. We can continue negative behavior because someone hurt or abused us.

Or, we can take the positives that we have been given and use those to make our world and the world a better place. It's up to us to decide which we want to focus on and put our energy into.

This is not to gloss over real pain and issues; we can work on those and heal from what needs healing. But we don't have to limit ourselves to what's wrong with us either.

Challenges are most often handled by mind over matter. Just ask anyone who has ever achieved something truly great and see if they didn't struggle at times with self-doubt or limitations that could easily have kept them from achieving what they did.

We decide every day whether to move forward, backward or stay the same. Some days we are up to the challenges and give it our all to move forward, some days it's all we can do not to move too far backward. In the long run, choosing forward momentum and believing in ourselves will take us to great places where we will find and use our gifts.

Decide who you want to be and move in that direction.

 જી

March 7
Fear Destroys Drive
"Fear is that little darkroom where negatives are developed."
—Michael Pritchard

Fear manifests itself in different ways for different people. For me it's a gnawing anxious feeling in the pit of my stomach that makes me want to either self medicate or curl up in the fetal position and hide.

Sometimes fear is a good thing because it keeps us safe from outside forces. It's a normal reaction to something new or stressful. But the fear that I'm talking about is not fear of something physical happening where our natural fight or flight instincts come into play, it's something on another level, something or some things out of our control. It's negative what-if thinking and it sucks the life right out of us. It can immobilize us completely.

We cannot function at 100 percent of our capabilities if we are in fear. It takes too much energy. What we can do is let go. Letting go of that which is out of our control will melt away the fear. And we do it as many times as it takes as often as it takes.

We stop thinking about negative what-ifs and think positive thoughts. Not unrealistic thinking, just half-full rather than half-empty. Better to think positive and be disappointed than think negative and never do anything.

If we are fearful about performing, we realize that we don't have to be perfect in what we do. If we fear being accepted or loved by other people we remind ourselves that we don't have control over what other people think or do and whatever happens will happen despite our fears and worry.

We can think of "what's the worst thing that can happen" if we do or don't do a particular thing. Then we weigh the worst thing with the best thing and decide if the fear is valid.

Don't let fear stop you on your journey.

 જી

March 8
Decision Making: Somebody Has To Do It
"I believe the single most significant decision I can make on a day-to-day basis is my choice of attitude. ...When my attitudes are right, there

is no barrier too high, no valley too deep, no dream too extreme, no challenge too great for me." —Charles R. Swindoll

Making the right decision about things can be a very difficult process and may take us through the gamut of all of our issues because each one screams out at us during the process. Fear, anxiety, codependency, low self-esteem — these are just a few of the things that come into play when we have to think something through and pick a side or make some sort of possibly life-changing decision.

We may worry about what other people will think, we may have concerns over commitments made previously and not want to go back on our word, we might be stuck right in the middle of something because most things aren't black and white; they are some form of grey.

What we must do is process the decision. We may need to make a list of the "good" and "bad" or right and wrong; however we want to label each side of the decision.

For instance, if looking to take a new job we'd have one column of pluses and one of minuses, maybe the pay would be better at the new job, but the hours would not be the ones we like to work. Or the new job is exactly what we've always dreamed of doing, but the pay is not quite what we are used to.

Whatever the decision and whatever the "good" and "bad" things are, we can make the choice and know if it is right or wrong for us. We can discuss it with others but ultimately we must be the decision makers since it's our life. Sometimes we may think after a while that we've made the wrong decision. If that happens we can always start the process over again.

Letting go of commitments, changing jobs, getting married or divorced, these are big decisions and should be considered fully before moving forward, and may take quite a struggle from us with all of our issues screaming.

Try to quieten the things in your head that are unreasonable so you can listen for the real answers.

∽

March 9
Home Plate
"If you put yourself in a position where you have to stretch outside your comfort zone, then you are forced to expand your consciousness."
—Les Brown

Our lives are like baseball. In baseball the goal is to hit the ball and run around all the bases until stepping on home plate. Once there the runner is safe and scores a "run."

In life when we are having a difficult time we can head out for the day and all we want to do is return home safely. We have certain things we have to do, our bases, until we can get back to our safety zone. This is okay, often in baseball the runner does not get around the bases and home safe, he has to go back and try again later. We may live this way as long as we need to, until we no longer worry about being in our comfort zone. We feel safe out on the other bases as long as we have to be there, until we can get back to home.

The more we face the fears and challenges out there, the less we will experience those fears or feel that doing certain things are a challenge. Sometimes the "bases" aren't so scary, it's just that we don't want to be away from home plate because that's the only place we feel totally safe.

In order to grow and expand our lives, we must take risks, which means we won't always feel safe. Making changes is not usually comfortable. If it were easy for us to change at a moment's notice we would likely never get in ruts or be bored. But changing and growing and moving out of comfort zones often feels icky and sometimes downright scary.

Doing things differently, facing our fears, moving out of a comfortable place into an unknown realm may take many attempts, but in the end we will be glad we stepped up to the plate, took a swing at the ball and ran as hard as we could to successfully reach our goal.

Step out of your comfort zone as fast or slowly as needed, but do it.

❧

March 10
Insides Don't Always Match Outsides
"If you compare yourself with others, you may become vain and bitter, for always there will be greater and lesser persons than yourself."
—Max Ehrman

It's never a good idea to compare our insides to other people's outsides. Since we never know what is really going on with other people, appearances can be very deceiving. And comparing the unknown with our own situations can set us up to feel "less than" in many ways.

And if we think too highly of ourselves we run the risk of becoming a snob because we think we are smarter, richer, and prettier than the next person.

Someone who has a bigger house, a nicer car, a boat, etc., may be in huge debt and on the verge of bankruptcy. Or the stress of their bills may be causing them to lose sleep at night or might be giving them ulcers.

And another person who appears to not have much in the way of material possessions may be the happiest person in the world because they have joy in their heart and plenty of love in their life.

We just never really know what goes on in other homes and lives. People tell us what they feel safe to say and if there are major problems, they probably don't feel safe.

What we must do is work on our own issues and be happy and proud of what we do with what we've got. Life isn't all about money and things. It may be for some people, but not those of us who are working on our insides.

When other people appear to have it all, they just might, but you can't have their life. You have your life and your own journey. Your self-esteem is dependent upon you believing in yourself not in comparing haves and have nots with others.

Your insides are all that really matter when it comes to happiness.

᠔

March 11
Exercise is Invaluable
"Movement is a medicine for creating change in a person's physical, emotional, and mental states."
—Carol Welch

No matter if we're trying to lose weight, get over stress and anxiety, clear our minds or solve a problem, exercise can offer a solution. It's not just an emotional salve; it has chemical properties in the brain that makes us feel better. Think "runners high," although we don't have to run to feel better.

A brisk walk where we get our blood pumping and exert some energy and sweat can be a fabulous way to let off steam or think. Sometimes getting up and doing it are the last things we can imagine doing. If we do it anyway, we reap the benefits soon after hitting the streets, gym, trails, etc. It clearly can't hurt anything to give it a try if you've never experienced it or if you feel too out of shape from not exercising for a long time, although going easy is best if it's been some time since exerting yourself.

Another added benefit is if we can get out and about on a nice day with sunshine during the time of year when it's dark more than light and the sun doesn't shine a lot of days. We get out on a cold brisk sunny day and soak up the rays while breathing in fresh air instead of that which has been circulating through our homes and offices for days.

We also may find new, fresh thoughts replacing the stale, ugly thinking that's been swirling in our minds for hours, days or forever.

Exercise is a healthy de-stressor.

❧

March 12
Listening for the Answer

"Prayer is when you talk to God; meditation is when you listen to God." —Diana Robinson

The last of the Twelve Steps of Alcoholics Anonymous begins with, "Having had a spiritual awakening …." On first glance before working the steps we might wonder just what that means. But those of us who have had a spiritual awakening, either because of those steps or some other way in our lives understand what that means, although it is difficult to explain to others.

I experienced something that brought the words "having had a spiritual awakening" to my mind.

I asked God for something and I got an answer. Not only did I put it out there, when the answer came I was aware that I had gotten an answer to prayer and I felt connected to my Higher Power, whom I choose to call God. I didn't make the prayer too specific, but it was specific enough that when the answer came I didn't doubt that it was an answer.

Often we pray for things and don't remain alert for the answer so when we get it, we "get it." This is something to be mindful of when we do throw out prayer, to remain alert for the answer, even though the answer may not be exactly what we want, it is still an answer.

For those of us who aren't religious it's a spiritual connection, knowing that there is a power greater than us, someone to turn to and to turn things over to. When we know that we aren't in control of the world, that there is a Higher Power, we can take some of the weight off of our shoulders and let that Higher Power, whatever name we give it, take control.

If you pray, remain alert for the answer so you don't miss it when it comes.

❧

March 13
Freedom from Pain
"The burden which is well borne becomes light."
—Ovid

Sometimes in our recovery process we remember things we have buried deep inside. Hurtful things that we discover are the root of an issue that may have been causing us difficulty for years.

Sometimes we can spend lots of time discussing our lives with counselors, therapists, friends, or family and still not pull everything out as fast as we'd like. Then one day we find that some huge occurrence that caused an issue that was buried below the surface comes out in a conversation when we weren't even trying to work on our issues. That thing that caused us to have a particular fear was the root cause of our issue and now it's in the light where we can think about it and work on it.

Knowing the basis of an issue doesn't immediately make it go away, but it does help us to process it. We can talk about it with someone. It's always good to bring those buried memories and feelings to the surface so that they can see the light of day. Somehow they don't seem as bad when we can talk about them and take some of the weight of the burdens off.

It's kind of like carrying around a big sack of potatoes on our back. If every potato is an old issue that we haven't dealt with, we can one by one get rid of a potato until that baggage becomes almost weightless. Our spirits will be lifted and we'll feel more freedom to be. We'll have more to give to others. We'll be happy and happiness will be drawn to us.

Freedom from some of our old pain and issues is available if we can let it go. But we have to be willing to go through the process of getting those things out in whatever way we know to do that. Sometimes, as mentioned above, it comes out in a surprising way when we aren't expecting it. Sometimes it comes with lots of work and effort. The important thing is to find a way to shine some light on the monsters hiding in the dark.

Bringing our stuff out in the light makes it less scary.

◈

March 14
Garbage In Garbage Out
"To keep a lamp burning, we have to keep putting oil in it."
—Mother Teresa

Experts have theorized that children become more violent because of video games and movies that are watched. And while others discount this idea, we know we have been desensitized to death and violence because we see so much of it on television and in movies.

What we feed into ourselves is what we become. If we feed our spirit with spiritual things we will become more spiritual. If we feed our minds with positive thoughts we think positive thoughts. If we educate ourselves we become educated and then we can teach others.

"Garbage In, Garbage Out" is a phrase used in the field of computer science. But the words can be used in regard to what we put into our minds, bodies and spirits.

Spending time in prayer, meditation, reading uplifting things, listening to music that feeds the soul; all of these are good things we can do which produce peace in us and carry us through our days.

We must be active in our recovery in whatever way we know works. We take into ourselves that which is healing and that which produces growth. This is how we continue down the road of recovery. It's okay to not always think about growth and recovery. It's okay to let ourselves play sometimes. It's not all work, this recovery process, but we need to be mindful about how much "garbage" we take in and balance that with productive, healthy input.

Healthy in, healthy out.

৵

March 15
Give Up On Control
"For peace of mind, resign as general manager of the universe."
—Unknown

For some of us this sounds like such a great answer, but we are only able to do it for brief moments in time. We should do it anyway.

It's difficult to keep all of our own plates spinning without having to manage the whole world around us. When we realize that we really aren't in control of much it's easier to let go. We cannot control the weather, another person's reaction or behavior, our boss, children, partner, employees, or anything else in the universe.

Once we let go of the false belief that we just might have control over these things we start to feel a bit of freedom from the mental strain it takes to figure all of the logistics of the universe out in our minds. We find space in there for pleasant thoughts. We find relief for our tensed up muscles. We sleep better.

There's something about knowing that we don't even have to try because it's useless to try anyway to control everything around us.

Some peace comes instantly upon having the thought that we are powerless over something. Then we actually put that into practice by not trying to control whatever it is. We do this situation by situation, thing by thing, until we start to find that it is so much easier to not try to make everything work, to let it just happen.

Stop trying to control everything and see how simple life becomes.

❧

March 16
Growing in Recovery
"I am not now what I was."
—Unknown

With just a short time in recovery we change quickly. Some of who we are will always be who we are, but oftentimes we grow into something better than what we were before.

The fears we felt before, perhaps about being alone; going without drugs, alcohol or some other addiction; taking positive action; whatever the fear was may not be there anymore. We have changed.

We should stop from time to time in our lives and evaluate who we are, especially when we are working on changing ourselves. We may find that we have changed and that the fears we still think we have are not even there anymore, we are just accustomed to the fear being there and continue mistakenly to live as if it were.

Stop and evaluate to see if you are the same today as you were before. Most likely you are not who you were.

Pause to check out who you are today; you may be more free than you know.

❧

March 17
New Eyes Open Our World
"The voyage of discovery is not in seeking new landscapes but in having new eyes." —Marcel Proust

There are times when we discover that what we've been searching for is already there. The new job, the relationship, healing, love, it's there waiting on us to be open enough to receive it. We must let go of our old thinking and look at things in a new way, with new eyes, not rose colored glasses, but with clear vision, new vision, different vision.

When we push too hard the answers don't come. We block our own vision by locking ourselves in boxes and trying to always figure out logical answers for that which is not always logical. Love isn't logical. Healing isn't logical. Relationships can be illogical. Our lives don't neatly fit into tidy packages where we never experience highs and lows, or at least they shouldn't. And if they are we aren't experiencing life as it was meant to be experienced. We'll miss the sound and smell of the ocean, the beauty of sunrises and sunsets, the comfort of hugs, and the ecstasy of love, if we don't see the whole of life.

The world is a wide open place where we are each on our own path of discovery. Often we are on our path with blinders on and heads down. We trudge through the days always looking ahead to the next thing or the weekend. We miss so much.

Look up and around with new eyes and find what you've been longing for.

❧

March 18
Let Your Light Shine
"And as we let our own light shine, we unconsciously give other people permission to do the same. As we are liberated from our fear, our presence automatically liberates others."
—Marianne Williamson

The quote above may bring back memories of the song that goes like this: "This little light of mine, I'm gonna let it shine; let it shine, let it shine, let it shine," that many of us sang as children either at church or camp.

We can let our light shine whether it's our knowledge of God's love, our freedom from oppression or fear, or maybe it's having had a spiritual awakening. It could be we feel better about ourselves after working on self-esteem issues. Anytime we overcome some challenge set before us we have the opportunity to share that victory with others.

When we share our lives in totality with other people, we allow others to be enlightened and strengthened. When we tell our stories whether that is in a Twelve-Step meeting, church, over the water cooler at work, or some other way, we allow other people to share our experience, strength and hope.

Our fear may be one shared by a whole segment of society. Remember it only took a few to open the way for women to vote and for Blacks to have equal rights.

Whatever fear you have overcome, share that with others. You can open a path for those who follow. Someone, many people, in fact, may be watching you without your knowledge. We find God's message, and we find strength in others in many ways. Someone needs your light to shine today.

Sometimes we lead and don't even know it. Let your light shine.

March 19
Give Others a Chance

"We are afraid to care too much for fear that the other person does not care at all." —Eleanor Roosevelt

One of the things we may need to work on is not letting past relationships affect future relationships in destructive ways. We try not to put up walls that keep other people at arms' length. Although at times it's a good idea to be protective of ourselves going into any relationship since it takes time to really get to know another person.

We all bring so much "baggage" into relationships, especially as we get older and have more experiences. No matter how much we try going in not to carry the baggage from one relationship to another, we do, because it's part of who we are and part of what made us the person that we have become.

Our perception about how much others care for us can be skewed by our own issues. We must strive to not shut people out who we "think" are feeling a certain way about us, because we just don't always know what they think. We seek balance in caring for others. We strive not to be codependent in relationships. We try to give and take. We don't control and we don't allow ourselves to be controlled.

We need to keep in mind that the other person also has their own baggage that's brought into the relationship, and be willing to be patient with them as they see if we are a fit in their lives just as we do with them.

Take time to see if your baggage is compatible with their baggage.

❧

March 20
Struggles Make Us Stronger

"I trust that everything happens for a reason, even when we're not wise enough to see it." —Oprah Winfrey

We are rarely able to see the reason why some things happen in our lives. Sometimes weeks or years later we look back and see that what happened made us stronger, or caused us to do something good, something healthy, that we otherwise would not have done had we not experienced what we did.

We gain compassion and understanding for others after we go through a difficult time and experience compassion and understanding from someone else. We learn patience from things that cause us to struggle with trying to be patient. We learn to let go when we have a broken heart. Most of it is not fun, but the learning process is there for a reason in our lives.

It's a good idea to sit down sometimes and think back, to work back through what got us where we are. For some of us we may have hit bottom and turned our lives around by returning to and finishing college. Maybe just getting clean and sober was enough of a better place and we didn't need anything further but to continue growing in sobriety.

Think back through some of the major events in your life and see how if one thing hadn't happened that another would not have either. Some of them are easy to spot and some of them take a lot of wisdom.

Some of what we go through is hellacious and we may not want to think it through. That's okay too, but if we are able to trace our lives back to some of our struggles we will see that they got us where we are today. Maybe next time we are in a struggle we will realize the lesson is being learned we just don't know what it is yet.

Struggles teach us along the way.

∽

March 21
Seeing Growth

"Whatever we are waiting for — peace of mind, contentment, grace, the inner awareness of simple abundance — it will surely come to us, but only when we are ready to receive it with an open and grateful heart." —Sarah Ban Breathnach

It's not always easy to see where we've grown and we may not see it until we experience it. Perhaps we've been trying to let someone go with love. We care about them, but our relationship is unhealthy. We work on it and pray over it, maybe even fight letting go. And one day we see that person, we spend time with them and we realize that we still care for them, but we do not feel the same way, it's a healthy love and not a needy love, or an attachment, nor a painful love; it's just an honest caring for that person.

We may even discover that not only did we grow and that relationship is healthy now; we may find that our work has affected change in us so that we don't get into unhealthy relationships anymore. Our work, all of the pain and struggle is paying off and we didn't realize that until we were in a certain situation where our particular issues came into play. This is just one example of the many ways we grow and can see how far we have come.

Often other people can see our growth before we can. And often we will find that if we work on a particular issue it affects other struggles we have in life. Every part of who we are — mind, body, and spirit — is connected to the other parts. We focus on healing our spirit, and our mind gets healing. We work on our spirit and we become more spiritual, but we also find our mind cleared of some of its junk. When we take care of our physical self, we have clearer thoughts.

You will see your growth through later experiences, sometimes when you least expect it.

❧

March 22
What Brings You Joy?
"Sometimes your joy is the source of your smile, but sometimes your smile can be the source of your joy."
—Thich Nhat Hanh

Those days when we feel good, when we have pep in our step or a swagger as some refer to it, those are the days we long for. And sometimes they seem to appear for no reason and regretfully disappear as fast as they came.

One of the answers to our happiness is to figure out for ourselves what brings those on and what makes them go away. Often it could be something that happened outside of us, someone giving us a literal or figurative pat on the back. It could be a small success that on any other day would have no affect on us. It might be internal joy over a small or large accomplishment.

Often we know what to do when we get down and have to work our way out of a depression. But do we know how to get the joy when we are having a regular time in our lives, when we are simply dealing with our day to day self-esteem issues?

The confidence that we have in the moments when the swagger is there is something that would be nice to bottle and keep for future use when we aren't feeling so good. If we can figure out what makes us feel confident, we will be more successful at having the pep and swagger.

What brings you joy? Figure that out and you'll find you have it more often.

❧

March 23
A Fresh Perspective
"Life is a continuous exercise in creative problem solving."
—Michael J. Gelb

On any given day we may experience some problem for which we do not have an answer. We struggle and fight to come up with a solution on how to handle a particular matter at work, with friends, with our children or partner. The more we try to figure out a solution the more upset we get.

When that happens we can leave the problem or issue for a while and do something else. Often the answer comes when we aren't trying to force it. The more we struggle, the more upset and anxious we become. Our mind becomes filled with too many options or no options and only fear or anxiety. Walking away from the problem often will bring an answer while we are thinking about something else.

Go take a walk or do something different than what you are doing and see if the answers come. Wash the dishes, do the laundry, do a different task at work, read your child a book, take a drive, pray, meditate, sleep, go to a Twelve Step meeting … try doing whatever you are not doing at the moment that is not working.

Sometimes even doing a different physical activity won't bring the answers we are looking for, but at least we get a break for a while. Sometimes the answers come when we are just still and quiet. Forcing an answer is useless.

The answers will come when you stop trying so hard to get them.

∾

March 24
Patience is a Virtue

"One moment of patience may ward off great disaster. One moment of impatience may ruin a whole life."

—Chinese proverb

I remember one time when I was young receiving as a gift a small plaque that had the Holly Hobbie dolls on it and the words "Patience is a Virtue." The gift was from my aunt and I asked her what it meant.

"You'll find out when you get older," she said. That's when patience became a conundrum to me and unfortunately, it tends to remain such.

It's difficult to be patient. Standing in lines, getting stuck in traffic, waiting for a Web page to load, or a day to end, all require patience. But what about the big things: waiting on an answer to prayer. Waiting to meet and fall in love with your soul mate. Waiting on word that your book proposal has been accepted for publishing. These are a lot tougher.

What does it mean to be patient though? We don't have much choice in some instances but to wait, but how we wait is the key to patience being a virtue.

Some words that are synonyms of patience include: endurance, composure, stability. It implies qualities of calmness, and persistent courage in trying circumstances. Sometimes we just don't want to be stable and show courage and composure. But it's just that calmness that will keep us sane during times where great patience is needed.

We can live our lives impatiently, but we won't be able to have serenity. Patience takes a lot of letting go. It takes strength to see that we can't control the outcomes of every part of our lives.

Give patience a shot; what choice do you have?

∽

March 25
Laughter is the Best Medicine
"You have to laugh at yourself, because you'd cry your eyes out if you didn't." —Emily Saliers

We take ourselves and life way too serious sometimes. We worry about tomorrow and yesterday and forget all about what we are doing at the moment.

Have you every done anything really silly? Maybe something that you cannot believe you would do by letting yourself be out of perfect control for one minute? Did you live through it? Did the world come to an end? Of course not.

And the best part is that when we do make mistakes or do something outside our ordinary boxed in perfect little lives and we can laugh about it, the world is a happier place because we've let go, even if only momentarily, of perfectionism.

Someone said, and it's been repeated often, that laughter is the best medicine. A good old deep belly laugh can be one of the most healing moments we can have. We don't have them enough, but if we think back to the last one we had we can see where it helped. Most likely we had tears streaming down our face and could not control the laugh or the tears.

It's not always easy to get to that place. In the movie "Steel Magnolias" there's a part where two usually crabby older women have just attended the funeral of a young, vibrant new wife and mother. They argue a bit and before you know it they are laughing. I did the same thing watching the movie; cried and then laughed. Both crying and laughing can bring healing tears.

Find something to laugh about every day.

March 26
Be Ready for the Lesson
"When the pupil is ready the teacher appears."
—Old English saying

Lessons come to us all the time, even when we don't think we're ready. Somehow, though, we find that we were ready because we've made it through a particular lesson we faced or found whatever tools were necessary to get through the process.

We don't plan our growth lessons. If we did there'd be nothing to learn. Things come along in life the way they are supposed to for whatever reason. Or maybe they just happen randomly; certainly philosophers have debated this for centuries.

We get a lot of our learning experiences when we are in the process of trying to grow and learn. If we are just living a life of getting through each day, counting down the hours, and not doing any kind of work on our spirituality, mental and emotional state, or relationships then most likely we won't get many lessons. Why? Because we won't take advantage of the thing that does come along to teach us whatever we need to learn. Instead we will just bury the difficult stuff and never even grasp any good that comes out of a situation.

Knowing that when presented with a growth opportunity we can use it to our advantage helps when we really would prefer not learn a particular lesson, or rather, we'd prefer not to have to go through the process it takes to learn it.

Be ready when the teacher appears. Do what needs to be done to learn the lesson, to grow, to face whatever challenge is presented. This is where we become strong like a tree with deep roots that does not blow over the first time a storm appears.

Be present and grow.

March 27
Stop Fear with Action
"The most difficult thing is the decision to act, the rest is merely tenacity. The fears are paper tigers. You can do anything you decide to do. You can act to change and control your life; and the procedure, the process is its own reward."
—Amelia Earhart

Fear can be a paralyzing thing in our lives. Many times it's simply fear that keeps us from moving forward with an idea or goal. We fear failure and we fear success. We fear what others will think about what we do, we fear an outcome that may differ from our goal.

Without challenging our fears and moving forward we will never accomplish much. If we have ever faced a fear and walked through it to the other side, we can use that as a guide, an example of how it is possible to face our own fears however real or imagined they may be.

Fear can be experienced when faced with beginnings as well as endings. Sometimes we are in a relationship, job, or situation that requires great strength to walk away from or end. We can have as much, or more, fear in endings as we have when we have a dream of starting something new.

If it's time to move on we can face our fears and make a plan. Just as we sit down and plan starting a business, or family, or anything new, we can sit down and plan an ending to something. Write down the plan. Pray about it. Talk it over with someone. Take action.

Don't let fear paralyze you into staying in a bad situation. Don't let fear stop you from the beginning you dream of in starting something new either.

In every ending is a beginning; don't let fear stop either.

∽

March 28
Life is What We Make It
"Plant your own garden and decorate your own soul, instead of waiting for someone to bring you flowers."
—Veronica A. Shoffstall

I imagine many of us have already found out that we are our own best friends or worst enemies. The knight in shining armor that we thought would ride up on a white horse and carry us away never showed. The Cinderella slipper did not fit our foot. And most of us never won a lottery.

But just because the fairy tales didn't come true, that does not mean that life cannot be good. It's just reality. Even if we became a movie star, a Grammy winning singer, or the quarterback for the Super Bowl winning team, there would be lots of work involved in getting there. We probably would have received a lot of rejection of our talent by the time we became a huge success. We probably would have worked long, arduous hours too.

Life is what we make it, good or bad. We are each given lots of challenges along the way. We get joy in there too if we are able to be alert for it and not live in the doldrums of despair thinking that life is all bad.

I know people who are suffering with cancer, yet they don't complain. I know someone who is HIV positive and rather than giving up on life, he is energetic and giving back to the community. The attitudes of these people encourage me to endure and discourage me from complaining about having a bad day or bemoaning something trivial that did or did not happen in my life.

Life is not always fun, but it's always worth living.

ॐ

March 29
Freedom from Addiction

"I want freedom and I can't have freedom and be addicted to anyone or anything." —Anonymous

Any addiction we have is one in which we are kept from being free. We can be addicted to many things: sex, food, drugs, alcohol, people, places and other things.

Addiction doesn't just come in the form of the homeless alcoholic lying on a park bench, or a crack addict holed up in an abandoned house. Sometimes our addictions aren't that striking to us or the world around us. But they are addictions just the same.

If we are being controlled by a substance, behavior, or person then we aren't free. If we are in a relationship where we are constantly walking on eggshells to keep from conflict we are addicted too. Codependent relationships are not freedom. Smoking cigarettes is an obvious addiction that won't land us in rehab, but is tough to give up nonetheless.

In my recovery I've given up different addictions at different times. Sometimes the thing I was addicted to came back into my life in a non addictive way. The physical addictions were sometimes easier than the emotional or psychological addictions, especially with certain people. I once told someone I cared about that it would be easier for me to let go if she died because then I had to let go. It doesn't sound like a nice thing to say, but it was an honest statement of a feeling.

On occasion I did not completely give up my addiction the first time I tried. Smoking cigarettes is like giving up heroin, so I've heard, and just as difficult, they say. I never tried heroin so I don't know, but giving up nicotine has to be up on the list of the most difficult addictions to break, and it took me a couple of tries to quit.

Giving up an addiction is not easy, but the rewards are great. We may need to seek support and advice from others while breaking addictive behavior. We can find help if we look for it.

Freedom from addiction is available with great effort.

March 30
Peace

"I do not want the peace that passeth understanding. I want the understanding which bringeth peace."

—Helen Keller

Peace in this world is not an easy thing to find. Everywhere we turn there is controversy, fighting, and even war.

What one of us might see as peace another may not. Holding and cuddling a baby might bring a sense of peace to some and fear to others. Spontaneity can bring anxiety to those who have fears based upon past experiences, but being spontaneous to some is a form of peace. Letting go of judging of self can be peace provoking. Letting go of anything can bring peace.

The ability to sit calmly in the middle of a family fight or a one-on-one argument with a partner or spouse can be a sign that we have peace. Not worrying over every little thing in our lives brings peace. Not trying to control the world is another place peace can be found.

There comes a time when we realize that worry and stress over things do not solve problems. We can worry about the smallest things until they become huge. If we let life happen as it's going to happen anyway, without worrying to extremes, we will find peace. For instance, if we have plans for an upcoming weekend and the weather reports show unfavorable conditions worrying about it will not bring us peace or change the weather. Making alternate plans around the weather will bring us peace.

We ought to each have places where we can go and sit calmly in peace; a church, on a mountaintop, near the ocean or lake, watching a sunrise or sunset, in our favorite chair with a hot cup of coffee or our favorite pet, anyplace where we can relax and be calm and at peace.

Find what brings you peace and remember to go there.

March 31
Letting Go of the Good

"There is a time for departure even when there's no certain place to go." —Robert Frost

Letting go doesn't always mean giving up the bad stuff or things that are wrong for us; it can also mean letting go of someone or something we care for deeply. Just as parents have to let go of their children as they grow in order for the child to become independent, we too must let people go sometimes so that we may move forward in our growth or they in theirs.

Sometimes we let go of a relationship and it changes into a different type of relationship than what it was when we moved on. And at other times it's a final farewell. If we are growing in our lives we will encounter lots of these moving on times. Some people we meet will become lifelong friends we keep in touch with, others will be in our hearts and thoughts only, and yet others we leave behind will soon be forgotten.

It takes great courage to walk away from something that isn't bad for us, but we know it's time to move on — in order to continue to grow we must let go. At times we must be gently pushed from the nest if we are in a nurturing relationship that has reached its potential. Or maybe we are the nurturer who must gently let our baby birds fly off into their own growth and wide open worlds.

It can be scary to make the leap of faith in these endings. It can hurt as badly as breaking up with a romantic love. Endings bring beginnings, but we don't usually know what that beginning is until we have closed the door on that which we are leaving. It will come though, the next thing, the next person, growth.

Letting go of a good thing is difficult; the outcome is determined by what's meant to be.

≈

April 1
Waiting Does Not Always Mean No
"What is delayed is not denied."
—Kay Yow

Things in life work out the way they are supposed to if we remain open. Even though at times it seems we can't have what we want at the moment, the day will come when we will see why it didn't happen now and we'll see that what we got was better even if different than our desire.

We experience what we experience so that we can evolve. Only when we remain open to the lessons of life do we get those lessons. Our Higher Power moves us along even when we don't see reality because we are blinded by what we desire.

Many times we can look back on our lives and see why we didn't get the job, the girlfriend, the boyfriend, the new car, the dream house we picked out, and on and on. It's often said that when one door closes another one opens. But we can only walk through the open door when we are able to fully close the one behind us and when we are willing to accept that things are not always as they seem and that we don't always get what we want when we want it.

And it may work out that we get exactly what we want it just happens at a different time than we expected, most likely because there was a lesson during the wait. Something like patience or faith could have been the lesson.

Always remember that not getting an answer to a prayer today or getting what we want at the moment, is not a final answer. It's either a: no, there's something better; or not now, but we will get an answer sooner or later.

We get what we need when we need it.

April 2
Shine a Light on the Monsters
"Unless I accept my faults, I will most certainly doubt my virtues."
—Hugh Prather

We all have things about us that we don't like, that we would change if we could and we do try to change when we can. We may be greedy, dishonest, or bigoted. We may have problems with jealousy, or we may get too needy with those we are in relationship with too often. We may lie when the truth would be easier to tell. Some of us may have fears that we try to hide from others, even perhaps from ourselves.

Acknowledging our defects of character is always a healthy option for us. Once we acknowledge a defect of character we can bring it into the light and lessen its power. We can pray about it and take action over it. We also understand that this is part of who we are just as our loving, nurturing, generous or other good qualities are part of us.

When we live our lives in an open way we will find the defects shrink because we no longer work so diligently to try to keep them hidden. The Twelve Steps, used by Alcoholics Anonymous and other groups, walk us through this process. Many of us have already worked the steps, but may need to revisit them. We can do this at AA or at other groups, such as Al Anon. There are other ways we can work on our character issues too, including speaking with clergy, a therapist, or a friend.

Pretending we don't have any faults is not being honest with ourselves or others. And it only serves to keep the issues not rid ourselves of them. When we keep our less than admirable parts hidden it means being less than who we are, which makes our self-esteem suffer.

The important thing is to acknowledge our light and our darkness so that we can be whole.

Shine a light on character defects and watch them disappear.

∽

April 3
Let Shame Go
"A nightingale dies for shame if another bird sings better."
—Robert Burton

Guilt and shame are two areas that are often confused. Some of us grew up believing that we were not good enough. Some of us did something that was wrong and we feel bad about that.

There is a difference in shame and guilt. Shame is thinking that who we are is not okay. Guilt is feeling bad about something we did. We can feel guilty for eating too much cake, and we can feel shame for being black or gay or sometimes for existing at all. It's the shame we must let go of.

Do we have a choice in how we come out of the womb? Did we choose to have brown skin, to be female (which is still considered "less than" by many), to be gay, to suffer from depression or some physical disorder? If we were born with something that others consider less than normal, we can let go of the shame of being who we are and who we were meant to be.

Another way shame hinders us is when we feel bad for being anything less than perfect. Maybe we have particular issues that we work on in relationships, we may have a drug or alcohol problem, maybe we have an eating disorder, or we are overweight, we may be greedy, or have anger issues. These are part of us and if we are working on them, on overcoming them, there is no shame there.

There is no shame in being human, especially since no person is perfect. Don't let others cause you to feel shame for being who you are. Each of us is unique and we were put in this world for a reason. Cherish who you are and what you give. Don't let others manipulate you by bringing up your faults. It may be that your faults are what lead you to help someone else.

Let guilt guide you to not repeat mistakes. Let shame go.

∽

April 4
Life is Not Static
"Lessons repeat until learned."
—Unknown

Almost with the sound of trumpets we experience a situation in which we think we have "done it." We have solved this problem in our lives never to face it again. It may be a situation with family, friends, or work related. It may be a personal growth issue. It could be anything that we have faced numerous times only to think that now we have achieved success.

Then something happens and we realize that the lesson may be learned, but similar situations may be faced over and over in our lives. Maybe we are just part of someone else learning a lesson and have to be present so they can master it.

Life isn't static. What we resolve today may strike us at another time in another way. We may have moved past a situation where people were saying and doing things we didn't approve of, yet we forgave them and decided that it wasn't about us, that those were their issues, and we have moved on, only to find that they are still stirring the pot. Or we may have conquered a fear only to be faced with it again under a slightly different circumstance.

Does it mean we didn't learn the lesson or grow when this new confrontation caused us grief? Not so much. It depends on how we handle it. Does the situation flare up like it did before or do we just take a step backwards where we'd taken giants steps previously in this area?

Don't look at the fresh episode as something that sets you back, look at it and see that this time it didn't blow up so badly and that while it was discomforting, it wasn't as severe as before and you handled it more maturely this time. That's growth. It is progress not perfection as the AA slogan says.

We do learn our lessons, but we still may get to revisit them from time to time.

∽

April 5
Random Acts of Kindness
"The true measure of a man is how he treats someone who can do him absolutely no good."
—Samuel Johnson

It's always a great experience when someone comes along who is kind who has absolutely no ulterior motives. Sometimes we are helped by friends and sometimes an unknown "angel" appears to help us when we most need it and least expect it.

We can be a Good Samaritan to others. We can be angels to people we know well and those we don't know at all. Sometimes the smallest thing can mean the world to another. A smile, holding a door for someone, helping another carry packages to their car, it doesn't have to be a huge effort on our part to bring a little bit of good into another's day, with no expectation of pay.

At other times we may give or receive a larger gift; someone to sit with us when we are sick, a friend to hold our hand when we are grieving, a bill paid when we aren't able, mowing the neighbor's yard when they are unable. Any number of things can be passed from person to person with compassion.

And we'll find that when we show kindness to others, kindness will be shown to us. Not every time, with every person, but what we give out usually comes back to us in some way when we least expect it.

Try one day just smiling at people you pass on the street, in stores, in office buildings, at your job. See how many smiles are returned. And see how much better you feel each time you smile and are smiled at. It's catching and it's so easy.

It is in giving that we receive.

∽

April 6
Be 100% You
"The greatest justice in life is to be who one is."
—Vanna Bonta

Any time we pretend to be something other than who we are, not only do we not fool other people, we show ourselves to be dishonest. People often know about things in our lives even when we don't think they do. And if we put on a front and pretend to be anything other than what and who we are it really does hurt us and any chance to have real relationships with others.

There are people who will talk to us and act as though they are perfect human beings. We allow them to hurt our self-esteem because we compare ourselves to them, even though we know in recovery that it's not a good idea to compare ourselves to other people, especially their outsides.

There are those we look up to, we may even have them placed high on a pedestal, only later to find out that the person has been withholding certain things in their lives from us which show some of their imperfections.

If the people who look up to us know the truth about all that we are, does that tarnish our relationship, or make it stronger? How can we expect to be a role model or teacher to someone if we don't let them know our imperfections?

Just remember when we act high and mighty, as if we are better than, there is usually someone around who knows the truth. We are at our best and most available to others when we simply are who we are; no more, no less.

Let others know the whole of you.

≪∿

April 7
Unselfish Living

"... grant that I may not so much seek to be consoled as to console; to be understood, as to understand; to be loved, as to love ..."
—Prayer of Saint Francis

It truly is a wonderful experience when we step outside of ourselves and are able to connect with someone else on a new level, one in which we aren't seeking self-gratification, but rather one in which we are open to giving.

When we stop trying so desperately to be accepted we are able to give to others all of the things we have been grasping for in our lives. We often seek someone to nurture us when we need that; someone to understand our shortcomings; and someone to love us. When we learn to do all of those things for ourselves, we are able to give them to others.

The key to the prayer above is to "not so much seek" to get these things, but instead to think first of giving these things to others. We can give the gift of caring to other people; those we know and those we don't. And it can be in very small ways or in great big ways. Each situation calls for different measures.

As the Prayer of Saint Francis continues from above, "...for it is in giving that we receive, it is in pardoning that we are pardoned, and it is in dying that we are born to eternal life."

We, too, will be blessed when we seek to comfort, love, understand, and just be there for others.

≪∿

April 8
Dreams Trump Fear

"There's a moment when fear and dreams must collide."
—Josh Groban

Do you have a goal or dream to do something "more" with your life, but you are afraid that you will not be successful, or that it will have cost too much money or time? But still you think of it all the time and you know in your heart you really must do it.

This is when fear and dreams collide. It's when a decision is made that to not follow the dream is worse than following it and possibly failing. And sometimes even if we fail at the attempt, there are other things learned along the way so it's not in vain.

Not doing something, not using a God given talent, is wrong. We can always find excuses if we look hard enough. In fact, the excuses are often easier to find than the courage to face the fear and move forward with our dreams.

Every now and then we just have to take the plunge and hope that we are making the right decision. If we are following a dream, but we fear failure, and we fear lots of "what ifs" but we move forward anyway, that's how we succeed to our full potential.

If our dreams are to become reality in our lives, they will, but only when we step out of fear and all of the negatives about something and look at the positives and take a chance.

To really do anything difficult or new we are going to have fear, but the dream will propel us into action and will supersede the fear if we allow it.

If you want something bad enough you will succeed in getting it.

∾

April 9
Try a Little Gratitude
"It is impossible to feel grateful and depressed in the same moment."
—Naomi Williams

Gratitude is a most valuable tool when we remember to use it. And usually during the times when we are the most troubled, our darkest hours, we forget about it.

There are days when none of us feel grateful for anything. Those are the days to try some gratitude like the following.

I'm grateful:

• I dated that idiot because now I know what I don't want.

• I lost that job because I hated it anyway, and then I got a better job.

• That life threw me that curve ball because I learned from it.

• For the illness because now I can be empathetic to others who suffer from the same thing.

• That my childhood wasn't perfect because it made me stronger, and

• My husband left me, he was cheating on me and I didn't know what to do.

Those examples are for when we are grateful for things we'd just as soon not had to suffer through. When we feel grateful, when it's easy to have an attitude of gratitude, that's when we can be positive and grateful for all the good things that have happened in our lives, the things that are easy to show gratitude about.

It truly does work, though, the gratitude thing. Whether we mean it when we say or think it, it still works. And it is impossible to be depressed when at the same time you are grateful. Try it. Remember to use this tool on those days when you wake up on the wrong side of the bed or when something truly is wrong in your world. It won't make real problems disappear; it just makes them easier to get through.

Find something each day to be grateful for. If you are alive, that's a good start.

∽6∾

April 10
Not So Random
"Thanks for crossing my path."
—Sarah

Sometimes seemingly random things happen in our lives, but they really aren't so random. Things come into our lives when we need them. People, healing, thoughts, money, whatever it is will come to us.

It may not always seem that way though. Often it doesn't seem that way. But there are times when it happens and it's so unlikely that we know that a power greater than us made it occur. We can't explain it to anyone else usually, and it's in those times that we cannot put the event or action into words that we know it was not a random event.

The important thing is that we are aware enough to know when we get the message. Because that thing we are in need of may come to us in ways we didn't expect. We may feel lonely and want to have a date, but instead a friend comes into our lives and fills that loneliness. We may need a self-esteem boost and not even realize it until someone comes along and gives us a compliment. Maybe we feel as if our life doesn't matter much until someone makes a comment that we are important to them, or that we've touched their lives. Or a person crosses our path, ever so briefly, whose simple presence gives us a spark or connection that we need at that moment.

"Thanks for crossing my path," was written to me by someone whose writing I had read on the Internet. I complimented it and showed her some things I'd written and it touched her enough that she thanked me for crossing her path because she had been having a difficult time and it helped her. We have never met, yet we were both touched by the encounter.

Our lives are intertwined whether or not we realize it. I believe that when we recognize these types of events as coming from a Higher Power our faith grows. Then when darkness comes into our lives we have slivers of light (hope) that shine through the darkness and remind us of events in the past that were not so random.

We never know from where our help will arrive.

∽

April 11
Don't Give Up
"When you get to the end of your rope, tie a knot and hang on."
—Franklin D. Roosevelt

Life can be grueling and disappointing, especially in recovery when it seems there is always something to work on. But things do get better. They will get better. We will have bad days as well as great days as we go through our journey of life.

Some days many of us will admit to having thoughts of giving up on recovery, or even on life. But don't. The next good thing that comes along, the next good day or moment we will see that the struggle was worth it.

Even when we reach a point in life where we know we have learned a lesson — a big lesson sometimes — we still aren't done with the game of life. Our Higher Power will help us through each and every stage if we ask for help.

The lessons keep coming as we grow. Some things are more painful than others, but there is more joy too as we proceed through them.

It takes great strength to keep moving forward in recovery and at anytime when life seems to be too difficult. Sometimes we sit still for a while until we find that strength again. We may even move backwards from time to time, but we will move forward again when the strength is there if we just hang on.

Don't give up there is more joy to come.

∽

April 12
Taking Care of My Side of the Street
"The best years of your life are the ones in which you decide your problems are your own. You do not blame them on your mother, the ecology, or the president. You realize that you control your own destiny." —Albert Ellis

Taking responsibility for our self, our accomplishments as well as our failures, is important for recovery and spiritual growth. We will never grow and evolve when we continue to blame our mistakes or misfortunes on something or someone.

No matter what happened to us in our lives, and truly we do have bad things happen, it is still our responsibility to take care of our self. As long as we use the excuse that "they" made us do something, we give up all of our power to that person or thing.

Excuses keep us locked in our misfortunes, not in our accomplishments and future goals and endeavors. Owning our power to take care of ourselves and our lives gives us strength to move forward. We really can do it. We don't have to lay the blame elsewhere anymore. We are moving forward, but only when we stop giving others our power.

We won't move forward until we know that we are able to, and we won't know we are capable of standing on our own two feet if we continue to attribute events, either good or bad, to others. We can take care of ourselves. We can grow and mature. We will when we start taking responsibility for ourselves and stop waiting on other people to do for us.

Once determined to stand strong there's no turning back.

༄

April 13
Stop Beating Yourself Up
"Who would you see if you saw yourself walking your way?"
—Chester Davidson

How do you see yourself on the inside and out? Are you totally flawed, or just normally flawed. When you make a mistake do you wallow in it for days or weeks, or do you pat yourself off and move on?

We can be our own best friend. It's time to stop beating ourselves up for past mistakes. It's time to see that nobody is perfect and whatever we do that is less than perfect is still okay.

Look past the mistake. As one woman's college basketball player learned anytime she made a mistake it negatively affected her game and caused her not to play her best. She would hang her head and now when she looks down one shoe says "Next" and the other shoe says "Play."

When we make a mistake we cannot afford to get bogged down in that error, rather we should learn from it and move on to our "next play."

Everyone has struggles even though it may seem as though we are alone in ours. We go through our lives wishing that we didn't have to go through this or that and wondering why us. And we think other people handle things better or don't suffer through some of the growing pains we do. But the reality is, we all have issues that we either work on or we don't. If you're reading this you are most likely one of those people who chooses to work on your issues to grow and become all that you were meant to be.

But in doing so, don't be so hard on yourself. Lighten up. You can get so stuck in the mire of mistakes and disappointments and beating yourself up that you forget all about being happy and having fun.

Go easy on you. Treat yourself as you would your best friend if they were having the same issues as you. Hopefully you'd treat them with dignity, respect, and love. Hopefully you'll treat yourself that way.

Next Play.

◈

April 14
It's All in Your Head

"If you are distressed by anything external, the pain is not due to the thing itself, but to your estimate of it; and this you have the power to revoke at any moment." —Marcus Aurelius

As much as we hate to hear the phrase, "It's all in your head," it is true that most things are a matter of perception. The good news is that we can change our stinking thinking.

How we look at our situations, problems, and shortcomings, determines our level of happiness and serenity. We have spent a lifetime learning how our parents or other people dealt with external situations, often without realizing that their solutions were not always the best, we just never thought to look at different options.

Gratitude is a great way to move out of the ruts we get in as well as moving out of anger, sadness, depression, and other issues. Gratitude changes our state of mind; it can change our mood.

Smiling and laughing can give us a new perspective just by the emotional lift they bring. Prayer, letting go, can move us into a different place.

We can write out our issues in lots of different ways. We can journal, make lists of positives and negatives of certain situations, or write letters to others that we may or may not intend to send.

A great way to see things in a different light is to talk about it with someone else. Time and time again I am amazed at how two people can have totally different takes on the same event or situation. We may not agree with the other person, but nonetheless it is always good to talk things out with someone else.

Sometimes just walking away from something for a while and returning later will stop us from obsessing about it or trying to make something work when it's not. And often the solution comes to mind while we aren't trying to find it.

It may be all in your head, but you have the power to control what you think.

⇛

April 15
Dealing with Difficult People
"Throughout life people will make you mad, disrespect you and treat you bad. Let God deal with the things they do, cause hate in your heart will consume you too." —Will Smith

We all have experienced dealing with those who are difficult to be in contact with no matter what the situation. They are the non-communicators, the people who are usually less than honest when honesty would be easier. They are closed minded and stubborn. They are unable to make eye contact or listen without trying to cut us off. And no matter what we do, they don't change.

How we deal with them depends upon our relationship to them. It differs if it's a working relationship as opposed to a member of our family. Or if it's someone we do business with as opposed to a friend.

We always have the option of walking away, although in work and business relationships we may not be able to make a move as swiftly as we could if the person was a friend or someone we encounter who doesn't have power over us because they are our boss or business associate.

If it's a family member it can be even more difficult because walking away may not be a viable option, although we never have to stand for abuse.

Boundaries help. We can set boundaries in each situation and when those are crossed we step away. We can continue to be honest and communicative even when these people aren't and hope that some of what we say gets through to them even when it seems they don't listen. We can make a decision to move on if it's someone in work or business who we just can't seem to make progress with and it is affecting us too much.

One thing we must keep in mind though is that we cannot change these people so we might as well remember step one of the Twelve Steps as it's applied to recovery groups other than AA, "We admitted we were powerless over people, places and things," and just maintain our sanity in whatever way is best for each situation.

Let go and let God deal with the things they do ...

❧

April 16
We Recover Over Time

"Behold the turtle. He makes progress only when he sticks his neck out." —James Bryant Conant

Often we think of turtles as the slow ones, the ones the hares beat in races as we have seen over and over in cartoons. But slow isn't bad. Recovery takes time and during our recovery we recognize that over the months or even years we change gradually. We can't just decide to change and have it happen immediately. And we have to move out of our protective shells from time to time to proceed too.

So many times we become impatient when we work on particular issues. And then we suddenly realize that what we were trying to change, our growth, has occurred. It's a process in which time is involved. Most likely the turtle approach is best in almost every instance of growth and recovery. It's not a jackrabbit paced thing.

We did not get into our addictions overnight and we don't recover from them that quickly either. Our issues, most of them carried over from childhood, were forged in us over many months and years; these too take time to heal from.

Most of life's lessons are learned through a daily effort of turning our lives over to our Higher Power while taking the actions we need to grow. Very rarely do we get answers immediately. It is often that during the process of getting the answer that we learn other things as well.

Change and growth too aren't always in straight line movements. We move forward and backward on the path. But eventually, like the turtle, we do get there.

Slow and steady wins the race.

❧

April 17
Spiritual Experiences

"Sincerely touching the soul of someone else can tap the well of happiness within each of us." —Anonymous

When the moment occurs that you realize you have touched another person's soul with words or actions, it brings a remarkable sense of oneness with God. When what you do or did affects another person deeply and you are able to witness it, even briefly, you will know that you know that you know there is some power in this universe that is in control and it is not you.

When we exercise our gifts and talents we will find God there because others will reflect our work back to us and we will "see" the face of God. For some this need only happen once, and for others, we don't "get it" until we have had this experience many times. It is something so deep that it is impossible to put into words. The translation from heart to words loses the depth and awe of the experience with God.

When what we do is remarkable, when we know that we didn't do it on our own, that is another way that we know a higher power was there, is there. And we will never understand what a spiritual awakening is until we have one for ourselves.

Most of the time our experiences aren't the burning bush type described in the Bible; not literally anyway. To us they are as significant and so real that we cannot deny them. But to understand what one is, it has to be experienced, and no describing by another will bring us to fully understand.

If you have not had a spiritual awakening, stay open and keep working on your spirituality in whatever way you do that and it will happen … in God's time, of course.

You will know that you know.

∽

April 18
Obstacles Teach Us

"I have learned that success is to be measured not so much by the position that one has reached in life as by the obstacles which he has overcome while trying to succeed."
—Booker T. Washington

Never in life are the easy things appreciated like those we have achieved by continued perseverance, tenacity, and failure. Yes, failure. A lot of what we learn comes through failure and trying again, sometimes over and over.

How we react to things is often a lesson in itself. If we learn patience because we have to wait or because we keep trying and failing then the patience we learned is a success.

Any obstacle in the path of whatever goal we are trying to achieve that we are able to handle successfully, is a lesson learned. Often it is along our journey that we discover small, yet significant pebbles of wisdom that we might not have found had we not been on that particular path.

We can know that whatever our goal is there will most likely be obstacles that we must overcome or endure in order to get the final prize. And usually when we get that prize, it's not the end of our journey anyway so we need the wisdom gained along the way.

Our journey continues our whole life. What we learn along the way helps us with every step of that path. That's success. We still strive for goals; there's nothing wrong with that, but we realize that our position in life is not all that important.

Smooth and steady paths teach you nothing.

∽

April 19
Understanding Love

"You will find as you look back upon your life that the moments when you have truly lived are the moments when you have done things in the spirit of love."

—Henry Drummond

Love is described in many different ways. It's not easily understood by some of us. Those who have codependent issues may have a distorted view of love. People who were abused or neglected as children may not understand what healthy love is.

We can start with where we are with love of others both in giving and receiving. If it feels right it probably is love. Otherwise it is most likely not a healthy way of being. Love is not smothering, nor demanding. The Bible says love is patient and kind, and that God is love.

The first step in learning about love is learning to love our self. We simply cannot love anyone else if we don't love who we are first. It's not selfish or silly, it's vital to loving others. We can only be open and honest with others when we can love our self.

When we give of ourselves in unselfish, healthy ways without any expectations, it is love. When things are done in the spirit of love, we will know that we truly are loving others. It's not easy to explain, but it's easy to feel when we are in it.

We can all give and receive love no matter where we've been.

∽

April 20
Manipulation Not the Best Way
"If you're sincere, praise is effective. If you're insincere, it's manipulative." —Zig Ziglar

Manipulation, not saying what you truly mean, is a subtle form of control. Many times we say what we think the other person wants to hear or what we think they need to hear, in order to effect some change in that person that we want, or for a reaction that we seek from that person.

If we give a compliment by saying, "You are so pretty," only because we really want the person to respond with a similar statement about us, it's manipulative.

One thing that we need keep in mind is that anytime we aren't speaking from the heart about such matters, we have ulterior motives. If we truly believe someone is pretty and we tell them, there's no issue in that, but if we do it seeking any kind of response or change in their behavior we are using manipulation.

In relationships sometimes we may be manipulative because we hide part of who we are thinking the other person won't like that side of us. It doesn't mean that we don't watch ourselves and ensure that we don't act out on some of our insecurities; it means we don't try to change the course of the relationship or universe with less than honest means.

It's manipulation to be anything other than who and what we are when we are trying to build real relationships. Eventually the other person sees the real us anyway.

Directness is the best way to get what we want, mostly because it works more quickly than manipulation, and too, because it's honest and that is the right way to handle things.

Try the truth over manipulation and see what happens.

April 21
Communication is a Two Way Street
"Good communication does not mean that you have to speak in perfectly formed sentences and paragraphs. It isn't about slickness. Simple and clear go a long way."
—John Kotter

Communication is one of the most important things we have when it comes to our relationships with other people. And it's one of the most difficult. No matter how well both parties do it, there are still times when we just don't get the other person.

Then there are people who have no communication skills at all. Communication with someone who is not able to communicate effectively is difficult at best, especially if this person is a boss or someone who you have little choice about walking away from.

All of us have experienced people who won't make eye contact, won't talk to us, and yet expect us to have a working relationship. Sometimes we encounter these situations outside of work and they are easier to get away from, but what do we do when we are stuck in a situation where we need to communicate, but the other person is not capable?

There is no simple answer. However one thing we have to do is stay true to who we are. Anytime we compromise that we are not at optimal capacity for anything. We must continue to say what we mean and mean what we say even when the other person does not. It's frustrating, but giving in to poor communication just opens up more problems down the road.

Be honest when you speak and hear when you listen.

❧

April 22
Solitude Can Be Golden
"Loneliness expresses the pain of being alone and solitude expresses the glory of being alone."
—Paul Tillich

Once we grow into a place where we love who we are and know that we can be alone, we find that more and more we seek that solitude. Of course, it's impossible to enjoy solitude if we are lonely, but being alone and loneliness are not the same things.

When we love ourselves we love the time we can be alone. If we are not comfortable in our own skin it is highly unlikely we will enjoy being alone. And it's probable that others won't find being around us too much fun either.

Loneliness occurs both when we are alone and in a crowd. There really is not a more lonely place than to be in the midst of people and to feel totally isolated. It really boils down to self love.

Once we get to know who we are and what we enjoy, void of any people pleasing behaviors, and able to spend time alone, we begin to long for solitude. It offers us so many opportunities that we cannot have in the presence of others. We grow spiritually and emotionally both with others around and alone, but we grow in different ways with each.

We can see that we have grown when we can be alone and not be lonely. We find too that when we discover this, we find the solitude golden.

Grow into healthy solitude and discover something wonderful.

April 23
People Pleasing

"I don't know the key to success, but the key to failure is trying to please everybody." —Bill Cosby

None of us will ever successfully please everybody. In fact, we may not please anybody most of the time. We all have our own agendas, responsibilities, and issues. Since we cannot read minds, we can never know exactly what someone else expects from us so therefore we're going on our own ideas anyway.

We might as well be true to who we are and do what we know is the best and right thing for us and hope that we at least please ourselves. If we succeed in honestly doing the right things in our hearts and minds, most likely others will be pleased too.

Where the problem lies is trying to please people when they have conflicting ideas about what we need to do. Or they have different values from one another so that if we're involved with both, it's impossible to please them. Even taking the middle ground will not please either of the two.

Not trying to people please may seem lonely sometimes because we may end up not spending as much time with folks who want us to do for them. But we can use that time to learn what pleases us about ourselves and what we want out of life.

When our hearts are in the right place we will please others.

April 24
Reactions Come from Past Experiences

"Most of your reactions are echoes from the past. You do not really live in the present." —Gaelic Proverb

Everything we go through in life is a lesson whether we realize it at the time or not. How we respond today is built on many yesterdays. We need to keep that in mind when we react to something someone else does and wonder why it affects us so much.

It is often something in our past or even childhood that brings up a response as adults. It can be amusing to figure out why when a person does something we are bothered by it. I can attribute some of my strange reactions to my family of origin, and other things to events and relationships that occurred after I moved out of my family home. A lot of my reactions I have yet to figure out.

What's important is to recognize when we are overly affected by something another person does that really has no impact on what we do. If someone eats too fast and we start to worry they will take our food, that's most likely an unreasonable reaction and we might want to think about it, find its origin and maybe the next time we won't be affected so much.

Sometimes other people don't talk the way we think they should, or wear the clothes we would wear, or some other outward thing. It's really not our concern what other people do, but a lot of our reaction is tied to something that has happened to us. Most likely we'll continue to be bothered by these behaviors until we find the root of why they bother us.

Today's responses are built on many yesterdays.

ക

April 25
Don't Lose Who You Are
"Now I think everyone should ask, 'Am I going to be able to be the person I want to be in this relationship?'"
—Ali MacGraw

Any time we enter into a relationship with another person, especially one with the potential to be a life partner, we compromise. What we want to be aware of is if we are compromising who we are and what we want in order to please the other person.

Compromising on which restaurant to go to, whether to stay in or go out, which movie to go to, or what to watch on television is not major stuff. But losing ourselves in the relationship by going against what we are to be with the other person is not healthy for us, them or the relationship.

It's not often easy to set boundaries early in a relationship when we want to spend lots of time with the other person. We want to please them, but those of us in recovery also are intent on being who we are now and we don't compromise that for anyone.

If someone comes into our life we can know that our Higher Power has a purpose for us meeting, but the reason may not be what we think it is. We can't put any parameters on that and think just because certain things may occur that we know the reason for that crossing of paths at the moment.

God, with time, will show us what that person's place in our life is. It may very well be what we expected or it can be the opposite. We can only stay true to who we are and let the rest happen.

Staying true to you is one of the most important things in a relationship.

∽

April 26
Hope Carries Us Through
"Hope is the thing with feathers that perches in the soul and sings the tune without the words and never stops at all."
—Emily Dickenson

When we get down on life, love, or happiness, having a little hope will always help us look forward to what's to come next in our life. We don't have to live in the future and out of the moment to have hope. Hope is intangible. It's built on knowing that our Higher Power is there for us and will carry us through when we don't always feel like going on. Hope is faith.

We only need to look back on our lives to yesterday, last week, last year, or maybe a few years ago to a time when we may have lost hope and something happened, something unexpected and good, and we once again were on our feet. We didn't have hope, but we learned that things can change in an instant. God can change things for the better; sometimes when we least expect it. Therein lies hope.

Hoping in times when you may have anything but hope will carry you through.

∽

April 27
Living in the Moment Brings Serenity
"Yesterday is gone; tomorrow is but a dream. Only today is truly ours for the taking." —Anonymous

Ah, living in the moment. It has to be one of the more difficult things to do. With our busy lives and burning the candle at both ends, we really do need to plan ahead a lot of the time to keep up with obligations.

If we can ever get to a place where we are able to slow down, we can get out of the tailspin and begin to live a more serene life; one where we live in the moment. It does take an effort to do, but we reap the rewards when we are successful.

As with many things we learn in recovery, it is progress not perfection that will take us to what we want and need. Living in the moment in a healthy way is something most of us have to learn because we may not have lived that way since we were children. We may even need to think about a child and watch a child live in the moment to see how it is done.

The innocence of children who are in healthy families allows them to not worry about things in the past or future. Some of us may have skipped that by living in dysfunctional families where we did worry about what would happen next and plan how we would handle that. We probably also lived for the moment when we were grown and out of the house only to find that was not a solution just the next phase of our life and growth.

We ought to try our best to live in the moment and not worry about what we did yesterday or how we will handle tomorrow. There is serenity in that place.

Live in the moment; it's where real living is.

≪

April 28
Time to Get Centered

"A mind at peace, a mind centered and not focused on harming others, is stronger than any physical force in the universe."
—Wayne Dyer

When we feel out of sorts with life and those around us, it usually means we have been spending too much time running in the circles of modern life and it's time to get centered.

Being centered means we know who we are and what we want. It is an inner peace that we have and we know it when we are there. We can return to that place when we do what we know works for us.

Some of us get it in prayer and meditation. Others find it during a long run or walk. Perhaps it can be found in recovery meetings or church services. Sitting on a mountaintop or hiking through the woods may be a good place to return to our center.

However we get there, we must remember to do it for it is what keeps us healthy and whole on an emotional and spiritual level. Additionally, poor emotional and spiritual health affects our physical health.

We cannot give what we do not have so working from a scattered place will produce scattered results. When we get out of balance and off center we also become unfocused and expend a lot of energy uselessly since what we send out's direction is uncertain. It's in this place that those who are clean and sober relapse, people with anger issues lash out, or those who overspend blow money, to give a few examples.

We tend to spiral more and more from center until we crash in some way. If we can catch ourselves before the crash, we have the quickest success at getting centered again. It's never too late to stop and get centered before hurting ourselves or others.

Being centered is necessary for healthy living.

∽

April 29
True Validation Lies Within

"People spend a lifetime searching for happiness; looking for peace.
They chase idle dreams, addictions, religions, even other people,
hoping to fill the emptiness that plagues them. The irony is the only
place they ever needed to search was within."
—Ramona L. Anderson

Those of us who suffer from self-esteem issues often seek validation outside of themselves. But there is a solution to that: we can validate ourselves without waiting on others to do it for us.

What we do is monitor our self talk. We treat ourselves as we treat those we love, with kindness, respect, dignity, compassion, and honesty. When we begin to have a consciousness about how we treat ourselves we begin to see where we may be failing. It takes practice to break old habits, and being unkind to our own self is a bad habit that will most likely take a lot of practice, trial and error, to overcome.

We accept the things about us that we cannot change and we change the things we can. But no matter where we are we can love all of us as we do those in our lives who we love. We begin to believe that we deserve the best life and love has to offer and we start to live in that mindset until it becomes reality.

We find that we validate ourselves and seek less and less support from those outside of us. We are stronger and more loving when we love who and what we are.

Try showing love to yourself as you show it to those you love deeply.

∽

April 30
Surrender

"We must determine whether we really want freedom — whether we are willing to dare the perils of rebirth. For we never take a step forward without surrendering something that we may have held dear, without dying to that which has been."

—Virginia Hanson

Surrender is a common term in any Twelve Step program. It is giving up our control or lack of control actually, over some person, place or thing that causes us problems. We give it over, surrender it, to our Higher Power.

Many times we are able to see and feel relief soon after we let go of our strong grasp on something and allow God to have it. We let go of false beliefs. We let go of control. We surrender.

Sometimes holding on to something so tight makes it like those toys that squeeze right out of your hand if you get a firm grip on them, but if you just hold them gently they remain still in your hand. When we are anxious and keep a firm grip on something we really squeeze the life out of it. If we are meant to have something we will have it, otherwise surrendering it will allow it to be what it's intended to be.

If we've tried and tried to make something work it may be time to surrender our powerlessness of that person, place, or thing and do as step three of the Twelve Steps tells us to do: "Made a decision to turn our will and our lives over to the care of God as we understand Him."

Surrender can actually get you what you want.

⤖

May 1
Protect Yourself from Harmful People

"Beware of false prophets, which come to you in sheep's clothing, but inwardly they are ravening wolves. Ye shall know them by their fruits." —Jesus

There are people in this world, including those in recovery, who claim to know what's best for us because they have "the answer" or some sort of formula or insight that nobody else has or at least that nobody has given to us yet.

Beware of these people. Oftentimes they are only seeking to make a buck or to stroke their own egos. Many, many times it's happened with big churches where the pastor constantly asked for money and claims to have "heard the voice of God" that one should do such and such. Time tells all because these same preachers were found to be having illicit affairs, stealing money, hiring prostitutes, and other various "sins" that they preached against.

There are those in the fitness world who will tell you what is best for you and then go home and smoke a pack of cigarettes and drink a twelve pack of beer every night. In addition there are some therapists who are sicker than the people they seek to help.

We can get input from others and we do need that. It's certainly an important part of Twelve Step programs for those who attend meetings, but we need to be careful about who we listen to and how much we take from that.

If it feels wrong in your gut, heart, mind or in any way, it's probably not right for you. If red flags fly when you are given advice from someone, seek advice elsewhere. If someone is trying to critique your every move see how they live and how much work they need to do on their own self before you trust them as your guru.

People can help, but they can harm too.

∽

May 2
Sabotaging Relationships
"Trouble is part of your life, and if you don't share it, you don't give the person who loves you enough chance to love you enough."
—Dinah Shore

Some of us have issues in our past that may cause us to unconsciously sabotage relationships. We may be afraid on some level to enter into new relationships and that fear can manifest in different ways. We might not even realize that's what it is, but when we overly find fault with others and things start to change drastically in how we feel about another person, with no apparent reason, we need to look at what is happening.

If we grew up in a dysfunctional family, we most likely have carried many issues into our adult lives. Our issues are carried over into any relationship we have no matter how intimate or casual. Some of our behaviors, many we learned as survival techniques, simply aren't healthy in adult relationships.

In order to have healthy, fulfilling relationships we may need to look at our "failed" relationships and see what part we played in each of the endings. We can do this in different ways by talking or writing about the issues we had with the other person. We may discover that we are doing things that we aren't even aware of. It takes some time and effort, but an inventory of ourselves is always a good thing, as long as we see positive and negative and not just the negative.

It's important to learn as much as we can about who we are and how we operate if we want to have intimate, lasting relationships with others. Being open to feedback from others is a good thing too.

Look within to find answers to relationship problems.

May 3
Repeating Messages
"Life will teach you the lessons it is up to you to learn them."
—Unknown

When we keep getting the same message from different sources that's a clear sign that our Higher Power is trying to tell us something, especially when that message comes from the places where we least expect it.

If the message to love keeps being offered up to you, love more. If forgiveness is what you are hearing, time to forgive. If you see the message to work on your spirituality, do that. Sometimes God has to keep telling us to do something. The message may start out small and from one source until we keep ignoring it and it ends up like a drumbeat in our head we hear it so much. We hear it from people, we see it in the books we read, we get the message in church or at a recovery meeting.

It takes what it takes for each of us to move into a new area of growth, or to work on something we haven't spent much time on, or to return to the same old "thorn in our side" issue once again.

We most likely will still be sent the "problems" and messages to work on the areas we need to work on until we do something about them. Life, God, the Universe, whoever is your higher power will move you to action.

Listen to the messages and heal.

❧

May 4
Boost Your Self-Esteem
"Fake it 'Til You Make It."
—Unknown

Any time we are trying to do something new and on occasion bold, it calls for confidence. We can gain some confidence by believing in ourselves and even by "faking" our confidence if necessary.

Many talk about how important it is to believe in ourselves. In the midst of great struggle or growth it is necessary to believe we can do it. We may have to pretend we are confident which can increase our confidence. If we don't believe we can do something we can't do it, so believing we can will give us an added edge.

We don't fake having money in the bank and write a hot check on it. We don't fake doing our work at our job. It's not that kind of faking it that the slogan suggests. What we fake is more of an inward talking to ourselves.

It's saying to self: "I'm good enough. I'm smart enough. I'm handsome enough." One woman told me about pretending to herself she's a movie star when she lacks confidence. It's okay to have good self talk.

Whatever healthy behavior it takes to move us forward with confidence is a good thing.

∽

May 5
Do What You Love
"You can only become truly accomplished at something you love. Don't make money your goal. Instead, pursue the things you love doing, and then do them so well that people can't take their eyes off you."
—Maya Angelou

It may not be a viable option to drop whatever job or career we have at the moment to suddenly pursue what we love as our main income source, however we can pursue what we love doing anyway.

We may start out taking a few classes to get a new degree or a first degree. We may learn to play an instrument with no intention of starting a musical career, but simply because it's something we love and want to do. Perhaps we truly love to work with children; we can find a place to do that.

Life is full of opportunities. Working at a job we are not happy with will drag us down in every area of our lives. Finding something fulfilling to do with the other hours of the day may help until we can leave a particular job and enter into a career we love. Or maybe we'll have so much fun outside of work that we start enjoying our job more.

If you do what you love and love what you do you will find a lot of joy. Whether a thing pays a lot of money or a little money, or none at all, it is worth doing if we find it fulfilling. If we are fortunate enough we will be able to earn a paycheck doing what we love, but we won't get there if we don't do it.

Love what you do and the rewards are plenty.

∽

May 6
Growth Opportunities
"To exist is to change, to change is to mature, to mature is to go on creating oneself endlessly."

—Henri Bergson

Those of us who are living our lives from the inside out, trying to grow, to be all that we can be, continually work at it. And then even with all of that occasionally life will present us with growth opportunities that we didn't expect.

We are asked to step out of our comfort zones to do something that we probably would not choose to do out of fear or lack of self-esteem at least. But if we take on the challenge and get the thing done successfully, perhaps even with great success, we can see that we did it and we will carry that level of growth from there forward.

It's easier to say "no" sometimes and not do a thing, but when we are sincerely working on ourselves and living life to its fullest, those opportunities come for a reason and we usually feel that turning them down isn't a good option because we wonder if we would miss the growth opportunity and never get the chance again.

Usually when presented with these opportunities we can look back and see that they are answers to prayer. We probably didn't specifically pray for a certain event, but maybe we prayed for our job situation to improve and we're given a work assignment that is out of our comfort zone. Then we do such a great job with it that not only is our self-esteem increased, but our coworkers and bosses look at us with new respect too.

We often don't know what is going to happen, but God does answer our prayers in ways that we couldn't have planned or expected.

Accept the chance to grow and you will reap the rewards.

May 7
Forgiveness Gives Us Peace
"Resentment is like taking poison and waiting for the other person to die."
—Malachy McCourt

If someone has hurt and/or angered us and we are ruminating in it, there is only one option to free us from it. That one thing is called forgiveness and it is not easy.

Forgiveness doesn't mean we forget the sometimes terrible things others did to us. It doesn't mean what was done to us is okay either. What forgiveness means is that we let go of it, we understand that others are human, and that holding on to it only hurts us. We allow others to be less than perfect and we move on from and heal from the issue that we are forgiving them for.

As long as we hold on to the anger we have for the other person, for the wrong done to us, we are holding ourselves back. We are unable to heal. We cannot have peace. And many times it will keep our addictions active.

And just because we forgive someone, it doesn't mean they have to be our best friend. It is more for us than them. Sometimes those who wronged us haven't even asked for our forgiveness anyway. They don't have to be told we forgive them. Our energy may tell them, or they may never know. It isn't about them as much as it is about us and our well-being.

Forgiveness simply allows us freedom and a chance to love more than we do when we hold onto our resentments. As long as we hold onto resentments, we are poisoning ourselves and wallowing in our anger and perhaps self-pity.

Forgiveness opens the door to freedom.

May 8
Stop and Think First
"In the midst of great joy do not promise to give a man anything; in the midst of great anger do not answer a man's letter."
—Chinese Proverb

It is so easy when anger is present to spout off and say things that we may not mean and certainly don't want to vocalize if we do mean them. In those times when our temper flares and we are not able to be as calm as we would like it is always in our best interest to not say what we know we will regret once the words are out of our mouth.

It's much easier said than done, but any time we can stop in our tracks when angered it will give us time to cool off and get ourselves in a place where we won't say the wrong thing, or say something the wrong way.

In this gadget filled age that we live in, we sometimes have too many ways to communicate and some of those ways aren't really the best. E-mails and text messages are two things that can be too convenient to spout off on, and to be misunderstood to boot. How many times have we had a disagreement because the tone was not properly read by the other person because it's so difficult to read tone?

Likewise promising the moon when we really can't give it is not a good thing to do. We may get caught up in a moment sometimes where we say we will do something before thinking it through because it we may really want to do it. However, we may have just been caught up in the moment or maybe we are just flattered to be asked and say we will do the thing out of that moment of joy. Stopping to think before saying yes can keep us from getting into something we will regret later.

Sometimes we just need to stop and think before we speak.

∽

May 9
Self-care is a Must

"I define comfort as self-acceptance. When we finally learn that self-care begins and ends with ourselves, we no longer demand sustenance and happiness from others." —Jennifer Louden

Taking care of ourselves is the key to many things in our lives. Physically taking care of ourselves can lead to better mental health and improve our spirituality.

We may not realize the importance of the simple things about truly caring for ourselves. Think of caring for a baby or child and all of the ways we care for them. We feed them when it's time to eat and give them milk, juice or water when it's time for that. Would a good caregiver ever withhold these necessities from a child? We should not keep the basics from ourselves either.

We have to care for ourselves before we can help others. And self-care may mean we have to pull away from others for a while to rejuvenate ourselves if we haven't been caring for us along the way.

We need sleep. We need rest and down time to relax. We need to eat when it's time. We may need to take a break from our routine sometimes and take a nap rather than going to the gym to workout. Maybe we need to go to the gym instead of taking a nap; too much of one and not enough of the other are both mistaken ways of living life.

Or we might need to learn how to say "no." We don't have to do everything we are asked to do. It's okay, absolutely okay, to say no if we don't want to do something. Someone else can do it or it won't get done. Too many times we fall into the "must do" mode when involved in charity or church work.

It's about balance. Sometimes it may feel selfish, but it's important to be able to care for ourselves in healthy ways. It helps us to be independent, healthy, happy, and whole.

Taking care of you keeps you from falling apart.

∽

May 10
It Really is Okay to Say No

"Saying no can be the ultimate self-care."
—Claudia Black

Many of us who have spent our lives trying to please others may find saying "no" a difficult thing. We may say it when we don't feel like going out, or we may pass on yet another volunteer opportunity, or maybe we just don't want one more assignment at work.

Sometimes we say no because we just have too much on our plate, even when we really would like to spend the day doing something fun or giving in some way. Sometimes we just need to fill back up before we can give anything because we've given until there's nothing left.

We may even say no just to see if we can. People will pressure and guilt us into things very often that for some reason they need us to do even if it really doesn't do anything for them. It doesn't mean that we don't love someone when we say no to them. It just means that we love ourselves enough to do what we need to take care of ourselves in that moment.

Falling into saying yes when we want to say no can be a codependent behavior. It's definitely a people-pleasing behavior. Many times when we first begin to use the no word with those used to us saying "yes" we cringe awaiting their reaction. Often we don't get much of a reaction and they just move on to someone else. Or they say something like, "Well, it's your loss if you don't do ___." Maybe it is our loss. Maybe we did miss an opportunity for something. It's still okay that we said no.

Sometimes it is ourselves we have to say no to. And we are gentle with ourselves along the way. We may need to be patient and kind to those we say no to if they react in a negative way. We do what we need to do to take care of ourselves.

Saying yes when you mean no can become an unhealthy habit.

✑

May 11
It's All in the Follow Through
"It was character that got us out of bed, commitment that moved us into action, and discipline that enabled us to follow through."
—Zig Ziglar

In many sports, including golf, tennis, and basketball, the follow-through of the swing, serve or shot is taught as part of the move and just as important as any other part. As with sports, the follow through on what we say we will do is just as important as the idea.

Making a decision to do something and actually doing it are worlds apart. Starting and not finishing and never starting are both problems. And if we tell someone we will do something, it's important that we do it, lest they lose confidence in our word.

If we say we'll do something once and we can't "follow through," but we usually do, then it's forgivable, but if it keeps happening over and over people will soon just never make plans with us or expect much from us.

Understandably we start things that we don't finish. Sometimes things are just not meant for us to do, but to rarely follow through will get us nowhere quick. It's progress not perfection just like everything else we do, especially if we've made it a habit to promise more than we can give.

No follow through will cause you to miss your shot.

∽

May 12
Allowing Ourselves to be Human
"In order to go on living one must try to escape the death involved in perfectionism." —Hannah Arendt

Allowing ourselves to be human lightens us and allows us to do the same for others. We seek perfection, but we aren't so blind as to think we actually ever get there. We need to remember that we won't ever reach perfection and neither will anyone else. This keeps us humble and able to relax.

Some of us get so worked up in trying to do everything and be everything, that we expect that from others and lose our inner peace. By freeing ourselves and others of the mode of perfectionism, we learn to love ourselves and others, and others are able to love us. It is in our imperfection that we are able to embrace one another. When we truly understand that striving to be our best is good enough, we understand that expecting perfection just causes us trouble within ourselves and how we interact and view others.

Letting go of perfectionism allows us to not only love others, but to forgive them when we feel they have wronged us. If we don't allow others to be human we won't have many people in our lives.

Set yourself and others free by getting rid of perfectionism thinking.

∽

May 13
Love is Our Purpose
"For one human being to love another; that is perhaps the most difficult of all our tasks, the ultimate, the last test and proof, the work for which all other work is but preparation."
—Rainer Maria Rilke

Loving others seems like an easy task, but it isn't always easy. It's not difficult to love some people, especially those who love us and are kind and gentle with us. But how about loving those who are not nice, who don't treat us well?

We begin with self-love. If we love our self we can love others and we allow others to love us. Many of us have struggled with self-love and thus love of others our whole lives. There are reasons we are in recovery for the various issues you read about here. Addictions, low self-esteem, codependency, adult child issues, and many more which can all be benefited by learning to love ourselves and others.

Those who are Christians will know that the one message from Jesus was to love others.

Loving those we see as unlovable is a difficult task. We can begin by praying for them. And as we learn to love ourselves it becomes easier to see good in those around us, even the dirty beggar on the street is loved by Jesus. And whether or not a person believes in the Bible or Jesus, many lessons can be learned by his teachings.

We are all fallible. Many of us in recovery have hit bottom so we know that no matter where we are in life, we really are no better than those we look down upon who aren't living life as well as we are. We also know that we could be in that spot too. And most likely we had someone love us while we were down and out to help us along our journey to today.

Love for those we don't wish to love holds many rewards.

May 14
Be Yourself
"Always be a first-rate version of yourself, instead of a second-rate version of somebody else." —Judy Garland

There's never anything wrong with being exactly who we are, even if we have problems and issues that we would rather the world not know about. What we ought to do is be honest about who we are with those we are close to.

If we are in pain and need the support of friends or family, telling them we are "fine" when they ask will be dishonest and will not get us the help we need. Every person in this world experiences up and down times. And everybody needs support from time to time. If we have friends we can turn to them. Or perhaps there's a family member who we feel will listen without judgment. If we don't have either of these we can seek help from a therapist, group or member of the clergy.

Pretending to be "fine" when we really aren't is pretending to be someone other than who we are. This does not mean we have to go around and tell every person we encounter how miserable we may be or trust every person with issues about ourselves that the world doesn't need to know, what it means is that we have people we trust and we are honest with them.

None of us can be everything to everybody, but we can be who we are. Pretending to be other than that will keep us from truly sharing our lives with others. Not being who we are and trying to be what we think others want us to be will cause our self-esteem to suffer too.

Be honest about both the good and bad in your life.

May 15
Live and Let Live
"To live and let live, without clamor for distinction or recognition; to wait on divine love; to write truth first on the tablet of one's own heart — this is the sanity and perfection of living."
—Mary Baker Eddy

To live and let live is one of the most freeing things we can do. It's letting go of our attempts to control others and our judgment of how other people live their lives.

Life becomes easier when we grow into this way of living. Thoughts may pop up from time to time about another person when we wonder why they are doing something a certain way or not doing it the way we would. We can just think to ourselves, "It's not my deal," and go on about our business.

For those who have never had control issues surrounding other people, this concept may seem foreign. And it will probably seem foreign to those who have not had this awakening. But once we have it, we know that it is the way to be. And if we haven't we can strive to get it.

We know we cannot control what other people do. We cannot control our children, coworkers, siblings, parents, friends, or neighbors. When we really grasp this concept and set forth to live, really live our own lives and let them live theirs, we will find a peace that we have not had before.

When we learn to live this way we have more peace and we are better able to love others without trying to fix them to fit what we think they need to be and do.

When we let others live we free them and ourselves.

May 16
It's Not Time That Heals
"They say that time changes things, but you actually have to change them yourself." —Andy Warhol

It's often said that time heals all and answers come with time. But it's not just the passing of time that gives us the answers and healing; it's what we do during that time that brings us what we need.

When we need healing we do the things that we know to do to get that whether it's spiritual or physical healing that's needed. If we want the answer to something we must ask the question and wait, but while we wait we take action.

For spiritual healing we pray, meditate, go to a meeting or church, forgive, let go, whatever it is we need to do. For physical healing we take our medicine, visit a doctor, pray, meditate, rest, whatever is needed for our particular ailment.

It's true that it takes time to heal, but time is not the healer. The healer is the action taken and the answers to prayers. We change, grow and heal over time when we do the things necessary to nurture our bodies, spirits, and minds.

Healing comes with time if you do the work.

May 17
We Never Know Who's Watching
"Don't worry that children never listen to you; worry that they are always watching you." —Robert Fulghum

The way we live our lives shows the truth about who we are whether we claim to be something different or not. And don't be fooled into thinking that only children are watching — others are watching too.

Very often we are unaware of who is watching us; perhaps looking up to us, or maybe even judging us. Sometimes we find out that someone has been watching us, admiring us, and it may be a person we would never expect to be aware of us.

When that happens it makes us pause and quickly rewind the tapes of our lives hoping to determine if we did anything untoward that the person may have witnessed and wondering why they look up to us.

It's a self-esteem boost to know that others watch us, but we should never feel conceit about it. We all have people we look up to and hopefully those we can turn to when we need advice on a situation that we haven't experienced, but they have.

Use the knowledge that others are watching as a way to help keep actions in check. We live our lives, many of us, by both leading and following; we often just don't realize it.

Stop and think of those you watch and times you have found out that someone had been admiring you from afar.

You lead by example even when you don't realize it.

❦

May 18
Feelings on the Job

"If you have a job without any aggravations, you don't have a job."
—Malcolm S. Forbes

Things that occur at work are very much a part of our lives so it is essential that we take care of our feelings surrounding events there, just as we would the ones that happen at home.

Work relationships are different than those we encounter at home because there are different boundaries. At work we have designated roles that we are supposed to be in. And just because someone is the boss that does not mean they know what they are doing or that they are always right. On the flip side of that there are often those who try to be in charge who do not have the authority to do so.

Work places usually contain all of the unhealthy behaviors, including: lying, cheating, gossip, and backstabbing, etc. It's difficult when someone does us wrong at work and we can't do anything about it, or the only option is to go to the person's superior. However, the problem may lie with the superior and there's not even that option.

What we have to do on the days when we get overwhelmed is to walk away and let go. When our day is over we leave and try to detach from the situation at work. We care for our work feelings just as we do those we experience at home.

We also take care of ourselves at work. If we are not being treated fairly, we can speak up through the appropriate channels. We work through our issues on the job just as we do those at home.

What we don't want to do is ignore things at work as if they aren't part of our lives. We spend a great deal of time at work with other people, more time usually than we do our significant other, children, and friends. Just as with all other issues in our lives, not taking care of ourselves at work can turn into a larger problem, such as drinking excessively or some other addiction.

Taking care of yourself on the job is as important as any other time.

❦

May 19
When You Give Love

"When we are feeling unloved and depressed and empty inside, finding someone to give us love is not really the solution."
—Gerald G. Jampolsky, M.D.

Not only is finding someone to give us love not the solution, it's next to impossible when we are looking too diligently to find it. It's almost as if we push it away by wanting it so badly. It's often heard that when someone "gives up" on finding someone to love they will soon meet the love of their life.

What we ought to do when we feel unloved and perhaps depressed is work on our self-love and also see who we can offer love to. As St. Francis said in his beautiful prayer, "It is in giving that we receive," and the universe really does operate that way.

Any time we can do something for another we feel better. And once we've experienced that, we will continue to want to do it, not to get rewards necessarily, but the payoffs come anyway.

And if we learn to love ourselves love will find us. We may not find our soul mate or true love, but we will find love. We will begin to receive love from those we thought didn't love us before. Suddenly we feel loved, and it started with our own self-love.

We can learn to give up the chase with almost anything in our lives. When we do stop chasing it, we usually get what we've been trying to get by the use of control, only we get it from our Higher Power instead. There's something about giving up control, letting go, that opens our paths for so many things. It seems paradoxical but it's the way it works.

When you give love to yourself and others love will find you.

᷈

May 20
Honesty Starts With Self

"Honesty is the first chapter in the book of wisdom."
—Thomas Jefferson

Honesty with self is the beginning to finding a happy and fulfilling life. When we cannot be honest with who and what we are — mistakes and achievements included — we can't be whole.

All of us have issues we wish to recover and heal from. Some of our issues show up in overeating, drinking too much, or some other addiction. We may not be aware of the reasons we do the harmful things we do to ourselves, but as we seek to grow and heal, we do discover that many actions brought us to where we are.

Whatever our issues, we first must own them for ourselves. If we cannot be honest with self, how can we ever be honest with anyone else?

Often we discover our real truths while talking to other people if we are being honest. We may surprise ourselves and actually admit out loud to someone what is truly inside of our hearts and minds. Perhaps this happens by accident simply because we are opening up to ourselves and someone else.

It's part of the Twelve Step to admit to ourselves, God, and another person our faults, but also our goodness. It often occurs over time and with trust for other people, but it starts with us.

We may practice saying out loud while alone our truths, whatever they are, and realize that saying how we truly feel, the gut honest truth about our strengths, hurts, fears, all of what we feel, will set us free to grow and heal.

It works. Holding things inside hidden from light in the darkness of our souls will only keep us sick. Shining the light on fears and failures only lessens the pain it does not make it grow. And in the process we find out things about ourselves we didn't even realize because we couldn't be honest enough to ourselves.

Honesty sets you free to be healed.

ᚥ

May 21
Live the Possibilities

"Rebellion against your handicaps gets you nowhere. Self-pity gets you nowhere. One must have the adventurous daring to accept oneself as a bundle of possibilities and undertake the most interesting game in the world — making the most of one's best." —Harry Emerson Fosdick

We — all of us — have things that we could use as excuses to never do anything with our lives. We have fears, limitations, pasts, hurt, anger … you name it we have an excuse for every situation if we choose to live our lives that way.

But those of us who choose to be the best we can be, to make the most of our lives, know that those excuses will limit us and hold us back from taking the risks living life presents. We can use the excuses. We can if those are the limits we wish to put on ourselves, but if we choose to move boldly forward we must put them aside one by one and forge on with our heads held high into the unknown world of taking risks.

The risks I mention aren't dangerous risks. They are courageous things we do so that our lives are what they were meant to be. It means we use our God given talents despite what our circumstances say we can or cannot do.

One simple example is going back to college. Some of us decided later in life to finish a degree we started earlier, or to start and finish one from the beginning. We may have had to borrow money to do this, or we may have had to dip into savings. Either way, we took a risk to get what we wanted. We may have used our financial limitations as an excuse for years before taking the risk, but most likely it paid off for us either with a better job or in the way we felt about ourselves.

Limiting ourselves by our handicaps gets us nowhere. Living our lives thinking of the possibilities of what we can do, and attempting the things that we feel led to do, will not only fulfill us, but will offer the world our gifts and talents.

Don't let handicaps limit your possibilities.

⤞

May 22
Seeing Both Sides
"Don't believe everything you think."
—Unknown

Often we go through our lives carrying old thoughts. We may have a head full of negative thinking that we have carried from childhood about who we are. Someone in our past may have had a great influence on us in a negative way and if so it's time to let that go.

Sometimes we don't realize what thoughts we have in our minds that aren't true. It usually takes soul searching and much thought to discover that we aren't necessarily what someone told us we were. Often we live our lives according to what we believe and those beliefs are based on false assumptions.

We must discover for ourselves what our truths are. Maybe we were told we were not smart enough either directly or in some non direct way. Or perhaps we aren't as handsome or as pretty as we would like to be. We may have failed in relationships because we could not trust another person since we never learned to trust.

Any of these things and hundreds of other things we think can be based on falseness. When we start to see ourselves in new ways we discover where these thoughts began and we can change our thinking. We don't think more highly of ourselves than what we deserve, but we also stop condemning ourselves to be victims and unworthy creatures.

We may need to write down on a piece of paper a list of both our good and not so good qualities. We do this to see that there are many positive things about us, and to see what we need to work on. When doing this, it's very important to list good things; we all have them so make sure your list has plenty.

Turn thoughts into truths about yourself and see your world change.

~

May 23
Success and Failure Go Together
"Success isn't permanent, and failure isn't fatal."
—Mike Ditka

It is good to remember that life is not stagnant and no matter where we are today, whether it's where we want to be or not, most likely that's not where we'll be in the future. That's not a gloom and doom prognostication for those who are right where they want to be now, it's just that things change, and we always want to remember that when we are in a rough spot of life.

Once we reach a specific goal we can't give up and say that we've made it and never move ahead. We made that goal and we set another one and move forward with it. If we fail, we realize that there are other options and chances in life and we try those. Just because we fail at one thing it doesn't mean we cannot find success in another.

Both sides of the coin of success and failure are important to our lives. We probably learned a great deal more from our failures than we ever did any successes. However, our successes are most likely what keep us trying even when we find failure at something.

You can bet on one thing, if you don't try you will never succeed unless your goal is to do nothing.

~

May 24
Loosen up, relax
"And you're feeling just a little too tense; gotta loosen up those chains and dance." —Dixie Chicks

Believe it or not the world will not fall apart if we take some time off to have a bit of fun. Most of us are so wrapped up in trying to keep all the plates spinning in our lives that we just don't let our hair down enough and enjoy life.

Whether it's dancing, laying by the pool, taking a nap, or numerous other things that often we don't allow ourselves to do, it's important to just be sometimes and stop doing. It's really vital to our mental health to let go too.

I took a vacation and was unable to get online for about four days. Before that I was never offline more than eight hours at a time, if that long. Amazingly enough the world, and even my world, didn't fall apart during that time and once I got online I was caught up within a few minutes. It was a nice lesson and a good break.

We don't have to be so wrapped up in our lives that we miss living. Juggling too many balls means we are so busy keeping them in the air that we miss out on lots of other things. Life encompasses a lot more than our jobs, our yards, housework, and even our children. We don't neglect any of those things, but we also take time to enjoy all of our life in order to maintain our sanity.

So loosen up those chains and dance if that's what you do. And if, like me, you're not a dancer, find some other way to loosen up.

You have more to give when at your best.

∽

May 25
Don't Forget to Say Thanks

"At times our own light goes out and is rekindled by a spark from another person. Each of us has cause to think with deep gratitude of those who have lighted the flame within us."
—Albert Schweitzer

As we go through our lives we all have people who have helped us when we needed it. Sometimes we don't even realize what a person's words or actions meant at a particular time, but later we see that they had a large impact on our journey. We usually see the big things, but sometimes the smallest thing we do for someone or someone does for us can mean a lot to our journey and theirs.

Often small things weave together to make our path easier and gentler. We just need to be aware of those things and remember to thank those people who were there in a moment of need. Sometimes it's as simple as a smile or having someone let us know they care.

Then there are those times when someone does something so big for us we don't feel that thank you is enough. Someone did something like that for me and I thanked her and asked how I could ever repay her. She said for me to just do the same for someone else. I can't do the exact thing for someone, but those words ring in my ears when I'm in a situation to help another person, sometimes when I'd rather not, but I've been placed in that moment to do that favor for someone.

We all interact in a constant give and take world. Just remember to thank those who give and the world will be a better place.

Always say thanks to those who gave you a spark on your journey.

❦

May 26
Don't Get Burned
"Holding on to anger is like grasping a hot coal with the intent of throwing it at someone else; you are the one who gets burned."
—Buddha

It's awfully difficult to let go of certain things when we get angry at someone, but we all know that when we hold on to it we are the ones who are getting hurt. People don't often treat each other with respect and kindness. And some folks are just downright mean about how they charge through life like a bull in a china closet.

When we haven't done anything wrong and we get treated in a bad or disrespectful way it's easy to hold a grudge against the person who did it. But it really gets us nowhere to be angry and hold onto it.

Anger can move us to action in good ways sometimes, but once we've wrung anything good out of a particular angry moment, it is time to let it go. How we let go can vary from person to person and from event to event, but we do it the best way we can. We may have to hit a punching bag, run several miles, work out at the gym, scream, pray, meditate, whatever gets that feeling out of us so that we are not holding onto it and causing ourselves sickness.

Sometimes there's no response suitable for what someone did. We have to learn from it and not let what happened repeat itself if it's avoidable in the future. First and foremost we take care of ourselves and do what we need in the situation.

Releasing anger frees us. It isn't saying what they did was okay; it's just forgiving them and moving on so that we are healthy and able to live our lives in a good way.

Don't let anger burn you.

❦

May 27
Everything's Changed and Nothing's Changed
"Change and growth take place when a person has risked himself and dares to become involved with experimenting with his own life."
—Herbert A. Otto

Those of us who are on the journey of recovery, whether it be from addictions, low-self esteem, codependency, abuse, or numerous other issues we've faced, know that we grow from the inside and it shows on our outsides.

A dear friend of mine invented a new word, "therapized" for those of us who have been in therapy for any amount of time in our lives. It does speak through us as some unknown language to others who have experienced therapy and the growth that comes with it. It's the same way for Twelve Step programs and those who've been involved with them for any length of time.

I used the words above to a friend saying how happy I am, "Everything's changed and nothing's changed." The reason for that statement is that there is no single outside change in my life today than from where I was a year ago. I have the same job, house, physical health, etc. But what has changed is how I see the world and those around me. It's an inside job.

And the amazing thing is that when we are happy on the inside our outside begins to match. However, no amount of outside pleasure and success can fulfill us when our insides are not happy and healthy.

The "therapized" kind of change does take an effort. It takes looking deep within and can entail many tears and brings up a lot of old pain, but in the end, on our journey, it's invaluable as a tool for growth and self-love.

Change inside and see the outside blossom.

May 28
Worry Solves Nothing
"Worry is a thin stream of fear trickling through the mind. If encouraged, it cuts a channel into which all other thoughts are drained."
—Arthur Somers Roche

If worrying ever kept a bad thing from happening it would be worthwhile, but worry does not gain us anything. If we have something of concern in our lives what is better than worry is to take action in some way. If the worrisome thing is something we actually have any control over, we take whatever action is necessary. If it's not in that realm we can pray about it; pray and let go.

Worry can keep us paralyzed by its fear and misery or it can motivate us to take whatever action we can. Our lives may pass us by while we sit and worry. If we try to think of one time in our lives that worry ever kept a bad thing from happening, we won't find it. Unless we turned worry into prayers and then the outcome would be affected.

It's human nature to worry, especially the way a parent worries about a child, but it really does nothing but keep the worrier awake at night and upset. It can drain our energy and cause us to miss out on life. And it solves nothing.

Stop worrying and live a little.

᷉

May 29
Setting Priorities

"The best things in life are nearest. Breath in your nostrils, light in your eyes, flowers at your feet, duties at your hand, the path of right before you." —Robert Louis Stevenson

Life is full of moments to both be busy and to relax. We are living in a fast paced world often doing more than one thing at once and never feeling as if we have time to do what we really want to do. But if we truly want to do something we usually make time for it.

What we must do is prioritize. We decide whether spending time in our garden is as important to us as watching something on television. Or is attending a meeting or worship service important to our well-being and/or recovery? We put our self first when we know that we need to regroup and get back to our center, even if that means that we have to say no to someone or something.

There are times in all of our lives when we realize that we've neglected some part of ourselves that needs to be nurtured. Perhaps our prayer life is suffering from neglect. Or we haven't spent enough time on our physical health. When we realize this need then it's time to make the changes necessary to right ourselves.

It's easy to get off track in our lives, but naming our priorities will get us back on track to do the things we truly know we need to do for our happiness and serenity.

Setting priorities keeps us on track in our lives.

᷉

May 30
Courage to Change

"Courage is the power to let go of the familiar."
—Raymond Lindquist

We have many opportunities to practice courage in our lives. Many people, when they think of courage, think about running into a burning building to rescue someone or performing some other heroic act, but courage is anytime we do something that we are afraid to do, something out of our comfort zone.

Simply facing change is an act of courage. Change is scary and while change happens all the time in our lives beyond our control, there are also ways we can change that take courage. Those who need to stop drinking have many fears to face. If we have issues in our lives that need to change it can be frightening. Those needing to end a bad relationship need lots of courage.

Whatever our issues are, we can find courage and strength. Prayer and meditation help. Taking our time with things, caring for our physical health, getting plenty of rest, eating right, we need to be in the best shape we can in order to handle difficult times.

Stepping out of our comfort zones is what allows us to grow. Often people stay in bad relationships or job situations because it just seems easier, but with a little courage getting out of something we don't want to be in can be life changing in a good way.

Ask God to give you courage to let go of the familiar.

∽

May 31
Relationships Need a Foundation
"Fine friendship requires duration rather than fitful intensity."
—Aristotle

Often when we first meet someone we are attracted to either for friendship or a love relationship, we make the mistake of moving too quickly and end up finding the end of the relationship rather than something long lasting.

When building any kind of relationship we need to form a strong foundation so when conflict occurs we still have something to work with. Building that foundation takes time, honesty, openness, getting to know each other's boundaries, and trust. We can never truly know someone in a matter of days or weeks and if we move too quickly we may end up in a place with someone that we don't want to be, such as living together or married even.

Any new relationship is exciting, if not we would never make new friends or life partners. But if we don't take it slow and easy it will fizzle out before we even get to know the other person. People are rarely what we think they are upon first meeting. That's not always a bad thing sometimes people have much better qualities than we think upon first impression. If we take our time in getting to know someone by listening and watching we will find true friends. We have time to see if what they say is really what they do. Actions always speak louder than words and people often don't match the two.

Give relationships the time and energy to be real.

∽

June 1
Truth Is There When We Are Aware

"When someone shows you who they are, believe them the first time."
—Oprah Winfrey

As we go through our journey of life we meet many people in various ways. We meet at work, church, recovery meetings, social settings, etc. And most of the time we try to get to know some people better than others.

If we are fully aware during out interactions with people and truly listen to and watch them, they will reveal to us a lot about themselves. If someone says, "I don't drink very often if at all," but every time we talk to them they are on the way to or from the liquor store, or talk about what they drank or what they are about to drink, then their actions speak for them.

Anytime someone says one thing and does another it sends up a red flag warning us that something is not right about the situation. The person may not even be aware of what they are saying and doing, in other words, they may be lying to themselves too.

Usually people tell us and show us who they are. Not so much in what they say directly, but what they say when they don't think about trying to impress us or when they let their guard down and the truth comes out. We need not learn a lesson about someone over and over again, once we find out the truth about them, we can let go of thinking that they will change. They won't. Their truth is their truth and people rarely change without lots of effort.

So if the person's faults are shining through and they don't show any effort to change, chances are they are stuck with that behavior. And if their actions are things that we cannot deal with on a regular basis, it's time to let go and move on gracefully from that person, before investing any more into the relationship.

If words and actions do not match, beware.

ॐ

June 2
Making Friends

"You can make more friends in two months by becoming interested in other people than you can in two years of trying to get other people interested in you." —Dale Carnegie

When living our lives most likely all of us have experienced times when we felt lonely or just in need of some friends and attention. And we may even have experienced trying to get other people to like us by doing numerous things, but never truly showing an interest in them other than a needy kind of desire.

There are times in our lives when we really need to be heard, but there are also times when we need to listen. If we want to make friends when we ask another person how they are we mean it and we listen intently to their reply. If we hear that they need help with something and it's something we're capable of doing, we help them.

All of us know people in our lives who never ask how anyone else is and they simply go on and on about what's happening in their lives. These are people we don't want to be around. We can use that as an example of what we don't want to be to others.

When we truly care for another it shows because while we do set boundaries, the relationship is not all about us, it's about the other person's needs as well. And this is where we make true and long-lasting friends, by doing what Dale Carnegie said in the quote above, by being interested in the other person.

It's about give and take. It involves setting boundaries. Friendship means we share honestly with another, and listen when the other person talks.

Your self-esteem depends on having people to love and being able to love others.

⋞

June 3
You Can Only Achieve What You Believe
"To be a great champion you must believe you are the best. If you're not, pretend you are."
—Muhammad Ali

Even if we are not trying to be the champion of something, we still have to believe to achieve. Our self-esteem is dependent on what we think about ourselves. It matters not if 100 people tell us how great we are or how well we've done something, if we don't believe it for ourselves it makes no difference to us.

Some of us suffer from social anxieties which means that most of the time in order to do things in public we must talk ourselves into going, and often once we get there we are fine and able to engage. But how many times did we not do things because we were too afraid?

That time is in the past and now we can go in confidence because we know why we are "shy" and we know that we can do it. For those who suffer from this anxiety hold your head high next time you are in a situation that you fear. Most of the time other people are more worried about themselves than you, they have their own anxieties about things.

Think of yourself as good enough, honorable enough, outgoing enough and go to that event or put yourself in that situation that you really want to be in, but are afraid.

No matter if we are trying to get up the nerve to attend a party or some other social event, or to get on stage to perform, we must believe we are good enough and strong enough or we won't be able to make it. Like the old saying, "Fake it 'til you make it," it's up to us to attempt things we fear.

Living a full life means that we often must face our fears and move out of our comfort zones in order to experience all that life has to offer.

If you don't believe you can do it, you can't.

⊷

June 4
Go With What You Know

"I feel there are two people inside me — me and my intuition. If I go against her, she'll screw me every time, and if I follow her, we get along quite nicely."
—Kim Basinger

Webster's states that intuition is "knowing things without conscious reasoning." Whether we know things without having to think them through because of some sixth sense, or because we've been there and done that before, it's the same thing — it's that we know something and we should go with what we know.

There are all kinds of people in this world who will manipulate and lie to us. And often we will let them do it time after time because even though our gut instinct is to not go there again, we think perhaps they will be different this time, or they need us, or wow, they are actually showing us attention. But often our thinking is as skewed as their behavior if we think of giving them the benefit of the doubt.

Sometimes we just know not to return to certain places with particular people. Our intuition, instinct, intellect, experiences, or something tells us what we should do. And we ought to follow that. We learn, over time and through experiences, that more often than not what we really believe about something is correct, especially as we grow in recovery and become more spiritual.

We learn to trust our gut. We learn that it's possible to err on either side of an issue, but better than to keep making the same mistakes.

Try following your intuition; it's more trustworthy than you may think.

⊷

June 5
Choice Can Be Power
"Any change, any loss, does not make us victims. Others can shake you, surprise you, disappoint you, but they can't prevent you from acting, from taking the situation you're presented with and moving on. No matter where you are in life, no matter what your situation, you can always do something. You always have a choice and the choice can be power." —Blaine Lee

We have all had someone ask what we regret in life. People want to know what we wish we had not done at some point in our lives and they also want to know what we wish we would have done differently if we could go back.

The answers to those questions can be easily thought of and at the same time dismissed. For those of us who endeavor to make our lives more meaningful, to live our lives to the fullest, and to give all that we have to give, we understand that it took all of our mistakes and victories and all of the situations in between to make us who we are today.

Take away a painful situation and whatever wisdom was gained would not be with us now. Remove a particular mistake, or certain way we lived our lives for a time and what strength and knowledge we gained from that would be lost. We would not be the whole of who we are today.

It's what we do with our pain, grief, joy, hurt, disappointment, love, broken heart, with every situation that we gain power; power that is ours and ours alone. And there comes a point in our growth where we know we have made it over that ridge, where we see the prize we have sought. It's our power, it's our self-esteem; it's ours and we earned it with every bump and bruise.

Your actions and choices give you power that nobody can take away.

∽

June 6
Seeing the Truth
"We do not see things as they are, we see things as we are."
—The Talmud

How many times in our lives have we argued with another person about something that we both know we are right about? And sometimes we are both right, it's just that what we see is through our eyes and they through theirs. What one sees as a burden another sees as a chance for growth. Where one person sees venting as a bad thing another knows that sometimes it's necessary.

A concrete example of not seeing things as they are, but seeing them as we are, would be looking at something through the eyes of someone who is color blind. Just because they see something in one color does not make it that color.

We can only know what we know and see what we see through the eyes of the person we are at the moment. What we know and see today may not be the same thing in a year. We may grow and see things completely different in a matter of time. And often we'll find that what we thought before, what we were certain about, was not so.

No matter how many times someone tells us "this too shall pass" or some other comforting thing, until we have had enough experiences for ourselves to know this as fact, we won't truly believe it.

And it's also true that we may see only the things we wish to see in situations. Sometimes we blame others for something we perceive as us being wronged, when it's our own incorrect thinking about what's happened.

You can only see things from the point at which you stand.

ॐ

June 7
Maybe the Problem's not Them

"People spend too much time finding other people to blame, too much energy finding excuses for not being what they are capable of being, and not enough energy putting themselves on the line, growing out of the past, and getting on with their lives."
—J. Michael Straczynski

Anytime we find ourselves having to learn a lesson again and again it may be time to stop blaming people and events outside of ourselves.

If we've failed at numerous relationships and the same problems crop up in each, we are attracting something to ourselves that doesn't work for us. If we don't change, the same problems will continue to come our way.

And if our problems involve work or business and we keep having the same issues that cause us unnecessary stress and agony, who needs to change? We have some reason to keep getting in these situations or not getting out of them soon enough.

We can stay stuck in our ruts of destruction that end with self-pity and loss of enthusiasm or we can look inside ourselves and learn why we keep getting into the same situations again and again.

Only we can break our own cycle of destructiveness.

The first thing we have to do is admit that it is our problem and that we are the only person who can get us out of it. Blaming the boss, parents, exes, current spouses, or anyone else is not going to get us moving and out of the situation.

Once we can admit that we have to do something, we can then take action and get unstuck and hopefully not have to keep repeating the lesson because we can't seem to get it.

Look inside to find the problem and the strength to overcome it.

∽

June 8
We Are Who We Make

"People often say that this or that person has not yet found himself. But the self is not something one finds, it is something one creates."
—Thomas S. Szasz

As we go through the days of our lives we are on a journey that offers many choices. It is our challenge and responsibility to determine which route to take when we hit that "Y" in the road.

We meet new people and we wonder if that person is worth investing time and energy in; is there something long-term we wish to carry on with that person.

We hear about a job somewhere that interests us and we start to consider if that's an option we wish to pursue. Or perhaps it's time to end something and we aren't sure what to do.

We create our own world. Sometimes we want more; sometimes we are content to stay where we are in our safety and security whether or not we are happy. And often we fear making that move, taking the next step, making changes, and taking risks in order to create something more for ourselves.

We can always keep in mind that even if we move forward into something new and that fails to be what we want or we are not successful in our endeavor life goes on and surely we have gained new knowledge and insight about life and ourselves. We've created more of us; more wisdom, knowledge, insight, and possibly self-love.

In order to create who we wish to be, we must take these chances. It's difficult sometimes because we've been jaded and hurt in our lives over relationships, business dealings, jobs, family issues, and other things. But each one of those things taught us something about who and what we are and made us who we are today.

We can take these chances when opportunities arise knowing that even if whatever it is ends in failure we gave it our best shot, we've taken a chance on life and love, and we don't have to crawl in a hole and hide from the world.

Take that chance on the next thing that comes along. You're strong enough.

∽

June 9
What Is Success?

"To laugh often and much; to win the respect of intelligent people and the affection of children; to earn the appreciation of honest critics and endure the betrayal of false friends; to appreciate beauty; to find the best in others; to leave the world a bit better, whether by a healthy child, a garden patch or a redeemed social condition; to know even one life has breathed easier because you have lived. This is to have succeeded."
—Ralph Waldo Emerson

Ever wonder when you are going to be a success? And do you think you're a failure because you haven't yet finished that Ph.D or landed at the top of the corporate ladder. And maybe you think you will never find that right person to spend the rest of your days on earth with.

Well, it's time to stop thinking like that. We who are living our lives with this kind of thinking are most likely successful well beyond what we imagine.

Anytime we give to someone — a hug, a listening ear, a meal, clothes, shelter, a smile — we succeed. When we cross our own difficult hurdles in life, we are growing and surviving and that's success. Caring for a child or loved one who is ill is a great thing. Making others laugh or helping them to feel loved is a huge accomplishment. Growing a beautiful garden or fixing our own automobile, those are successes.

There is so much more to life than attaining that top position at a company, or being the best musician in the world, or driving the most expensive car on the block. Success is not measured in dollar amounts at least not the kind of success that really matters.

We can all think back on those moments in life where we touched another person's heart in some way. If we can remember that feeling we can know what true success is. That's the kind of thing that is priceless.

How do you measure success?

∽

June 10
Don't Let Disappointment
Signal the End of Hope

"The sudden disappointment of a hope leaves a scar which the
ultimate fulfillment of that hope never entirely removes."
—Thomas Hardy

The loss of something we had hoped for can feel as disappointing
and hurt just as bad as actually losing something that is quite real.
When we have hope for something and that something is not quite ours
yet we already have grown an attachment to it. Thus when we don't get
it we feel disappointed and when that seems to happen over and over it
hurts and makes us wish we could just give up on ever having that
thing.

Hope, that courage, the going out on a limb to try again, we show in
the midst of so many losses and failures, can be lost as well. But it
doesn't have to be lost. We don't have to give up.

As we grow and try to extend our lives we do step out of our
comfort zones time and again. Sometimes the pain over a loss can
make us want to never go to that place again, but we eventually feel
pulled back. The pull is strong or we would not have felt so much pain
over our loss.

So we step out, we step up to the plate and take yet one more swing.
And hope beyond hope that we get what it is that is pulling us this
time. There is some reason we keep going through this thing, whatever
it is. We hope that in taking the step that the rug does not get pulled out
from under us; unfortunately though, it's very possible that's what will
happen.

It's life. And we can choose to walk out of disappointment and try
again or we can shut down and shut out the world and wallow in our
pain. We do have a choice. Choosing hope — again — is a struggle at
times. We can ask God to help, we can trust that there's a reason for
the disappointment, and we can risk loss, but at least we are living.

Hope keeps you alive.

❦

June 11
Offer Blessings Not Curses

"Bless those who persecute you; bless and do not curse."
—The Bible, Romans 12:14

When we are hurt by or angry with someone our first thought is
usually to curse them. We want them to feel bad. Sometimes we would
even like to tell them off. We want them to feel the pain that we think

they have bestowed upon us. It's a natural impulse. And whether or not we're a believer in the Bible, the teachings in it say we should offer blessings for those who hurt us.

Other religions teach this principle as well and in the Alcoholics Anonymous Big Book readers are given this instruction: "If you have a resentment you want to be free of, if you will pray for the person or the thing that you resent, you will be free. If you will ask in prayer for everything you want for yourself to be given to them, you will be free. Ask for their health, their prosperity, their happiness, and you will be free. Even when you don't really want it for them, and your prayers are only words and you don't mean it, go ahead and do it anyway. Do it every day for two weeks and you will find you have come to mean it and to want it for them, and you will realize that where you used to feel bitterness and resentment and hatred, you now feel compassionate understanding and love."

It's very difficult to be angry with someone and pray for them at the same time. And if nothing else there is a calm feeling when praying for them and thinking good thoughts. When we curse the person and wish bad things for them, we keep the resentment alive in our own heart and mind.

Bitterness eats away at the person who owns the feeling, not the person they are angry with. When you want to curse someone, stop instead and say "bless this person" and God will hear your prayer.

Curses just keep the anger alive, blessings bring peace and healing.

∽

June 12
Choose Peace

"Peace. It does not mean to be in a place where there is no noise, trouble or hard work. It means to be in the midst of those things and still be calm in your heart."

—Unknown

It's rare in life that all of our ducks are in a perfect row; all of our relationships are perfect, things at work and business are perfect, our children are doing just as we want, everything in our homes is working as it should, and our automobiles are running fine, we feel confident in ourselves and our place in the world. In fact, it's doubtful that all of that ever occurs at the same time, but even when it does things change and eventually somehow things get a little off center.

So how do we get to a place of peace and serenity? We get it because we have faith, because we have a relationship with a Higher

Power. We also know from experience that no amount of worry or fret will make things better, but turning whatever is wrong over to God will help bring us peace. Even if we have to turn it over and take it back dozens or hundreds of times, we still turn it over.

We can have peace in the midst of turmoil although it takes an effort. We have to choose peace over what's happening and do what we know works for us to get to that place. When we choose peace we make a conscious effort to get to that place and we do the work involved. If we love drama and turmoil that's what we will stay mired in, but if we want peace we can get that. It's usually easier to stay in the drama of life, but peace brings much more happiness.

Getting peace means choosing it and doing what it takes to accomplish it.

⋙

June 13
Fear and Faith
"We must take things one step at a time because we don't know the whole of a situation. God's the only one who has the whole picture."
—Jan Edwards

If we could see into the future and know exactly which twists and turns we would take in life. Or if we knew what calamities would come down upon us. Even if we knew the joys that we would be blessed with. Having all of this knowledge would limit us.

For some of us the unknown is what we fear more than anything. And don't we turn more to God when we are in fear than we do when we are full of joy? Taking bold steps down our path of life involves fear, faith, courage, missteps, falling down and getting up, and hope. We fear but we have faith that all will work out the way we want and if not, that we get something even better than what we hoped.

Many times we wish we knew why we could not have what we wanted in a relationship, or maybe we wanted a child and were unable to have one for any number of reasons, maybe we missed out on a job or promotion, or we can't have that nice house across town that we wanted and had to settle for the one we bought instead.

But along that path perhaps something came to us that we didn't expect. We met a neighbor who turns out to be a wonderful friend that we would never have met if we didn't live in the house we ended up in. And maybe we wound up going back to school to further our education because we didn't get the job we desired. Perhaps we now give our energy and love to lots of children since we don't have our own to care for.

Since we don't have the whole picture we can never know what the best thing for us is at any given time. We can trust God to know what that is since He does have full knowledge about what's coming our way. Faith is not an easy thing to have when we want to control our journey, but often it's the only way we can have any peace since life offers us a rocky path.

One step at a time, one day at a time, you can follow the path that God leads you on in life.

&

June 14
Toss That Thing Away
"Let Go and Let God"
—AA slogan

"Sometimes it's hard for me to give things to God, but I'm trying," a woman said. My reply to that was simple: "Do you think giving things to God is easy for anyone?"

Sometimes, rather, most of the time letting go of people, places, or things is so difficult. It is hard to know what action to take and where to let God step in. Because our Higher Power works through people we cannot just lay in bed and say, God take this problem, pay my bills, feed my children, mow my yard, clean my house, and take care of my pets.

One day I was playing catch with some boys. We were throwing a football. I pulled my arm back with a tight grip on the football and threw a perfect spiral to one of the boys. They were amazed that I didn't "throw like a girl." Another boy joined in, a teenager, and I did the same only this time I threw it even farther. "Wow!" he said.

A few days later I was trying to let go of something that was very difficult for me. So I decided to toss it to God like that football. I visually pulled back and threw that imaginary football as far as I could in a perfect spiral, just like I'd thrown it with the boys. It was a different way for me to do that than just saying it. And it lasted longer than my normal letting go, about an hour! So I did it again, and again, and again.

Letting go and letting God can work for a few minutes and we can do it over and over until it sticks. I figure He got tired of catching those perfectly thrown spirals, but I kept throwing them. Eventually I let go of that person, and she didn't go away. The relationship changed. Because I was able to let go of what I wanted, the person is still in my life in a different sort of way. The way she was meant to be.

Letting go isn't easy, but it works.

❧

June 15
Taking Care of Self

"There is a connection between self-nurturing and self-respect."
—Julia Cameron

In order to be a giver in this world we have to have it to give it away. Whatever "it" is we can only give what we have or what we know. We cannot love without first loving ourselves. We can't offer hope to another if we have no hope. We won't be able to truly nurture another if we have given too much and have no more left to give.

Some of us put ourselves last by thinking that it's selfish to think of ourselves first. But to truly be there for others we must be whole within us. Sometimes this means we have to say no. We have to slow down, pull away, regroup, pause, and nurture ourselves in whatever way we do that. We may have to go away for a while to regroup, or we may just stop within our current situation and take a break from everything to recharge our batteries.

It's really very simple but often overlooked that we must fill up in order to give out. An automobile cannot run without fuel, why do we think we can continue to operate without being energized? We might be able to go through the motions and think we are holding up the world in our hands, but we truly aren't.

To really love ourselves we must nurture who we are. Some of us learned to nurture ourselves because we had nobody else to do that for us. It was simply survival. Others may not have learned how to do that. And while there are numerous ways we can nurture ourselves and care for our own well-being, each person is an individual in how they accomplish that.

It's usually easier to take care of ourselves along the way on a daily basis rather than finding ourselves spent and having to fill up from empty. We can carve out some time every day to do that which nurtures and invigorates us. Journaling, meditation, prayer, exercise, reading, art, gardening, sleeping; all of these things and many more are available to us today to help us stay charged and ready for the troubles and joys of each day.

Taking care of self must come first.

❧

June 16
Wanting What We Cannot Have

"We always long for the forbidden things, and desire what is denied us." —Francois Rabelais

Wanting what we cannot have seems to be a great mystery for many of us. It seems we can spend hours, days, months, even years obsessing about a person we want to be in relationship with only to never achieve our desire.

Sometimes we wait because we are told to, that things are going to change and that person is going to come to us. Other times we just wait hoping they decide they want to be with us even if they have never said that. Some of us wait hoping they will suddenly see our value and come running.

But the reality is that if someone does not want to be with us or cannot because of circumstances we really don't need to wait. Why would we want to be with someone who does not want to be with us? We are deserving of all good things. The best things in life and love can be ours if we don't settle just so we are not alone. And the old saying holds true, "When one door closes another one opens."

Standing in between the closed and opened doors can seem to last a long time. And we may wonder why we have to wait and we want to know if the door will ever open. And sometimes the door is open, it's been open for a long time we just didn't notice because our focus was over there on that situation that we couldn't have.

It may be time to take a good close look at our lives and see what we do have. We may be overlooking wonderful things in our lives that are there being ignored while we long for what is just beyond our reach.

Today look at what you do have instead of what you can't have.

June 17
Look for the Lesson

"Are you focusing on the circumstances of your life instead of the lessons? Instead of asking why, learn to ask what the lesson is. The moment you become ready to accept it, the lesson will become clear." —Melody Beattie

Life can sure throw us some curve balls at times causing us to wonder why this or that experience came our way. We often can't see the reason why we got what we got, or didn't get what we wanted, or lost what we had.

We can continue to focus and live in the "why me" way of thinking or we can choose to do what Melody Beattie suggests above and look for the lessons in the circumstances. There are lessons in everything we do, usually more so in the difficulties in life than those things that bring us joy.

When we take the focus off of "why" and look for the lesson, it can also help us to let go of those things which are causing us pain. When we stop obsessing about why and step out of it as much as we can for the moment, it takes away some of the power of the situation. Stopping, even if we can only do it a minute or two at a time, and asking what the lesson is … focusing on that instead of "it" can help us along the way.

Often when we are in the grips of a painful situation the last thing we think of to look for is the lesson. However, if we begin now, with one thing in our lives, and start making it a way of thinking, a habit, we will begin to look for the lessons in all things that happen to us. The lessons may surprise us too; we may learn something we weren't even seeking to know.

Look for the lesson instead of asking "why me."

∽

June 18
Finding Freedom from Fear
"Ultimately we know deeply that the other side of every fear is freedom." —Marilyn Ferguson

Many of us probably have fears that we don't tell anyone about. I'm not talking about the fear of public speaking, or heights, or spiders or snakes. The fears that we most likely hide would include things like the fear of abandonment so we choose not to get close to anyone; the fear of failure so we just don't try very hard; we may have trust issues and just assume everyone lies to us a lot; or maybe we fear commitment so we stay alone. There are many fears that we hide behind in our lives.

There are all kinds of fears that we lock inside ourselves and ways we build walls of protection around us so that we don't even really have to face those scary invisible demons that hide in our thinking. Even when we know the only way to overcome a fear is to face it head on and go to battle with it if that's necessary, we will still often choose to continue to live with the fear.

If we truly want freedom in all areas of our lives we must overcome that which holds us back. Consider all of the joy that's lost if we are walled off from the world because of fear. The fear's not bringing us joy, but perhaps if we could just work through it to freedom we would find a whole kaleidoscopic world of possibilities we didn't even know existed on the other side.

Sometimes our fear is simply that of the unknown and since we don't know what will happen if we don't have the fear anymore we cling to it as if it's a life raft instead of an anchor. We can overcome all of our fears even if we have to do it by taking baby steps.

As Mark Twain said, "Courage is not the absence of fear. It is acting in spite of it."

Find the courage to leave fear behind and you'll discover freedom.

⌘

June 19
Persevering Through Trials
"What seems to us as bitter trials are often blessings in disguise."
—Oscar Wilde

Trials and suffering are often the way we learn and grow. Sometimes when something is really difficult and we seem to be trying to swim against the tide it probably means that we aren't supposed to have that thing. Having trials and suffering is not the same thing as hard work.

Getting a college degree or beyond is difficult at times during the process, but we don't give up over that type of difficulty. The trials and suffering that may be telling us to give up and let go are of a different sort. They probably involve people and situations out of our control and may be things that we will never be able to conquer. And maybe that's because we never were supposed to.

And if the trial isn't teaching us to let go of whatever it is, then there's some other lesson in it. The Big Book of Alcoholics Anonymous teaches that nothing happens by mistake, and if we believe that then we get in the midst of trials and tribulations for a reason. Sometimes the lessons from things are our lessons and sometimes we are the teacher.

If we find ourselves in what seems to be a losing battle with a person or situation, we can take some time to really examine what is happening and try our best to determine if it's time to let go or fight harder for whatever it is.

Seeing trials as opportunities helps you move past the pain involved.

⌘

June 20
Open Up and Feel
"Honesty and transparency make you vulnerable. Be honest and transparent anyway." —Mother Teresa

For a lot of people being open and honest with others is one of the most difficult things imaginable because of the vulnerability. Some of us were told that who we were was not okay and we believed it. And others may have done things that were not okay and are ashamed or full of guilt.

But we are past those things now. To be whole we must be able to open up and let who we are shine to the world. Whatever pain we have buried deep inside needs to be felt and released. We do this by being honest with ourselves first and sometimes we need to talk about it with someone else.

During this time of healing we may feel extremely vulnerable, but once we move through our issues that cause us pain, we will begin to feel stronger and will come out of it with growth and a renewed spirit. As long as we hold onto the garbage we will continue to feel sick and lonely.

We each have our own gifts and talents that were given to us in order for us to use them. We can't offer our talents if we keep ourselves hidden behind an imaginary shield because we have shame or guilt.

If we can't be honest and open with friends or family we may need to seek help from a therapist or member of the clergy, or we may work through these issues within a Twelve Step program. The important thing is that we work through the issues so that we can live our lives to the fullest.

Most of us are truly capable of so much more than we know. Those of us who have been honest and open and have grown through our issues are testaments to the before and after lives of those who were suffering and now feel whole. We aren't without problems or pain, but we have become stronger and better able to cope with things as they come our way. And we don't have all of the baggage that we had before either.

Open your heart to healing and you will become whole.

૭

June 21
Living Life Fully Today
"Look to this day for it is life, the very life of life. In its brief course lie all the realities and truths of existence; the bliss of growth, the

splendor of action, the glory of power. For yesterday is but a dream
and tomorrow is only a vision, but today, well lived, makes every
yesterday a dream of happiness and every tomorrow a vision of hope."
—Ancient Sanskrit Proverb

So much of our lives are spent looking into the future or past that
we forget to live this day to its fullest. Each day offers us many
opportunities that can be easily missed out on if we are too focused
either on the past or the future.

Some days are meant for great things; a scurry of activities, large
spurts of growth, a new risk taken, or some other great feat. Other days
are simply days where we are just being who we are, where life is
moving along and we are giving what we have to give, accepting what
is presented to us, simply fulfilling that place in the world where we
are supposed to be for that day or moment.

We all have times where we suffer great pain and on the flip side of
that hopefully we all experience times of joy. The range of all of these
emotions is what makes us human. If we look at each day as we are in
it, we can see the beauty of our own growth or that of someone we
love; we can experience what comes along in our lives as it happens
and not miss anything.

But when we live in the past or future we aren't really living
because the moment is where we are and we must be present in that
moment to really get it.

Often we want to know the answer to something, especially how a
situation will turn out, but we can only know what we know in the day
we currently occupy. It's too easy to lose out on this day when we are
focused on any other time. The past cannot be changed and the future
is yet to occur, but today is where we are and where we ought to be
present.

Look to this day for it is life, the very life of life.

৶

June 22
Character Shows Itself
"Every man has three characters: that which he shows, that which
he has, and that which he thinks he has."
—Alphonse Karr

No matter how much we might try to convince others of how good
of a person we are, it's our actions that speak most loudly. If we do
what we say we will do we become trusted by others. If we fail to do
what we say often enough we show that we have no character and
nobody believes us.

There are times when we have legitimate reasons for not doing a thing, but when it's a habit to not do what we say we will do, that's when it becomes a problem because nobody believes us.

Are we kind to those who are unkind to us? Do we talk badly about others when they aren't around just to put them down and build ourselves up? There's a difference in venting and getting our feelings out and just downright gossip.

The words we speak about others and the things we do in our lives are huge character giveaways. It really doesn't do any good to gossip about what we see as defects of character in others. Those are their issues. Our issues are to be true to our word and to be positive in our actions.

Character requires that we keep our word; that we say what we mean, and mean what we say. Those with great character are honest and trustworthy. When someone asks for their help, they know that they can count on that person to do what they promise.

Those who don't have much character may think they are fooling others, and they may for a while, but it doesn't take long for a person's true character to show.

Examining your character from time to time is a good idea to keep on track.

∞

June 23
Controlling Outcomes

"I do believe that when we face challenges in life that are far beyond our own power, it's an opportunity to build on our faith, inner strength, and courage. I've learned that how we face challenges plays a big role in the outcome of them."
—Sasha Azevedo

Rarely in the journey of life do we absolutely peg the outcome of particular paths and challenges that we face. We may desire things to turn out in one way and have the opposite happen, or things might turn out much better than we could have ever imagined they would.

Often when we are in the midst of something big in our lives we start projecting; thinking thoughts about the future. "What ifs" can drive us crazy if we allow ourselves to get out into tomorrow. We can start obsessing about the craziest things that might happen.

What does happen when we so desperately want to know the outcome is that we miss the journey. And as is often said, "It's the journey, not the destination." There's a whole lot of life going on right this moment that we are absolutely going to miss out on if we are fretting about tomorrow, next week, next year, or our whole lifetime.

Turning the outcome of a thing over to our Higher Power helps us to let go of it and enjoy the moment. We really can't control outcomes much. We can put our energy into something and give it our all, but we don't have the final say in what will happen.

It's very easy to get caught up in the "what ifs" and lose sight of the now. Usually the "what ifs" are not very pleasant because they are fear-based feelings. Turning the outcome over to God gives us more ability to let the "what ifs" go and turns our thinking into positive thoughts instead. And who knows, positive thinking might be better for the outcome than the negativity that comes with fearful "what ifs."

Live the moment and leave the outcome to God.

∽

June 24
Knowing the Answers
"If you wait to do everything until you're sure it's right, you'll probably never do much of anything."
—Win Borden

Everything we do in life involves a certain amount of risk and it's very rare, if it happens at all, that we know for certain that what we are doing is the right thing.

Starting or leaving a job; beginning a love relationship or ending one; making a move across the country or staying in our comfort zone at home; or going back to college are just a few of the big decisions we face in life, but there are numerous smaller choices we must make every day.

What happens if we make a decision and it turns out to be "wrong" for us? Most likely we have learned something from it. And if we were careful in moving forward with our decision it's unlikely that it's going to be impossible to recover from it. What's important is not moving into any big change too suddenly unless it's thrust upon us by nature. We must take our time and go through each process with as much knowledge as we can ascertain.

Maybe the event in question is something that God put before us because it's time for us to move on from where we are. Perhaps we can't really grow anymore where we are and need to broaden our horizons. And it might be the lesson we learn is to be happy and content with what we've got by staying right in or where we are at the moment because sometimes we just don't realize how good what we have is.

We just don't always know what the right choice is. What we need to do is pray about the big decisions, the small ones, and every one in between. Our answers will come as they should if we allow ourselves to hear them. The answer is probably already there just waiting on us to find it.

To grow is to continue to step out of your comfort zones.

June 25
Feeling Pain

"Given the choice between the experience of pain and nothing, I would choose pain." —William Faulkner

None of us wants to feel emotional pain. We don't set out to find it, we avoid it when possible. And we hope to never experience it when we care about someone.

However, pain comes with truly living. We can avoid most pain if we avoid relationships, but not being involved with people, being reclusive, only means that we aren't truly living our lives. It would be easier to just never experience pain, but without going to places where that occurs also means that we won't experience joy either.

Living a full life involves the whole gamut of emotions, the good with the bad, joy with pain. We limit ourselves when we don't allow ourselves to take the risk of love because we fear the pain that so often comes with that.

We can look back over our lives and examine the times when we were hurt. We may have thought at that time that we would never live through it because we hurt so deeply. We may have planned to never allow ourselves to be exposed to pain like that again. Yet we find that we are drawn to love even with the knowledge that we can end up in pain.

It's certainly a scary process. It's one in which we would rather shut down and wall ourselves off many times rather than experience the vulnerability that living life fully offers us. And we never know how others will react when we become involved with them. They may shut down and shut us out with no warning signs leaving us to feel the sting of pain abruptly and with full force.

But to live in fear of the pain that can come with loving may also lead us directly to the pain. Our fears can become reality simply by letting them consume us until we shut the other person out. It might be simpler to remember that we will live even if we get hurt and stop expecting the pain to arrive, since we may think our way into it.

Living life fully brings pain and joy.

June 26
Expecting Perfection

"People throw away what they could have by insisting on perfection, which they cannot have, and looking for it where they will never find it."
—Edith Schaeffer

Amazingly enough as much as we know there is nothing perfect in this world, we often go about our lives as if things should be perfect. We tend to find the imperfect things in jobs, relationships, families, ourselves and in other situations, and overlook the wonderful things that are available in these areas.

By thinking of the imperfections we often throw out the baby with the bathwater. We have a problem at work and think we must have a new job. Or we encounter some obstacles in a relationship and our first response is to get out of it. Perhaps we make a mistake and think that it would be better just to give up on ever trying.

But life is full of imperfection. And loving life and those we share this journey with is what's important. Always seeking perfection will result in being miserable. Seeking love, laughter, joy, and opportunities to share those gifts we do possess are what makes life happy.

We don't have to expect ourselves to be perfect any more than we expect that from others. If we can learn to laugh at our imperfections we will also stop expecting others to fit into some pre-determined mold that we have designed in our heads for how they should be. When we do this and allow freedom within us and also for those in our lives, we find reality which itself contains all the joy and love we need.

Always looking for what's wrong will help us find just that, but learning to appreciate the differences in people, places, and things from what we perceive to be perfection, will help us to embrace life instead of finding fault with it. When we want sunshine and it rains, we adjust our plans; when someone can't love us as we expect, we love them anyway and seek what we need elsewhere; when we encounter difficulties we use them as tools to grow.

Remember that just as we can't expect ourselves to be perfect, we cannot expect others to be that way either. Live and let live ought to be our motto when dealing with those we encounter on the path of our journey.

Expecting perfection only brings disappointment.

❧

June 27
Positive Self-Talk
"If you had a friend who talked to you like you sometimes talk to yourself, would you continue to hang around with that person?"
—Rob Bremer

Most of us have likely battled with our self-worth over the course of our lives. And we are usually very hard on ourselves when it comes to our past mistakes or current standing in life. Some of us may have things we've done that we cannot forgive ourselves for, or maybe we struggled with those things for years before we did let go. We also have daily smaller things that we deal harshly with ourselves over. During times of self-doubt and struggle we usually talk to ourselves unlike we would to any other person and it's not pretty.

What we believe about ourselves we become. What we believe about who we are guides what we say to ourselves. Finding positive things about who and what we are and praising ourselves can only be a good thing. We don't do it out of conceit, we do it until we believe it; we do it until we can love ourselves.

Sometimes we have to fake it; we may even have to struggle in the beginning to find something positive to praise ourselves for. At the start of our journey it's difficult. But it becomes easier as we find one thing then another and another. We build our self-worth brick by brick, thing by thing, especially at those times when we have hit bottom and we are climbing out until one day we discover that we not only dug our way out, we are standing tall and strong. It's well worth the work once we find enough about ourselves that we are truly able to love who we are.

The gifts that follow our discovery are immeasurable. Because we love ourselves we are able to love others and that love flows back to us. Life becomes a new creature with the peace and joy we have never known. And even when pain and difficulties are upon us, we have wisdom and serenity from our newfound realization. And it started with simply talking ourselves up instead of down.

You become what you think you are.

June 28
Create Healthy Habits
"Excellence is not a singular act, but a habit. You are what you repeatedly do." —Shaquille ONeal

Many very talented people got to be that way with hard work and lots of practice. Ask anyone who teaches a musical instrument about learning and they will tell you that the most important thing is to practice. Some of the greatest talents in the world, including those who invented things we take for granted, spent abundant time and repeated tries at becoming the best or finally inventing that thing they sought after.

We don't become great at anything if we don't spend time with it. We also don't have good relationships with our families, friends, or partners if we don't nurture those relationships.

Becoming what we want to become doesn't just happen to us; we create it by making it a habit.

Those of us who work out regularly know the importance of the routine and we don't like to skip working out on our scheduled days because it's easy to skip again if we skip once. Making something a habit causes us to be able to continue to do it, even when we'd rather do a hundred other things.

Being a kind and gentle person can be attained with practice. Learning patience may be achieved when we repeatedly work at being patient when confronted with certain situations. Being punctual rather than late all the time can become a good habit to have. Eating right and skipping certain foods or bad eating habits can become routine.

It's all about doing the things that get us where we want to be. If we want to lose weight, we have to do certain things to attain that. Maybe we want to stop having bad relationships and we need to break our old patterns and form new ones; this takes practice.

Habits can be healthy or unhealthy. It's better to repeatedly do the healthy things in life than those that are bad for us. Once we replace the bad patterns with good ones we find we don't have much time for the bad.

Whatever you do you become; make your rituals things that help rather than hurt.

&

June 29
Finding Joy
"Joy is but the sign that creative emotion is fulfilling its purpose."
—Charles Du Bos

Our lives are often filled with busy days and nights. We work too much, we do volunteer work, we care for our children or our parents, we have things we must get done before we ever feel like we can just do what would bring us joy.

Jim Croce's song "Time in a Bottle" sums it up in a few words: "But there never seems to be enough time to do the things you want to do once you find them ...." And it does seem to be true that even when we know what will bring us joy and pleasure we have difficulty getting to it.

And sadly some people don't even know what would make them happy. If we don't know what brings us joy, it's time to find out. Look for what brings you joy and do that. Some people find it growing things in a garden, or building a deck, others in rocking a baby, or perhaps singing in a choir or learning a new instrument, and still others might create a drawing or painting. Whatever place that joy can be found it's important to go there.

Even if someone told us we couldn't have fun in life or we have always thought that we had to be serious all the time and only work hard, it's time to let go of that thinking and find some joy.

Joyful people are more loving people because they love themselves. If a person is filled with joy they cannot help but spill that over onto other people.

Life does not have to be all about work. It's okay to have fun. It's okay to laugh. It's okay to find pleasure and have joy.

Find what brings you joy and do it.

∽

June 30
Moving Forward Despite Fear
"The purpose of life is not to get rid of the butterflies in your stomach, but to make them fly in formation."
—Unknown

Stepping out of our comfort zones into new realms of our lives often causes us to become anxious. Do it anyway. Most things that are worth having require effort, fear, and anxiety. Almost anything new we attempt is going to bring us some feelings that we may not necessarily like.

Fear and anxiety ought to not keep us from moving forward or from trying new things. The things in life that we had to work the hardest for most likely mean the most to us now. What we have that came easy is probably taken for granted.

What we can do is realize that anxiety and fear are normal parts of living. We learn to deal with them and take care of ourselves when they strike us. Just because we are scared, we don't give up on something that we want, at least not until we've given it our best shot. Sometimes we aren't meant to have something, but to give up on it because we have butterflies would be a mistake. If we are honest with ourselves we will know when it's time to give up or move forward and it won't be determined by the amount of fear we have.

Fear and anxiety can have a strong grip on us; they can keep us paralyzed and stuck in places that were fine for a time but that no longer suit us as we grow and evolve. We can look back and see many things we did that got us where we are today that probably caused a lot of stress for us, things we had a lot of fear about, but we walked through that and came out on the other side.

Unless we were spoiled and given everything we have, we have gone through a lot of fear and anxiety in life. Just keep those times in mind and see the victories that came with the effort when we trudged along through the muck of fear, stress and hard work.

Let the butterflies flutter they just mean you are alive and living fully.

✄

July 1
Communication is a Necessity
"The way we communicate with others and with ourselves
ultimately determines the quality of our lives."
—Anthony Robbins

When we can effectively communicate with others we will have more solid and deeper relationships with those who cross our paths. We let others know where we stand and what we need; and we let them know what we won't tolerate.

If someone hurts us or does us wrong in some way, we always have the option of letting them know how we feel. And we tell them in a direct way, not partially or by making them guess, we just communicate with the other person so that they know the truth. Not saying what we feel or lying about how we feel is a form of manipulation. If we feel angry we can say that to someone. Angry feelings don't have to end any kind of relationship, but if we fail to communicate the reason for the anger, that may cause an ending.

Part of taking charge of our lives includes setting and keeping boundaries. Sometimes our boundaries are not told to others, but we still have them. At other times we must let someone know when they have overstepped our boundaries. We can communicate this directly and honestly, without anger or out of a need to control the other person, but in order to take care of ourselves.

Every type of relationship involves communication. The level of that communication for all parties concerned will help determine the success or failure of that relationship. Sometimes we have difficulty articulating what we mean. We should still do our best to say it. And other times we just don't know what to say, we can say that too.

There are also times when we know that our issues with a certain situation are more related to our relationship history which triggers a reaction within us. We may need to tell the other person that so they know that our reaction may have nothing to do with them. This allows us to feel our feelings and still be honest.

It's all about communicating the truth. Being open and honest in our communication will bring us to deeper levels in relationships. Without communication we are left with guessing or assuming which can both be off the mark.

Communication is utterly important in all kinds of relationships.

∽

July 2
Beware of Jealousy

"Jealousy is simply and clearly the fear that you do not have value. Jealousy scans for evidence to prove the point — that others will be preferred and rewarded more than you. There is only one alternative — self-value. If you cannot love yourself, you will not believe that you are loved." —Jennifer James

It's probably pretty normal to have little twinges of jealousy from time to time, but the type of envy that is destructive is not healthy. Having someone you love show attention to another can cause a bit of jealousy, but obsessing that the one you love is having an affair based upon no basis of truth is hurtful and will probably cause the relationship to end sooner than later.

Jealousy often says, "He/she must be paying someone else attention because they are better in some way than me." It puts us down and places someone else above us in status, either by looks, financial standing, brains, wit, charm, and on and on.

When we care enough about who we are, when our self-esteem is sufficient, we won't go to unnecessary places of comparison with others. We will realize that they are who they are and we are who we are. And if the person we care about wants to be with us they will be with us. Do we ever really want someone in our lives who doesn't want to be there?

If someone gives us reason to be jealous by not being honest about our relationship, then it's time to look at moving on, but to be jealous simply because we are insecure is reason to look within and work on what's inside of us, not what could be happening that's probably not.

Having good self-esteem gives us a better chance in relationships because we won't doom them with jealousy and other insecurities. It means we choose people to spend time with who are good for us and if we find out with time that they aren't, we move on. Yes, we still get hurt when relationships end, even when we love ourselves, but loving and losing are part of life. The only way to protect our hearts from hurt is to never allow ourselves to love anyone. That's not a solution.

Jealousy can rob us of healthy relationships if we allow that to happen. Loving ourselves first and taking care of ourselves helps us not to be jealous without reason.

Jealousy can be a deal breaker.

∽

July 3
Setting Boundaries
"It is impossible to have a healthy relationship with someone who has no boundaries, with someone who cannot communicate directly, and honestly. ... It is our responsibility to take care of ourselves — to protect ourselves when it is necessary. ... It is impossible to learn to be loving to ourselves without owning our self — and owning our rights and responsibilities as co-creators of our lives."
—Robert Burney

In order to take care of ourselves in any kind of relationship including work, love, friendship, business and parenting issues, it's important that we set boundaries.

Sometimes setting and keeping boundaries can be very difficult, especially when others don't like them. But when we don't have any boundaries we open ourselves up to get walked on and maybe even abused. Usually people will respect our boundaries. Sometimes they may overstep them, but having boundaries makes us stronger and helps with our self-esteem issues.

We don't have to tell others what our boundaries are unless there's a problem. Our actions can speak for us, but there are times when we must let others know what our limits are. We don't have to do that in a condescending way, we can be pleasant and polite when we confront those who have somehow overstepped what we find acceptable.

It's not always another person's place to figure out what we expect from them because not everyone has the same limits. And some people don't know anything about boundaries so we can't expect them to adhere to ours if we don't let them know they have crossed over them.

We don't expect others to treat us with any more respect than the way we treat them or how we treat ourselves. If we say we are too busy to do something with someone, but we do it anyway, we should not tell them later that they didn't respect our boundaries or worse yet, complain to other people by saying that person took too much time from us. Going forward when we said no was a crossing of our own boundary, not them overstepping it.

When we make an issue about setting a boundary, it's our duty to uphold it, so we don't cause confusion in our relationships. If we cross our own boundaries we cannot expect others to respect them. That's not saying we have to be too rigid in our lives, it just means we should set reasonable boundaries and stick to them. It's not someone else's responsibility to ensure that we mean what we say and follow that, it's our issue.

Setting and keeping boundaries is good for you and all your relationships.

∽

July 4
Influence of Others
"You will be known by the company you keep."
—Unknown

Not only are we known by the company we keep, those we spend our time with have a great influence on us, although just what amount those around us affect us usually is determined by our maturity level and our self-esteem. Often in work and families we don't have a choice about whose company we keep. But in our personal time we do have choices.

Oftentimes, especially if we are malleable, others we spend time with can have a great influence. And here's where choosing is so important. Do we want to be influenced in a negative way or a positive way? It's simple, really. We can choose those who are good for us to be with and stay away from those who bring us to trouble and pain.

"If you hang out with the wrong people long enough eventually they will bring you down," a man said. He was referring to a pro football player who had been indicted for some very bad treatment of animals. The football player was charged along with a couple of other men. And what they were accused of doing involved making money, something that a pro football player certainly doesn't need in the U.S.

And it makes one wonder if this man was influenced by the people whose company he kept or if it was something he led them to. Maybe he was the bad that brought them down.

Most of us can remember a time when someone we called a friend led us into something we would probably not have done otherwise. It's best to keep an eye on the company we keep. It would be much better, given a choice, to spend our time with those who bring good things to the world, and to us, than those who inflict negativity and pain.

Watch what influences you, especially if you are easily influenced, and beware of those who might help bring you down rather than raise you up.

୶

July 5
Dealing with Frustration
"My recipe for dealing with anger and frustration: set the kitchen timer for twenty minutes, cry, rant, and rave, and at the sound of the bell, simmer down and go about business as usual."
—Phyllis Diller

Frustration is something that we all have in our lives and how we deal with it is important for our sanity and well-being.

An especially frustrating thing is dealing with other people when communication is not perfect, which it rarely is. Often our assumptions and expectations can cloud our thinking causing us to hear what we want to hear and miss the truth only later to be disappointed, hurt, and frustrated.

There are ways to deal with stress and frustration. We can go for a run, walk, a workout at the gym, take a nap, punch a bag, go for a bike ride, and on and on. Sometimes just getting away from the situation helps; when we can do that. And at other times we need to stay in it and talk it out with whoever is frustrating us.

Usually when we are frustrated or angry with another person, we end up saying things that we don't mean to say; the words come out and we can't take them back. So stepping away or out of the middle of something for a while and "simmering down" can be a very healthy thing and possibly keep us from further spinning ourselves into a hole with the situation.

We may want to cry, rant, and rave as the quote above says, and there's nothing wrong with that as long as we use it to process the situation and move on, rather than staying stuck in it. If only it was as easy as she describes above to move on from certain things.

We really have so little control over frustrating situations when they involve others. Letting go of our need to control the outcome goes a long way in lessening our frustration level. Turning it over to our Higher Power is a great solution.

When frustration hits — do something — so the hole isn't dug deeper.

✍

July 6
Living with Rejection
"Human beings, like plants, grow in the soil of acceptance, not in the atmosphere of rejection." —John Powell

Most of the time when we are rejected it's not so much about us as it is about the person who is rejecting us. We can only be who we are and who we are is good enough. If someone does not want us to be a part of their life then we ought to honor that.

What's especially difficult though is when rejection comes from those within our family. It's not easy to know if we should walk away when a parent, for instance, rejects us. We have some responsibility to family members that we don't have in other relationships.

Discerning where to draw the line when rejection occurs within a family is not an easy task. And we don't have to do it perfectly. Those dealing with dysfunctional families know that sometimes no matter what you do it's wrong in the eyes of those who choose to be martyrs. It's that "damned if you do, damned if you don't" situation.

The bottom line when handling rejection whether it's a family member, friend, business associate, or love interest is to take care of ourselves first. If someone cannot or does not love us, that does not mean we are unlovable. If we have done nothing to harm the other person, if we have done nothing wrong, yet we are rejected, we must hold our heads up and move forward. We are loveable maybe they just don't love themselves enough to love another.

Becoming a victim after rejections is not the answer. Hanging our head and having a pity party won't solve anything. We must look within and find the resolve to realize that who we are is okay, no matter if everyone agrees or not.

Rejection is painful, but it does not mean we are unlovable.

✍

July 7
Finishing the Race
"It's a marathon, not a sprint."
—Jason Priest

When we decide we want something or want to be able to do a new thing it's difficult to have the patience to achieve it or to wait to get it. The quote above is something my guitar instructor has said to me several times in only a handful of lessons.

Yes, I want to know how to play now. But in order to start with zero knowledge and achieve a decent level of playing ability there is a lot of groundwork that goes into the learning process. It takes countless hours of practice playing scales and finger exercises, among other things, before one can even play a song.

As with many things in life though, it's the long enduring journey rather than just deciding upon something and having it. Many times we give up before we get whatever it is we are trying to have.

Attending and graduating college is a good example of something that takes time and endurance. We take classes that we have no idea how they will help us with a particular job. A lot of it feels like a waste of time, but it's just part of the deal. If nothing else, a college degree shows that a person can stick to something long enough to finish.

Most of what we have in life that means something to us took a lot of work and effort. It takes that in relationships, learning an instrument, getting a degree, building a house and numerous other situations. Things that come easy rarely give us a whole lot of pleasure or self worth.

Also to achieve the things we desire we must often compromise something else. If we want to get a degree, for instance, we may have to give up something that we enjoy while we attend classes and study. If we want to build a long-term relationship with someone we might have to give up certain things sometimes to spend time with that person. Just as with learning an instrument, relationships take patience and time.

If we truly want to achieve or have a particular thing we will do what it takes to do that. If we don't care much one way or the other, it will show and eventually we'll let the thing fall to the wayside. Most of us lead busy lives. Yet we want to do new things and stretch who we are. We may want to find someone to spend our life with, learn a new trade, or learn something for fun, like a musical instrument. Most likely that will take compromise. We have to decide if it's worth giving up something else to fit in what we say we desire. If not, then we really don't want it much.

If we truly desire something we will compromise and do what it takes to have it.

❧

July 8
Entertaining Good Thoughts

"Put love first. Entertain thoughts that give life. And when a thought or resentment, or hurt, or fear comes your way, have another thought that is more powerful — a thought that is love."
—Mary Manin Morrissey

It is very difficult to have a thought that is love when someone has hurt us and we hold resentments toward them, or we are in fear over something, but loving thoughts do have strength.

Thoughts are powerful. When we offer blessings not curses for those we think have wronged us, we begin to feel better. Sometimes the relationship takes a turn for the better too, without us ever speaking a word to that person.

If we stay in a negative frame of mind, we will become stuck in that. Negativity breeds negativity. Just as a positive, loving outlook produces happiness and love. If we constantly live in fear we stay in that place, but if we can break the cycle we will see that we have been bogged down in it so long we didn't even realize how it controlled us.

Living with positive thoughts as much as possible may appear to be a bit silly, but trying it for a while will prove it to be a good thing. When thinking about two possible outcomes for a situation, we often choose the negative, most likely because we would rather think of that than be hurt or disappointed.

However, thoughts become actions. So if we think of negative outcomes more than likely that's just what we'll get. And maybe it won't hurt as bad because we didn't have much hope, but we will still not find much happiness and joy in life.

Thinking about positive outcomes will breed positive actions. So what if we get disappointed. Negative thinking would bring us to the same place, and perhaps we might just get the unexpected.

Entertain thoughts that give life and love and see good things happen before your eyes.

∽

July 9
Healthy Relationships

"To wait for someone else, or to expect someone else to make my life richer, or fuller, or more satisfying, puts me in a constant state of suspension." —Kathleen Tierney Andrus

We have many people in our lives that have an effect on what we do and the decisions we make. And that's part of living; it is part of being in relationship with others. Parents, siblings, spouses, partners, preachers, bosses, friends, children, teachers — each person in our life has some influence on us.

The problem lies in waiting and putting our lives on hold for another person to do something. We must go about our lives living from the inside out, taking care of our self first and then our relationships. If we are true to ourselves and honest with the other person the relationship will take care of itself.

We ought to not do more than we know is right to do in order to win another's approval. At our jobs, for instance, we should not work excessive hours of overtime trying to please the boss to gain his/her praises all the while neglecting our other responsibilities. It's not healthy to do too much for another in any relationship hoping for a reward of some kind … love, gifts, affection … whatever we seek.

Our lives are rich and full when we are real, honest, and do what we really want to do, not when we do what someone else thinks we should do when that's out of line with what we know is the right thing

The key is being honest and true to our self. If we want to do something for another we do it. If we want to say no, we can say that. But we don't put our lives on hold waiting for someone else, nor do we neglect everything else in our life to do for another. When we do that we build up resentments.

Taking care of self is working on a relationship.

৯৯

July 10
Parental Control
"PG - Parental guidance suggested"
—Motion Picture Association of America film rating system

While the above is intended for movies, in life sometimes it may be the parents who need the guidance. Very often parents have difficulty letting go, letting children grow up and lead adult lives.

Parents wield a great deal of control over their children, even when the "children" reach adulthood. Some use manipulation to try to tell us what to do by giving money and gifts or withholding such items. Other parents use affection and attention or the lack of to somehow try to get their offspring to do what they desire.

Yes we are adults now, but parents still have ways of at least trying to control us whether they actually do or not. We may go about our business and do what we want, but their little recordings play in our heads. And while we go about doing our own thing, they can bring us displeasure and cause strain in our relationships because we are afraid of what they will say or what they are thinking, or even if they will withhold something from us.

Some of us never much had support from our parents so we don't have as much "parental control" but there are still things that ring in our thoughts; things that we have carried for decades many times these negative thoughts still rule what we do.

And then there are those whose parents are very much involved in their lives although they don't approve of what the adult child is doing which makes life difficult for that child. They may use money or other "gifts" to try to control, but most likely they just get the information from the child which he/she chooses to give to them, not necessarily the truth.

It's difficult because they are always our parents no matter how good or bad they treated us and most of the time we still seek their approval whether we are willing to admit that or not.

It's time to loosen the hold they have on us. We are grown now. None of us are perfect, but we are who we are. And if you are reading here, then most likely you are working on growing and evolving in your life.

It's difficult to break our parents control over us, but we can do it one step at a time, one thing at a time, until we no longer feel the struggle against who we are and who they wished we had become.

Letting go of parental control allows you to be an adult.

∽

July 11
Thoughts Control Actions

"Every waking moment we talk to ourselves about the things we experience. Our self-talk, the thoughts we communicate to ourselves, in turn control the way we feel and act."
—John Lembo

We have a lot more control of what goes on in our lives than most of us realize. When our self-talk is negative, our actions will in turn tend to be more destructive than productive. By putting ourselves down all the time we are more apt to make poor decisions.

When we make a mistake or don't take an action we should have taken, beating ourselves up won't solve the problem. We ought to talk lovingly to ourselves and treat ourselves the same as we would hope others treat us, the way we treat others when we are kind and loving.

If we need forgiveness for something we ask for it from those we have offended, and we also forgive ourselves and move on. Constantly berating ourselves will not bring us growth or peace; only more disharmony in our lives.

We learn from our mistakes in positive ways. And our self-talk ought to be for positive growth rather than constantly bringing us down. Telling ourselves we are bad or wrong all the time will keep our mind on that rather than the lesson learned so that we can move on.

This does not excuse inappropriate behavior. It's just that we take appropriate actions to move on from our mistakes. And we treat ourselves with love. The more love we have for our self the less often we will be in situations where we do the wrong thing.

Do unto yourself as you would have others do unto you.

July 12
Stormy Times
"Talents are best nurtured in solitude, but character is best formed in the stormy billows of the world."
—Johann Wolfgang von Goethe

Sometimes we think we've finally got it. We find ourselves in a place that we have been working towards in our life. We have inner peace. Our head is on straight. Life feels good. And that's when the hurricane winds blow in and sweep us off our feet and throw us around like rag dolls. Our emotions feel like we are still back in that place before all of our growing occurred. But we haven't lost what we gained it's just hidden behind those icky emotions that have currently moved in.

It happens. But when we reframe it into the fact that we are building character through our difficulties it becomes much easier to deal with. We really never "get there" in life. It's a journey and for those of us who strive to continue to grow, the stormy weather of life will blow in and make us doubt our previous growth. If we ever actually got "there" wherever that is, we would then be stuck and life would become boring.

It's always helpful to remember that change is going to happen. Whether we are in that place of inner peace and think we have finally arrived, or we are on our knees begging God to take our pain away, whatever is going on will change with time. It may happen in an instant or it may happen in a month, but things don't stay the same.

We really can never predict when the storms of life will strike. But they will. Just as the times of happiness, peace, joy and all the good things come to us, so the trials and tribulations come too. And it's in the storms that we grow stronger. It's where character and faith is built.

The winds that blow through our happy times aren't curses from God or the Universe or anything out there, they are blessings in disguise. It won't feel that way while we are in the midst of the struggle, but when we get to the other side, we'll see that it was for our good.

When stormy weather blows in don't struggle with why — look for the lesson and growth instead.

July 13
Pain is Part of Life

"Pain and death are part of life. To reject them is to reject life itself." —Havelock Ellis

It's very easy after suffering an incident that caused pain, to just give up and say we won't ever go there again. Maybe it's a relationship issue and we just want to crawl into an imaginary shell and hide from the world and the thought of any future romance in our lives. Or it may be a member of our family who continues to hurt us each time we see them and we really would like to just cut off contact with that person, but they are our family so it's not always the best idea.

Pain can come from many sources and usually it hits us when we have been at our most vulnerable. And in order to get over the pain some time must pass and we will need to feel what we feel until it is gone. Feeling our pain is how we move forward. Shutting down and closing ourselves to future relationships is not the answer if we choose to live full lives.

One way to recover from a painful incident is to practice acceptance. We just stop fighting it and asking why it happened, why someone did what they did. What's happened is done and there's no going back in that situation to undo or redo. We accept it for what it is.

Another necessary recovery tool for pain is to forgive — forgive whoever hurt us and forgive our self if we need to do that. We may have been equal partners in the painful situation, or perhaps we are angry with ourselves for allowing our self to get in the situation that hurt us. Whatever the circumstance we forgive those who hurt us and our self.

It's okay to grieve. We can cry and scream if we have to, as long as we don't turn our pain onto someone else or turn it inward. Grieving is a process that doesn't fit into a nice tidy little package. We feel what we feel and stay away from medicating our pain with drugs, alcohol, or anything that we would use to keep us from feeling.

Pain comes when we live our lives fully, just as joy comes too.

July 14
Challenging Our Minds

"I could not, at any age, be content to take my place by the fireside and simply look on. Life was meant to be lived. Curiosity must be kept alive. One must never, for whatever reason, turn his back on life."

—Eleanor Roosevelt

Upon telling someone that I had begun to take lessons to play a musical instrument at an age well into my forties, I was asked: "Whatever made you decide to pick it up at this stage of your life?" And my answer was simply: "Why not? It's something I've always wanted to do."

Doctors say that when we continue to challenge our minds we are less likely to suffer dementia. Some say to work puzzles that challenge the mind, but truly anything we do that makes us think is a benefit. Just as exercising our bodies keeps us in good physical shape, using our minds keeps them sharp.

Living, being a journey rather than a destination, is about being able to do things that make us happy. It's not all about a dreary job that we may have to pay the bills, or the drudgery of certain chores, it's also about having fun, experiencing joy.

If we've dreamed of doing something but have put it off, it's not too late. Just because we may be too old to make a career of our particular interest, or to become great at it even, that doesn't mean we can't do it, or have fun doing it. And what if we just happened to find a hidden talent in whatever it is, at age 30, or 40 or even 60 or 70?

Life can be fun. We can fulfill a lot of our dreams if we just make the attempt and stop saying we're too old for that. If the alternative is to be bored and miserable because we didn't get to try something, we should just go for it.

It's never too late to try something you've always wanted to do.

❧

July 15
Living Now

"God made the world round so we would never be able to see too far down the road." —Isak Dinesen

Staying in the moment is not an easy thing to do. We are often either lamenting yesterday or worried about tomorrow. And more often than not we are trying to live our lives in the far off future.

When we stay stuck in the past we can't move on to the next lesson and most likely we are missing out on what we've been given for today. What happened before is best left behind. We do this with prayer, letting go, forgiving, asking for forgiveness if needed, and possibly making amends to those we have harmed.

To live in the future also causes us to miss the moment and the lesson at hand. Worry about tomorrow, next week, next year, or whatever outcome we are stressing over, will not make something happen the way we want. Worry never solved anything. In fact, worry may sabotage our best interests. If we are in a constant state of worry, most likely there are a lot of negative thoughts associated with that. And those thoughts can become reality.

To not worry about the past or future does not mean we don't take responsibility for what we've done or what we are going to do. It doesn't mean living our lives without any planning or goals, it just means that we focus on the facts of a situation rather than the crazy things our minds try to tell us.

One tool that is helpful when we cannot let go of a particular troublesome thing is to ask ourselves, "Will what I'm worrying about, or the outcome of it, matter in five years?" Often what we are so upset about is something that won't matter in five days, let alone down the road. But it could be something big enough to matter in five years, although worry itself won't make a difference in anything. If some future issue is causing us to worry, and the outcome does matter in the future, we can take the steps to work on the decision, and take the best actions we know of to prepare for and solve it ... all the while we can pray about it and turn it over to our Higher Power.

Life would be without growth if we had a fortune teller on hand.

July 16
Getting Through Grief
"Hope is grief's best music."
—Unknown

The grieving process is one that we would very much like to avoid, but it's an inevitable part of life. It can strike when we go through personal trauma or change, or when we lose a loved one, pet, relationship, job, home, or anything that means something to us. To experience grief means that we have opened our heart to love and joy and lost something, which is better than to never experience truly living.

The Elisabeth Kübler-Ross model shows that grieving has five stages, which are not experienced sequentially, but rather randomly and some are not experienced by every person who experiences grief.

The five stages, according to her model, are: denial, anger, bargaining, depression and acceptance.

Many times when a person is sad people will tell them not to cry, but it's cleansing to cry, and a part of the process. If we hold in our feelings they will come back in the future and manifest in other ways. We may have a lot of anger and not understand where that's coming from. We may experience a deep depression that we cannot seem to shake. No matter how the feelings come up, they will at some point. The best thing to do is feel what we feel now and move through them so that the grief doesn't interfere with our future relationships.

Grieving is part of life. We should never be ashamed for feeling a feeling. Our emotions are part of us. They mean we are human.

Also keep in mind that the length of time we grieve is not predetermined. It's a process that is not pleasant or fun, but there are some things that can help us through it including talking to friends and loved ones; exercising; counseling; joining a support group; eating right; listening to or playing music; and doing something fun when feeling up to it.

Most importantly we should be patient and loving towards ourselves no matter how long it takes to get through the process. We will get past a great deal of the pain with time and effort. The kinder we are to ourselves during our grief, the easier time we will have in moving on. The sadness we feel when we grieve feels like something we will never be rid of, but before we know it we will successfully be at a place where we can feel joy again.

Grieving is easier when you are loving and patient with yourself.

෯

July 17
You Deserve Your Love

"You yourself, as much as anybody in the entire universe deserve
your love and affection." —Buddha

Looking outside of ourselves to find a hero — or to find someone to love us to somehow justify that we are loveable — is not what we ought to do. Instead we start with our self. When we love who we are we will draw love to us as we give it. And it will be much healthier than what we are accustomed to as we have tried to find it outside of ourselves.

Loving ourselves is paramount to loving others. It really is that simple. If we can love ourselves we can love others, and if we don't love ourselves no amount of effort to love another will ever be successful.

A lot of the time we look outside of ourselves for encouragement and recognition. We wait for others to tell us how great we did something, or how handsome or pretty we look. Sometimes people just don't give out compliments. And it doesn't mean we aren't deserving of praise, but it may be that the other person is waiting on it too.

What we can do instead is pat ourselves on the back. We nurture us and give ourselves gifts that we deserve for a job well done. Maybe the gift we need is a day of rest. Sometimes we want to buy something or go out to dinner. Perhaps all we need is to hear a compliment. Any of those things we can do for ourselves.

If we set a goal to lose a particular amount of weight, run a 5K in a certain number of minutes, seek a new job, get the laundry done, whatever it is that we set forth to do, once completed we deserve praise. Give it to yourself. Waiting on others to fulfill our needs will never work. That would be codependent behavior and that's something we wish to avoid.

Sure, compliments from others are always nice, and very much welcome, but having them or not should not determine our level of happiness or love for ourselves. The problem is, even if someone praises us, if we don't believe what they are saying about us it won't stick anyway.

Love starts within.

∽

July 18
Staying Open
"When we close ourselves off from our friends, our fellow travelers, we block God's path to us and through us. ...When we close ourselves off from each other, we have destroyed the vital contribution we each need to make and to receive in order to nurture life."
—Karen Casey

Not shutting down after being hurt is difficult. Staying open despite our pain takes a great deal of effort. And we may need to shut down temporarily from time to time. But to stay shut off, to build up another wall each time we are disappointed and hurt is not the answer. Putting up walls and shutting down just adds to our pain.

If we are living a full life we are going through painful experiences. That's just how life is. We know that we grow through the tough times, we've already learned that. Then why do we get angry with ourselves and God when we find that we are in the midst of a painful growing situation? Most likely because we expect perfection from ourselves and wish we could have known not to go into the situation where we got hurt. We blame God because we don't understand God.

Some of our pain from a situation can be from prior relationships, issues from when we were still children, and low self-esteem. For instance, if we have a fear of abandonment and we are abandoned by someone, it's easy to see the pain of the current situation magnified.

Even when we feel a lot of anger in a situation with someone, we can know that the person that hurt us was placed in our lives for a reason. That may not be clear to us at the time of our intense pain, but hopefully one day when the pain has lessened we will see. And likewise, we were put in the other person's life for their growth.

Whenever we are hurting it feels as if the pain will never stop that we will never feel good again. But we will return to a better place. And we'll have learned something in the process. We will also be stronger. But the experience, the pain we felt, the growth, will only be worth it if we continue to live and stay open.

Shutting down is the only thing that keeps the pain present and keeps you from growth.

∽

July 19
Forgiveness
"Forgiveness means giving up all hope for a better past."
—Lily Tomlin

If we desire to rid our lives of resentment, regret, and bitterness, we probably need to work on forgiveness.

Forgiving others and ourselves is a way to move past those things that are blocking our growth and happiness. When we have a resentment because of something that was done to us, or when we regret something we have done, we are continuing to live in the past. And since we cannot change the past we must try another option.

Forgiveness is letting go. It's not necessarily forgetting something lest we have to go through the same situation again, but it also means we move on with the knowledge that what is done is done and we cannot change it. Holding onto whatever it is won't make it go away. Letting go of it will.

Sometimes we won't forgive someone because we are not ready to move on. We hold onto the pain at times because it's familiar or it's all we have left of a person or situation. Additionally, hanging onto resentment from the past keeps us in the victim status of life. As long as we don't forgive and move on from a painful situation we remain the victim. We can be stronger than that. We can move out of the misery that victim status holds by forgiving.

And while forgiveness means giving up hope for a better past, it also offers us a better future than we would have if we hung onto a hurtful issue. We must look within and find out why we are unwilling to forgive ourselves or someone else. It may be that we think forgiveness lets someone off the hook for having done us wrong, but it doesn't. And hanging onto our pain doesn't teach them a lesson either. Not forgiving ourselves keeps us living in guilt.

Forgiveness removes the roadblock to the future.

July 20
Coming Alive
"Don't ask yourself what the world needs; ask yourself what makes you come alive. And then go and do that. Because what the world needs is people who have come alive."
—Harold Whitman

Whenever we are really fired up about something we are doing in our lives we have all the energy in the world to do it. We are fully alive. And it shows because we spend the time on it to succeed. We have the drive and energy necessary to be successful in the endeavor.

On the flip side when confronted with tasks we'd just as soon not have to do we often must talk ourselves into those things. We procrastinate. We moan and groan about it. We feel tired and unenthusiastic. We probably don't do whatever it is very well even if we manage to do it.

Having a strong desire, a fire in our belly for something, is what moves us into action. When we have that, nothing can get in our way. Our mind is focused; other things are put to the side. So when we find ourselves with an intense interest in doing something or we remember a time when we did have the enthusiasm that made us feel alive, it's time to do that thing.

Sometimes what makes us come alive is not a task that would support us financially, but if it is such a thing we should do our best to make that our life's work. The thing that makes us come alive is a gift and no matter if it's income producing or not, we should share that gift with others.

No gift is unimportant. Every opportunity to use our talents is important. And once we discover what it is that makes us come alive we will find a way to do that anyway because it feels good.

Find what makes you come alive and then share it with others.

July 21
Having Swagger

"In college football, the swagger is essential for any team to win a national title. Nearly every great team in college football seems to have that air of invincibility." —Columnist J.P. Degance

Having high self-esteem and being in a place in life where we feel on top of the world gives us swagger. And while this word may bring to mind images of a peacock in full plumage strutting around, chest stuck out, head held high it doesn't mean having a swagger is a bad thing at all.

There's a difference in feeling good about ourselves and feeling invincible than there is in being cocky. When we have experienced having the swagger we know it is something we want, it's a place we want to be in our lives. But it isn't always present. Life happens. Trauma and tragedy happen. Disappointments happen. But we can get our swagger back.

If we keep doing the things we know to do — the next right thing — we can get our lives back on track if things have gone awry lately. And we can either return to our swagger or discover it for the first time.

When we have swagger, we feel like we can succeed at anything we do, and when we believe in ourselves we *can* achieve most anything we set our mind to.

Swagger, confidence, the feeling of invincibility can take us a long way on our journey. It can help us heal from hurtful situations or loss; it can give us the courage to face a difficult challenge; we may better be able to set and keep boundaries; and it might help us to go after a goal that we wish to achieve but have not found the courage yet to approach.

As long as we aren't boastful and conceited, having swagger isn't a bad thing at all, it's something to be cherished and held onto if possible. If having swagger can help a whole football team win a national championship, just think what we could do with it in our lives.

Don't ever feel ashamed of having swagger just be sure to use it for good.

❧

July 22
Powerless Over Others

"We admitted we were powerless over others — that our lives had become unmanageable."

—Step One of the Twelve Steps of Co-Dependents Anonymous

We cannot control other people. We can't control their thoughts, behaviors or actions. No matter how much we may wish to we will never be able to do such a thing. So the sooner we learn this and accept our powerless over others, the faster we can move forward with our own growth and ability to be in relationship with others. When we try to control others our lives will be unmanageable and we won't find peace until we let go.

We may have tried in our lives to help a partner, friend, or family member who has an addiction problem, only to find out that no matter what we did they didn't get any better because it's their issue and no amount of interference will stop a person until they are ready.

Sometimes in relationships in order to get along with another person we may try to control outcomes of interactions only to find our best intentions fall flat. We may try to say what we think they want us to say and that's not right. So we say nothing and that fails too. We let them make all of the decisions and that doesn't work either.

We simply cannot control another person, just as we cannot control any outcome. As soon as we can admit being powerless over others, we can begin to let go and move on. We can look at what we do have power over. We can walk out the door, quit the job, move on if need be. That's where our power lies, in what we can do, not what they do or don't do.

We can have more manageable lives when we learn to take care of our side of the street and leave other people to deal with their issues. It's not usually easy, especially when we care about someone deeply, but we can't have relationships with others the way we want on their terms only. We only have power over what we do and say and that's a big enough job without trying to control another person's behaviors.

Accepting powerless over others gives you power.

July 23
Facing Our Giants

"You will not be free, hanging on to things that hold you back and hurt that question all your worth, that make you feel afraid…"

—Christine Havrilla

We all have things that hold us back and hurt. Many of us have carried these things with us since we were small children. And some of us even after therapy and lots of emotional and spiritual growth cannot completely let the "things" go no matter how hard we try.

What we can do though is move forward despite whatever it is that is an obstacle for us. Even if we don't do it great and even if we cry and our hands shake all the way through it, we still only make progress by attempting, never by sitting still and saying we can't.

For me there are many of these things and mostly they are performance anxiety related. When I returned to college as an adult I was determined that I would take speech class and get it out of the way, and if I did that I could make it through school. Because I have such fear of public speaking it was very difficult. For my final speech I presented information about panic attacks because many of my symptoms when "performing" in front of others are similar.

And not only did I make it through that class, I got an A and I ended up graduating from college. I had to give a few more speeches in other classes and it never got any easier, but I made it through.

No matter how many times I've had to perform in some aspect in front of others, no matter how afraid I was, or how bad my hands shook, or even the number of tears I cried, none of that ever killed me or even brought me great shame. I may never get to a place where I don't have this level of fear, but if I don't attempt to walk through it I know I will continue to carry it with me.

We are all human. We all have obstacles that hold us back and hurt. What we choose to do with those will determine a lot about where we can go in our lives. Walking through our fears, facing the giants, gives us character and strength.

Progress comes with attempting, never by sitting still and saying I can't.

༄

July 24
Speak No Evil
"To speak ill of others is a dishonest way of praising ourselves."
—Will Durant

We are all guilty of speaking negatively about other people in our lives, especially if that person has hurt us in some way. And sometimes people talk badly about others because they are so lacking in self-esteem it is their way of trying to make themselves look better. The sad part is that when we talk about someone in a negative way it doesn't give us a lift at all, either from within or from those we are talking to.

There are people in our lives who probably deserve to be talked badly about. They may not be living life the best way possible for them. But it's not our place to tell them how to live and gossiping about them surely won't give them any guidance. We may be put in the path of another on any given day as part of their lesson but it's not our duty to decide what they need to learn.

If we are in relationship with someone who doesn't treat us right and we decide to move on, that's our right. Just because we see things that they need to do differently, in our opinion, it's still not our place to make sure they are getting the lesson, especially when they know why we left.

The responsibility lies in that person being honest with herself, and us taking care of our own lessons. If they didn't get the lesson while dealing with us, they will be presented the opportunity again. How many times have we had to be given a learning experience only to have to go through it again with another situation because we didn't get it the first, second, or tenth time?

It's okay to talk about someone to another if we are honestly trying to work through our hurt feelings and issues surrounding that relationship. We need to talk about it and get input from others. What's not okay is to continually put that person down to others to simply make ourselves look or feel better. Just because we may know the faults of others, it's not serving us or anyone else to spread that information to the world.

Speaking poorly about another person does not give us a boost in the eyes of others.

≪⑤

July 25
Being Vulnerable
"We all need somebody to talk to. It would be good if we talked ... not just pitter-patter, but real talk. We shouldn't be so afraid, because most people really like this contact; that you show you are vulnerable makes them free to be vulnerable."
—Liv Ullmann

To be vulnerable with another, to be truly open, raw, exposing ourselves to be hurt or ridiculed or loved is one of the most difficult things we can do. So much of the time we live behind the façade that everything is okay within us. We hide our pain, jealousy, anger, and fears behind the walls that we put up to protect ourselves from the world.

And when we feel brave enough to let someone see in, even if we only let them see through a tiny sliver of a crack of our armor, it can still feel like we've been peeled back and opened for all kinds of emotions to sweep over us. But we should do it anyway. We should find safe places to be vulnerable.

Sometimes we can do this with a really close friend, partner, sponsor, or in therapy. And when we do it we grow. We may feel as though letting someone see exactly who we are is so painful we'll die from the embarrassment, but most likely what we say to another isn't anything they haven't felt or done or experienced. It's such a relief to find out that others aren't any more perfect than we are since not a single one of us is perfect.

It's also an added boost when we are vulnerable with someone to find out that our letting them see inside our true self helps them to do the same either with us or with someone else whom they trust.

Sometimes we are vulnerable and discover that perhaps we would have been better off to keep the walls up with a particular person. When that happens it is still not the end of the world and the worst thing we can do is never trust another person to see inside us, we may just need to choose more carefully.

We are the same inside whether or not anyone else ever sees that person we try to keep hidden. We can find freedom when we let others see who we really are, when we stop using so much energy to try to make the outsides look the way we think they should all the while neglecting the reality of who we are.

Being vulnerable is scary, but it is important for our healing and growth.

ക

July 26
We Get What We Give
"To have peace, give peace. To be happy, make happy. To feel loved, love. This is very simple and is a part of all the world's inspired teachings. But it cannot be understood by a mind that refuses to pause." —Hugh Prather

This is a simple concept and one that we can easily see working when we are in a time in our lives that things are going well. When things aren't going so great we may not be as apt to "get it."

All we have to do is remember a day in our lives when it seemed like the world was our oyster. Life didn't give us any lemons that day, in fact, we probably got compliments from places we never saw coming and we felt really good. We smiled. Others smiled at us. We felt better still. We radiated love and we felt it come back to us. It truly does work. What we give we get back most of the time.

So too does it work in reverse. If we are down and having a pity-party, walking around with our shoulders slumped and our heads down we probably aren't getting smiled at and we probably don't feel very loved. If we have a chip on our shoulder and we're angry then others most likely will respond to us in a negative way.

It's very easy to be on the upswing of life when things are going well and we just feel good. And we should enjoy it for all it's worth and try to perpetuate that mood into the next moment which turns into the next day.

And when things aren't going well and we just want to go home and pull the covers over our head we ought to remember the up times and know they will return. And they will come back more quickly if we "make happy," and give love and peace. We don't always get what we give, but more often than not if we feel loved it's because we gave it out first.

What you get from others is often a mirror of what you are doling out.

◆

July 27
Knowing When to Walk Away
"You got to know when to hold em, know when to fold em, know when to walk away and know when to run."
—Kenny Rogers (song lyrics)

Knowing when to walk away can be a difficult thing for many of us. When we care about someone it's hard to make the decision of finality with that person, but often a clean and final break may be the best for all involved.

We should never let anyone treat us in a way we do not deserve. If we are being kind and loving and someone is being unkind to us, we should walk away. There's really no way to change a person who doesn't want to be changed. We may try for a while, but usually that person is not working on growth and change or they wouldn't continue to treat us badly. To keep hanging on to some hope that things will be different is a self-defeating behavior.

The person who is treating us badly may be acting out because they don't want to be in relationship with us and they don't know how to say it. So either consciously or unconsciously they behave in a way that makes us leave without them having to be the bad guy, which they are anyway because of their poor behavior.

Or maybe they just don't know how to be in relationship with another. Some folks are unwilling to compromise. Perhaps they are spoiled and unable to give of themselves because they are used to getting. But every relationship no matter how deep or shallow requires compromise in some degree.

We may need to examine why we hold onto hope for a true connection with someone when there's not one there anymore. What are we getting from the relationship that makes us think we cannot let go and walk away? Do we need that person's approval? Is being treated badly so familiar to us that we just can't let go of it? Do we want to be in relationship with someone who either isn't capable of mutuality or doesn't want us in their lives the way it was at one time or the way we want it?

Whatever the reasons we can't seem to let go, once we discover that we can safely move on and free ourselves of that person it's time to make the break. We will discover freedom. We will see growth when we love ourselves enough to cut from our lives those who do not treat us the way we deserve to be treated.

Loving yourself means letting go of those who treat you dishonorably.

∽

July 28
Watch Yourself

"Self-observation brings man to the realization of the necessity of self-change. And in observing himself a man notices that self-observation itself brings about certain changes in his inner processes. He begins to understand that self-observation is an instrument of self-change, a means of awakening."
—George Gurdjieff

As with anything familiar, we sometimes forget to observe our own behaviors and thoughts. But it is important to stop and watch ourselves, listen to what we say and think during our daily routines.

How do we treat others? Are we kind and loving, or do we just expect those kinds of behaviors from others when, in fact, we are being mean and hateful? Do we offer thanks and compliments to those who do things for us or who we observe doing things for others? Do we do simple things like letting someone into traffic or holding doors open for others? Are we constantly making fun of someone else or gossiping all the time?

How we behave is symptomatic of what's on the inside of us. And we may not even realize what's on the inside — our anger, fear, pain, etc. — until we see ourselves acting out in ways that are not how we really want to behave. If we observe our actions consciously we may be able to change something about ourselves right away, or what we see may trigger in us a new area we need to work on.

Another thing to be aware of is how we treat ourselves. Are we eating right and getting exercise? Do we get enough rest and sleep? Do we balance socializing with alone time? When we are healthy physically and emotionally we will treat others better. It's difficult to have good emotional or physical health when either one is being neglected.

Observing ourselves with honesty and without judgment is the best way. We don't do it to beat ourselves up, but rather to know what's really going on within us, which may answer some questions we have about what's going on outside of us. We learn from watching and from there we make whatever changes are necessary to be the person we wish to be.

Self-observation can answer a lot of questions and bring about change.

∽

July 29
Being Honest With Self
"Self-honesty is a prerequisite for self-discipline."
—Ellen Kaye-Cheveldayoff

There's a line in the Big Book of Alcoholics Anonymous which states that there are those "who are constitutionally incapable of being honest with themselves" and because of this inability to be rigorously honest they cannot achieve sobriety.

And so it is with life, really. We can walk through life, go through the motions, be reasonably successful, or not so successful, or even make it big in whatever we attempt. But in order to have emotional and spiritual success where we are capable of self-love and healthy relationships, we need to be honest not only with others, but also with ourselves.

When we are wrong we admit it, but we don't take blame when we have not done harm to anyone or been out of line. That would be dishonest. It means we are truthful to others and we don't deceive ourselves either.

Many times people think of "cash register" honesty when asked if they tell the truth. And while giving back the extra change from an attendant if given too much, or telling them when we are undercharged is a form of honesty, it still doesn't mean we are honest in other ways.

Another way we look at how honest we are is if we tell the truth when asked a question.

But the honesty necessary to grow and to have self-love is that in which we have pure motives and where we are sincere. It means that we don't lie to ourselves or rationalize poor behavior.

Self-honesty means we examine our strengths and weaknesses so that we can do the work on those parts of us that may need to be changed. We don't convince ourselves that we are just this way, or blame it on someone or something in our past; we admit to ourselves that we have something that needs some work.

It's easy to deceive ourselves. Some will say they are not an alcoholic because they only drink beer as if there's no alcohol in that. There are those of us who claim not to be prejudiced against a race other than our own, but our thinking and behavior says otherwise. We may try to lie to ourselves that we didn't eat all day when dieting because all we ate was a bag of cookies, no real meal.

Deception of self can take on many forms. But until we can be honest with ourselves we cannot be truly honest with others. And until we are capable of self-honesty we won't be able to grow much or have sustained self-love.

Honesty with self is necessary in all aspects of growth and love.

∽

July 30
Go Easy on Yourself

"Don't wait until everything is just right. It will never be perfect. There will always be challenges, obstacles and less than perfect conditions. So what? Get started now. With each step you take, you will grow stronger and stronger, more and more skilled, more and more self-confident and more and more successful."
—Mark Victor Hansen

No matter what areas of our lives we are working on, it's important to be gentle and loving with ourselves as we grow and change. Sometimes we make mistakes or take wrong turns on our journey, but that does not mean we are failures and should stop proceeding.

Perhaps those things we view as wrong turns or mistakes are actually parts of the journey that we'll look back on and cherish for the lessons they taught us. Most importantly we ought to be kind to ourselves when we are experiencing growth, change, grief, or even stagnation. Beating ourselves up never gets us anywhere healthy, it just gets us beat up.

Many of us will be hard on ourselves because while we made a decision that we're proud of, we berate ourselves because it took us so long, instead of focusing on the fact that we did it.

When we're grieving a loss we must understand that it takes whatever time it takes to get through the pain and we need to be gentle and loving with ourselves as we work our way through it.

Sometimes we get stuck in a place in our lives where we're straddling a fence over what to do next. We may want to make a career change, but we have reasons why we don't fully put our energy into looking for a new job. Maybe we have fear. Perhaps we are concerned about change. Whatever the reasons, if we are unhappy with something whether it's a job or a relationship, it's important to our growth to face the fears and hop over the obstacles to get where we want to go. And we can never do that if we are not kind and loving with ourselves during the process.

We can be our own best friend or our own worst enemy. It is our choice to make. Just remember that when something is loved and nurtured it grows and heals. And that's a gift we can give ourselves as we work through our own issues.

Growth and healing occur more quickly in a loving environment.

July 31
Do It Now
"Procrastination usually results in sorrowful regret. Today's duties put off until tomorrow give us a double burden to bear; the best way is to do them in their proper time."
—Ida Scott Taylor

Most of us have problems with procrastination. Usually what we put off are those things we just don't like to do, but sometimes we procrastinate doing things we enjoy as well.

One thing to keep in mind when putting off until tomorrow or next week, something that we could do right now, is to not allow things to reach a crisis mode. It is so easy for things to snowball into something big when we don't take care of them as we ought to.

A talk with a significant other about a problem if put off too long can escalate into a huge argument because we took on so much emotional energy over time when we could have handled it sooner and not had a fight. Sitting the children down for some parental guidance before there's an incident may fend off a crisis involving problems at school or worse.

Then of course there are physical situations that need to be taken care of before they turn into disasters. Or maybe we don't like particular things about our jobs and we put them off until the last minute and then have extra added stress that we could have avoided.

Some folks like to do the most disliked tasks first so they can enjoy the rest of the day. Getting out of the habit of doing things late or at the last minute is something that can ease the anxiety in our lives. When something is hanging over us that needs to be done it takes away from pleasurable things.

And often when we feel overwhelmed it's because we have let things build up until it appears there is no way to complete everything. Finding balance in our lives is dependent upon not taking on more than we can handle, but it also means doing what we need to do to complete those things we have taken upon ourselves.

Take care of things now before they reach crisis mode.

ॐ

August 1
Starting Over

"Keep on beginning and failing. Each time you fail, start all over again, and you will grow stronger until you have accomplished a purpose — not the one you began with perhaps, but one you'll be glad to remember." —Anne Sullivan

Each of us has been down a road before that we thought was going to be a rewarding and fulfilling journey, one which we knew was the right path. And while we were on that road we were happy and grateful, and probably relieved because we finally got there. And then something happened. It didn't work. We failed, it failed. It doesn't really matter. What matters in the end is that we don't give up and never try again.

We can start over. We can begin our day over. We can start a new job when one doesn't work out. We can go back to school if we didn't get the degree we sought. We can begin the diet and exercise program once more. We can try another relationship if ours ends in a breakup or divorce. We can start over. It's the doing that brings success.

It hurts to not find success, especially when we thought we finally had arrived at a place we wanted to be, only to have it pulled away. But we do grow from unsuccessful attempts at things.

There's the old saying that when God closes a door He opens a window. And really there are lots of opportunities for us in this world. We just need to remain open to them and not close ourselves off when we feel hurt, disappointed, and defeated.

People will lie. They will promise us things in business and in our personal lives that they never intend to give, or maybe they aren't capable of giving what they promise. We can't be responsible for the shortcomings of others. What we can do is keep beginning, and failing if that's what happens, and one day we may truly be on that road we just thought we were on before.

None of us wants to be the person who isn't honest and true to others; the one who promises what we can't give or misrepresents who we are. And most likely the people who treat us that way don't mean to be dishonest and hurtful either. We ought to always beware of carrying our baggage into the future lest we become that way.

But even when others do us wrong, or fate doesn't give us what we want at a particular time, we can start again.

Failure breeds strength; starting over is the beginning of success.

∽

August 2
Feelings Last

"I've learned that people will forget what you said, people will forget what you did, but people will never forget how you made them feel." —Maya Angelou

When a relationship ends we miss the other person mostly because of the way we felt when we were with them. Sometimes it's not the person we miss but simply that we no longer feel the way we did when they were in our lives. Many of us suffer from low self-esteem and even if it's not low, our egos can always use a boost. So when someone comes along and says nice things to us, and about us, we feel good.

And even if it's not a romantic relationship there can still be a spark between people. A meshing of hearts, minds, and souls that we don't have with everyone we meet. It's an electric feeling, a sensation of being fully alive, vibrant, whole, when we are in these kinds of relationships.

So it makes sense that when they end, we feel bad. As high as any drug takes us, the low goes just as far in the other direction and this can happen when we are involved with people.

Relationships end though. And it's not always someone's fault. We grow apart, or we move away because of jobs or family. We move into other relationships that require us to have less time for others. And sometimes one or both people in a relationship decide that they cannot do it, or are not capable of doing it and it has to end.

What we won't forget is how someone made us feel; good or bad. Most of the time if we are emotionally healthy we will seek out relationships that make us feel good. Sometimes though, when we are accustomed to less than healthy interaction, we may be drawn to those types of familiar relationships even though in our heart of hearts we know that it's not good for us and destructive even.

We must remember too that others won't forget how we made them feel. And feelings stick around longer than words. They permeate us. Our feelings are often what we operate from, no matter how much we try not to, we are emotional beings and our feelings effect our actions.

So take care when dealing with the feelings of others. Even if a relationship has to end we would rather another person have good memories of us than bad. We only do this in an honest way; we don't say things just to make someone feel good if we don't mean it.

Handling relationships with care is essential to long-lasting good feelings.

❧

August 3
Doing Good

"Do all the good you can, by all the means you can, in all the ways you can, in all the places you can, at all the times you can, to all the people you can, as long as ever you can."
—John Wesley

We aren't always rewarded for doing good in our lives. If we are giving of ourselves to our community and to those less fortunate, we are often asked to give more. And when we are good and kind to those who aren't nice to us, we often don't see any change or rewards. But regardless, we ought to do good anyway.

Doing good, whether it's being gentle, patient, and kind to those who don't treat us the same, or whether it's giving of our time, energy, and resources, is something that we do reap the benefit of, even when we don't readily see it. It goes along with the saying, "you reap what you sow." Sow meanness and likely it will return. Be selfish and most likely you won't get much from others.

It isn't always easy to "do good" when we'd rather not. Sometimes we do have to say no, and we do that without guilt. Because the ones who give are the first ones others come looking for when they need more giving. But better to be thought of as one of "those" than one who won't ever do anything for anyone.

In doing good, giving of our time, we strike a balance. In doing good rather than bad as far as our behavior goes, we seek to always do good even when we don't get that reciprocated. When given a choice of doing good or doing bad, the good must always win out. What will be the good in doing bad?

When frustrated by doing good, do it anyway. Doing good is loving and no matter what religion or philosophy we ascribe to, love is an integral part of it. Sometimes not doing bad is doing good. If we have been hurt by others, not hurting back is loving. Forgiveness is doing good.

Doing good is loving.

᪥

August 4
Denial

"Self-acceptance comes from meeting life's challenges vigorously. Don't numb yourself to your trials and difficulties, nor build mental walls to exclude pain from your life. You will find peace not by trying to escape your problems, but by confronting them courageously. You will find peace not in denial, but in victory."
—J. Donald Walters

No matter what we do in life we can either sugarcoat it into something better than it was, or curse all over it and turn it into something negative. Whether it's a thought, an action, a fear, it is what it is no matter if we're in denial over it or not. We deny the truth to make situations appear better than they are, as well as some sort of self-punishment to make things not seem so great when maybe, just maybe they are that good.

To deny our thoughts and feelings does not make them go away, in fact, holding our feelings inside can make us sick. Pushing down, internalizing pain brings on stomach problems, backaches, and headaches.

Denial is not noble. Courage to face our fears, feelings, and consequences of our actions is noble. Saying a thing is black when it is white does not make it white. To pretend, even to ourselves, that we are not hurt when we are does not make us free of pain. It is simply a temporary fix to a long-term issue, one that will be resolved when we are willing to be honest with our self and others in order to stop running from it and face it.

We all use denial as a defense mechanism for things that we find intolerable. Sometimes it is necessary for a while, but there comes a point in our "recovery" that we need to face all of the facts, feelings, and actions of our lives so that we may grow and heal.

When we learn to accept rather than deny we are better able to deal with life on life's terms. Life is not smooth and easy, it hasn't been for centuries and it is not going to be tomorrow. Living in denial about our difficulties doesn't make them disappear.

Denial only prolongs the growth from and solution to every situation.

∽

August 5
Living with Handicaps

"But just because you haven't led a normal life doesn't mean you can't lead a healthy life. Just because you have a reverse handicap — because you are special — doesn't mean that you can't be happy; it just means that it takes a lot of work to figure out how to do that."

—Jodie Foster

We all have some sort of "handicap." In comparison to those who have severe handicaps it may seem insensitive to state that fact, but it's all relative. People with severe handicaps often do things that those who are seemingly normal wouldn't attempt.

When faced with difficulties whether physical inadequacies, mental shortcomings, or emotional issues, what we do with that is what makes us who we are. It's what makes us either special or someone who just uses excuses to never be the person we are meant to be.

We often take our situation in life for granted. Maybe we had some lucky breaks and got where we are with little effort. In that case we are most likely not going to be very strong when something goes wrong. But those who have spent a lifetime struggling because they are different in some way; they know a strength that will carry them through when life presents a new challenge.

Some of us are handicapped by pain or regret. We may have taken a path that we wish we had not chosen and now pay for it with consequences. Some were born "different" with a learning disorder, a physical deformity or chronic pain, a race that is not respected, or a sexual orientation that is condemned by a portion of society. But those things are a part of who we are and those who are considered different, those who were born with what makes them not fit the "normal" mold, don't realize they are different because they just are who they are, who they were born to be.

Those who follow the teachings of the Bible would find that the people who are often condemned in this world are the same people that Jesus would love and embrace. Not to have pity for them, but because that's what love is.

Handicaps can be an excuse to do nothing, or they can propel you to greatness.

August 6
Inner Peace
"Do not lose your inward peace for anything whatsoever, even if your whole world seems upset."
—Saint Francis De Sales

There are a few things we can count on in this world and one of those is that sometimes we will have a bad day for no apparent reason, or basically that things won't always go the way we want them to no matter how hard we try or what we do.

But if we have true inner peace, when the storms of life hit us, we will be able to remain calm in the midst of it knowing that no matter what, we will be okay. We can remain peaceful knowing that no amount of anxiety or worry is going to change a situation.

Having inner peace is something that most likely has to be developed. It's based on trust and faith. Usually we have it after experiences have taught us that it is possible to be at peace when things get crazy outside of ourselves.

Many times when we feel like we are going to lose control, or our temper, or otherwise "freak out," we can be reminded that it is okay to relieve our stress in healthy ways. That won't make us lose our inner peace. We can cry and scream if we need to. Maybe we can work our frustration out on a punching bag, or go for a long hike or run.

Prayer and meditation have been proven to be effective means of gaining and keeping inner peace. Self-love — including a good level of self-esteem — and inner peace go hand in hand. We can't have inner peace if we don't feel capable of making good decisions or if we are behaving in unhealthy ways.

Some of the other keys to having and keeping inner peace involve forgiveness and acceptance. Knowing that others aren't any more perfect than we are and allowing them to be that way. We also understand our humanness and allow ourselves to make mistakes without being too hard on us.

Knowing our limits by having the ability to say no when we are overwhelmed and yes when that is a good answer for us will also allow for inner peace. Just as unexpected events can draw on our reserves, so too can things we knowingly put ourselves in the middle of. Being aware of what we are doing, living a conscience life is also essential to having inner peace.

There are things outside of our control and within our control that can take away from or add to our inner peace. It's up to us to decide if having inner peace is something we desire. If it is we will be willing to do what it takes to have it.

Inner peace takes effort, but so does its opposite.

৯৯

August 7
Self-image

"An individual's self-concept is the core of his personality. It affects every aspect of human behavior: the ability to learn, the capacity to grow and change. A strong, positive self-image is the best possible preparation for success in life."

—Dr. Joyce Brothers

What we believe about ourselves is what the world sees; it shows in how we live our lives. If we don't think very highly of our ability to love and nurture another person, we won't seek out relationships. And if we don't think we are smart, we won't attempt to do things that take an education. Or if we don't like our appearance, that can hold us back too.

The reality is that others rarely see us exactly as we see ourselves. Most of us are pretty darn tough on our self. We often hold ourselves to higher standards than we do other people. Or there are those who think so little of themselves that they just don't even try.

Having a good self-image is vital to success. And it needs to be an honest evaluation so that if we need improvement in an area we will take on that challenge and do what we need to do to better our image.

If our behavior is in need of correcting, we do that. If we have put on a few too many pounds we take the steps necessary to fix that. Maybe we've shut down emotionally because we don't think we are worth sharing our lives with another so we seek therapy or work with a program to learn how to be better able to allow ourselves to feel our emotions.

When we don't believe in ourselves, nobody else is going to either. We set the tone for our lives by our attitude which is directly affected by our self-image. Another person cannot fix our self-image because we won't believe what they say if we don't think it too.

Do what is necessary to have a healthy self-image and find your life improved dramatically.

৯৯

August 8
Getting Through the Tough Times

"I truly believe that we can overcome any hurdle that lies before us and create the life we want to live. I have seen it happen time and time again." —Gillian Anderson

We all have them, those times in our lives when it seems that things just are not going the way we want. Maybe our job is not good for us, perhaps we have financial challenges, or we have difficulty in our marriages or other relationships. But difficulties are part of life and love and getting through the hard times is what builds strength and character.

Sometimes we may not have any particular problems, but we just don't feel right emotionally or mentally. We may not be able to determine exactly what the problem is, which makes it difficult to solve. This too has an answer and will come to us when we are willing to ride it out and work on ourselves the best way we know how. Those in recovery programs go to meetings. Some of us read motivational books and daily meditations about growth and recovery. Some folks attend church. We give to others our time and listening ear. There are many ways to work through the tough times.

One thing to remember is something that we have learned from past experiences: just around the bend another "moment" is waiting on you to get there. When life seems gloomy and things aren't going as you want, just remember that it's not going to stay this way for long. Something will happen to change your current state of mind. It could be as simple as a smile from a stranger, or it could be as complex as a miracle from God. But the situation will change.

Hanging on when things are difficult is not easy. Sometimes we hang on when we should let go of certain things. That too is part of getting through a tough time.

Keep on living life and the answers will come.

∽

August 9
Beware of Isolation

"Solitude vivifies; isolation kills."
—Joseph Roux

There are many times in our lives when we just wish we could crawl into a cave and get away from the world and hide from our problems. And while solitude, in small amounts, can be healthy and enlivening, isolation is not good for us.

Something to keep in mind when we pull away from friends and loved ones for any length of time is that prisoners are often put into isolation as punishment. They are kept away from interaction with other people and it often promotes physical deterioration and mental illness in the inmates. This is most likely not what we seek when we choose to isolate.

Most likely we isolate because we feel we've failed, or because we don't think we can talk to anyone about what is going on with us either because they won't understand or because we just never learned how to open up to others.

As human beings we were created to be social creatures. We were given many abilities that animals don't have, such as language skills. Nature dictates that we interact with others, not just when we feel happy and upbeat, but also when we feel depressed and even needy. Often our problems are easier overcome when we talk about them, and usually when we hold in our pain or anger it just stays within us and grows.

It's okay to show ourselves to another, to bear our heart and soul to someone who is willing to listen, who cares. Most of us have friends and family who are willing to do this for us, but if we don't we may need to seek the help of a therapist, or member of the clergy, or for those in a Twelve Step program a sponsor can help.

Most importantly we don't continue to internalize our problems without asking for help. And we don't use the self-imprisonment of isolation as a remedy either.

Seek solitude when needed, but avoid isolation.

∽

August 10
Experiencing Relationships

"He who loves 50 people has 50 woes; he who loves no one has no woes." —Buddha

Upon first reading this quote, I thought of it in regard to love relationships and all of the breakups and arguments that can go along with those. But later it reminded me of something else too. When we are involved in groups, such as Twelve Step programs, or members of a church, or any other place where we make lots of friends and we lean on others for support, we also experience more sadness, including deaths and illnesses.

Sometimes it seems that all we do is experience letdowns, pain, and loss. If we never have relationships we won't experience much of that at all. But like the saying goes, it's better to have loved and lost than to have never loved at all. And it is.

We are who we are in part because of relationships. We do most of our growing in relationships too. So we can choose to be free of a certain amount of woes by avoiding any kind of intimacy with other people, or we can experience what life, what God, has to offer through other people.

It is easier in ways to live in our own world and be free of any closeness with anyone for fear of loss and pain, but to live life to its fullest it's necessary to share ourselves and be shared with. We will experience grief, but also joy, when we are available to others and when we allow others to be available to us. We can choose whether to live a full life or just exist by allowing ourselves to be in closeness with others. We allow our flaws to show and we do the same for other people.

Relationships can bring pain, but they bring joy too.

August 11
Showing Love
"We lavish on animals the love we are afraid to show to people.
They might not return it; or worse, they might."
— Mignon McLaughlin

Loving other people and letting them know it can be scary for some. Either we never learned how to show our love or we have been hurt and hold back for fear of more pain and maybe even embarrassment.

When we are afraid to love or to show that we care, we lose out on a lot in life. But there are ways to deal with this issue just as there are with all of the things that we struggle with. We do it a little at a time. We allow for real or perceived failure. We give ourselves the chance at success.

Loving another isn't reserved for romantic relationships. Some of the strongest bonds have been formed in friendships. Sometimes our lack of ability to show love involves family members. Loving another and letting them know it gives us a gift as well as the person we love.

We all have different ways of letting someone know we love them. Some people will show love by cooking a fabulous meal, others by doing extra chores around the house. Some who are affectionate will give hugs, others may write a letter. No manner of letting others know they are loved is any better or worse than another.

Today, or within the next week, take some time to show someone you love them. Maybe there's a family member or friend who you feel the need to share that with and haven't done it. Perhaps someone did something for you in your life that changed you in a good way, helped you down your path in a way that is memorable. Thank them for that. Even if you tell someone you love them often, sometimes doing it in a different way is good because it's fresh.

And if you show love to someone and it is returned accept it. If it isn't, just know that it may not be the time for that person to give it back; they may have blocks of their own.

Write a love letter or show love in a new way this week.

August 12
Attitude is a Choice
"I can't change the direction of the wind, but I can adjust my sails to always reach my destination."
—Jimmy Dean

We often don't have control over our circumstances, but we are in charge of our attitude. We choose how we wish to respond to the good that happens, the bad events, and all those in between.

We have every opportunity throughout the day to get irritated and frustrated when we have to wait in traffic, or stand in line to purchase our groceries, or make those dreaded calls to customer service where we have to go through minutes of recordings to finally get where we are trying to go only to be told that we have the wrong department. It is hard to maintain a good attitude when we have to wait.

Or what about maintaining a good attitude when our health fails? Knowing that we don't have a lot of control over our method of treatment if there's even one available is a strain on any person's attitude. And if the prognosis is not good, even for the most faith-filled person, it's hard to keep a positive outlook. But we can do it.

No matter what our battles are, attitude does have a way of helping us cope with what is thrown at us. Anytime we have a positive outlook on something we have more energy and are propelled forward, when we are in the negative mode of thinking we are tired and don't move much of anywhere.

And we never have to allow another person to choose our attitude. We don't ever have to allow anyone else to determine our mood or tell us that our way of thinking is wrong. If we have people in our lives that are always seeing the negative side of things, it may be time to find new friends. Having a good attitude keeps us moving forward where negativity just causes us to spin our wheels.

Life has ups and downs. When things don't work out the way we planned, we make adjustments and move on rather than getting stuck in the "poor me" mode of thinking. A positive attitude will make a difference in our actions.

You have the power to adjust your own sails no matter which way the wind blows.

~

August 13
Knowing Our Limits
"A 'no' uttered from the deepest conviction is better than a 'yes' merely uttered to please, or worse, to avoid trouble."
—Mohandas Gandhi

In life whether it is at work, in relationships, groups, churches, families, or anywhere we are involved with others, there are times when we are asked to do more than we can do. What is important is that we know our limits.

We need to know how much we can handle in our lives before we are overwhelmed and stressed out. And sometimes we may be able to handle more than at other times so it isn't always easy to know from month to month. Remember, too, that it doesn't matter if someone else can handle more than you, they may be overstressed and neglecting important things out of a need to please by doing so much.

If we are busy doing a lot of different things in our lives, activities beyond work and caring for our homes and families, and we feel like something is getting neglected because we are so busy, it may be time to stop some of our activities, and it's important not to take on more. It doesn't matter if someone thinks we would be the perfect person to fill a need, if we don't have time to do it and still take care of our current obligations we should say no.

Sometimes it is very hard to say no. We may be flattered that we were asked. We probably want to please whoever asked and those we would serve, but if taking on new tasks is going to cost us something that we are not willing to lose, then we must not do it. If we can give up one obligation to take on a new one, then that's a possible solution.

The important thing is that we take care of ourselves in this busy world. We get enough sleep, eat right, relax, have fun, and take care of all of our obligations. If there's room for other things in our life then it's not a problem, but taking care of our self must come first or we serve nobody. And when we get overburdened and overwhelmed we don't have much to offer anyone.

Know your limits and take care of yourself so when you do give it's out of a healthy place.

⁓

August 14
Taking Off the Blinders

"Miracles rest not so much upon healing power coming suddenly near us from afar, but upon our perceptions being made finer, so that for the moment our eyes can see and our ears can hear what has been there around us always." —Willa Cather

We can get so focused on a thing, a desire, that we lose sight of the big picture and often lose out on other things that come along while we put all of our energy into getting that one thing we want.

Perhaps we focus all of our energy on getting the attention of a particular person, either to be friends, or a romantic relationship. We spin our lives around that person putting lots of energy into finding ways to see them, or gain attention from that person. And once we get it, or maybe when we don't get it, we realize that there were dozens of other people we completely ignored because we had blinders on seeking to gain the love of one.

And maybe we do this too with our careers or other activities in our lives. We may have our goals set on one particular job and no matter what we do we either can't get an interview or never get hired when we do. It may be time to set a new goal, find a new place to put our energy.

This isn't to say we should never have goals or go after what we want. We should set goals and if we want something bad enough we usually get it, but sometimes that is not the case, especially when the outcome of a situation is not in our hands completely. We can't make another person fall in love with us, and we can't make someone hire us if they don't choose to do that.

We focus, we set goals, we strive to be all we can be, but in the meantime we don't overlook what opportunities are around us. A bird in the hand is worth two in the bush as the saying goes. There's a whole world out there and when we focus too much on a small piece of it we're bound to miss something. When the signs start telling us to give up on a person, place, or thing, maybe we should do just that and find something else to focus on.

Goals are good, but don't miss out on living a full life trying to make one happen.

August 15
Give Thanks

"As we express our gratitude, we must never forget that the highest appreciation is not to utter words, but to live by them."
—John F. Kennedy

Every day of the year we ought to stop and express our gratitude to God for the blessings we have received some of which may have seemed to be more of a curse, but nonetheless we see them in hindsight as opportunities for growth.

We all have many things for which we can give thanks and any time we can remember to be thankful for what we do have, it takes our focus off of the things we do not have. We may bemoan our jobs because we are not happy in them, but others are faced with unemployment. We might worry that our homes aren't nice enough, or maybe they are in the wrong neighborhood, but we have a home. There are millions of people in the U.S. alone who are living in the streets or out in the woods with no home and only scraps for food. We worry that someone with a better income than us will look at us as less than. And they just may do that, but it matters not in the grand scheme of things. Life isn't so much about what we have as it is about love.

Giving helps us to appreciate what was given to us. We, no matter what our financial status, can do for others, especially those less fortunate. When we spend time in service and giving to those in need we learn to be grateful for what we have.

Service and gifts to others, especially in their time of need, is a living expression of gratitude. It says that while we may want more and better than what we have, we are grateful for that which is ours and willing to give of our time and energy for others. It takes our focus off of the have not's and turns our attention to what we have.

Give thanks by serving those who have less than you and you'll begin to appreciate what has been given to you.

∽

August 16
Compromise

"One half of knowing what you want is knowing what you must give up before you get it." —Sidney Howard

Most of the time in order to attain something new we must give up something, make some sort of compromise, and this is too often something that many people will not do.

If we want a particular job but the hours aren't exactly the desired ones we have to decide if that's the job we really want and if so we work around the issue of the schedule. If we wish to have a committed relationship with someone we may have to give up some of our time with others, not all of it because that wouldn't be healthy, but we have to give up somewhat to make room for more.

In order to lose weight we'd have to give up our snacks and eat smaller meal portions, plus time would be given to exercise. But if we really want to lose weight we do what it takes to get it done. It's the same thing with learning to play an instrument, play a sport, a new hobby, anything we want to add to our lives may mean something else is taken away or cut back.

Giving up something to get another thing is not always necessary. But when it is we must be willing to consider what is at stake when we seek out the new. If we aren't willing to make the commitment to spend the necessary time with the new thing, especially if that's a relationship issue, then we ought to not start it so as not to hurt the other person because of our unwillingness to compromise.

Most new things in life do take a certain amount of willingness to make adjustments, to adapt to change, to compromise, but without making such efforts our lives may become stale and stagnant. So upon considering making a change or beginning something new, we must look at the costs of that situation as best we can estimate it and decide if it's worth what we give up to get it.

Growing, doing new things may mean giving up something else, but is often worth it.

∽

August 17
Choose Who to Be
"Begin each day by asking yourself what kind of person you want to be. Say to yourself: 'If I die tomorrow, how would I wish I had been today? Would I wish I had treated my child, my partner, and my friends more kindly? …Would I wish I had been happier and more aware? Or would I be content with having been preoccupied with petty values and distracted by foolish concerns?'"
—Hugh Prather

We can make the choice to be who we want to be. No, every action and reaction we have won't hit the mark we want, but the desire to be happier, kinder, and more aware is the start to getting there.

If we snap at our child, partner, co-worker, or friend, we can apologize and strive to not do that again in the future. If we spent part of our day gossiping about another we can strive not to do that, and stop ourselves in the middle of it. Maybe we aren't grateful for what we have and instead complain about the things we don't have.

If we don't know what type of person we want to be, then we don't have anything to strive towards. Those in recovery groups have a focused plan that helps determine their decisions. People who are active in churches learn about ways to be better people. We learn by trial and error sometimes, but mostly we need to have a place to work towards.

Life really does look different if you stop and think how you would live if you knew it was your last day, or last year. Most of us would be more loving, want to spend time with those we care the most for, and we'd want to have some fun as well. We can do those things now, whether we have one day or thousands left to live.

Be who you choose.

❧

August 18
Have Some Fun

"We've got to learn hard things in our lifetime, but it's love that gives you the strength. It's being nice to people and having a lot of fun and laughing harder than anything, hopefully every single day of your life."

—Drew Barrymore

Living life as we know it is busy. At times we find it difficult to get enough time to sleep. We move from one task to another, from one thing to another. We rush here and there and get caught in traffic jams. Life is stressful and harried most of the time.

We have to make time for fun. Having fun is healthy, it's a good thing. Taking time off to relax can actually invigorate us to move forward in our tasks and projects.

We may have spent so much time in our lives busy that we have forgotten how to have fun. Some folks enjoy a long hot bath, others love to go to a movie or live play, yet another may enjoy gardening and find that to be fun. What's relaxing and fun for some may be work for others, but the important thing is to find what it is that is fun to us and then make sure we do that thing.

If we're not having fun, most likely we are not getting enough sleep. We probably eat on the run, and stay under a lot of stress. Having some fun is like a release valve that allows some of the stress and tension to leave us so that we are better able to cope with the pressures of life.

We can have fun while we work if we allow ourselves to. And if the job we have is not conducive to having some fun while there, we either need another job or we have to ensure we get that fun when we are not working.

The world won't fall apart if we take some time off to laugh and play. Sometimes playing with a child can be the best release. Children don't have the worries of the world on their shoulders; they play and don't worry about what isn't getting done while they do it. For those who don't know how to let go and play, go watch children, join them if you can and stop worrying about life for a few minutes.

Find some fun things that release your stress and do them.

August 19
Doing Right

"That you may retain your self-respect, it is better to displease the people by doing what you know is right, than to temporarily please them by doing what you know is wrong."
—William J. H. Boetcker

Adults can endure as much peer pressure as children in school are exposed to. Some of us are easily swayed by what others want or in trying to please someone else that we may not do what we know is right at times, but instead we fulfill the desires of someone else. But not only do we lose our self-respect in such instances, we don't really make true and lasting friendships with others either.

We must strive to always do right even if what we are doing does not please others. We teach our children to do the right thing, to avoid peer pressure, so we too must do the same. For every conflict there are people on either side of the issue who feel as strongly that they are right as those on the other side feel they are correct.

Sometimes people will go along with others despite what they feel is the right thing in a situation. There are those who need so badly to feel loved that they will try to create that love in situations by siding with someone. We've probably all seen those people at work, in churches, or other places, who will chum up to someone on an issue and will not only turn on that person later, but will stab them in the back while they are at it. Taking the side that at the moment they feel will best give them what they want, not necessarily taking the side of what they know is right.

We have to make choices in our lives about big and small things. And sometimes our choices conflict with those we care about, but if we feel strongly about something that's what we must do. When we know in our hearts the right thing to do and we don't do it we lose self-respect, something that is of utmost value to everyone.

Do the right thing even when others try to sway you to do otherwise.

⌀

August 20
Staying Grounded

"A truly wise person will not be carried away by any of the eight winds: prosperity, decline, disgrace, honor, praise, censure, suffering, pleasure." —Nichiren

Life does blow us different winds over the years. Sometimes we can experience the highs and lows within hours or days. Of course when we are on the down side in decline, disgrace, censure, or suffering, it seems as if time stands still and we remain stuck in that place forever. Yet when we are honored, praised, full of joy, or prospering, it seems to only last for moments.

We ought to not get too absorbed in either end of the feelings of life. When we do something worthy of praise and we receive it, there is often someone waiting to shoot us down for whatever it was we did.

We do deserve to enjoy life when things are going well. And it's in the suffering and pain that we grow and learn. But what we don't want to do is let either end of the spectrum dictate how we live our lives knowing that every person experiences highs and lows and places in between.

If we were to get too carried away when we do something great our egos would become so big that nobody would want to be around us. And likewise if we wallow in self-pity all the time we won't have people knocking down our doors trying to spend time with us. It's certainly okay to feel good about ourselves when we have done a good thing. And when we fail in some way it's okay as well. We forgive ourselves and try to do better in the future.

There are also times when what we are feeling isn't true to what is happening in life. Or sometimes people aren't honest and true to us. They may offer false praise in order to gain our favor. And at other times we are beaten up and beaten down by those who are jealous or treat us badly for some other reason.

Whatever we are experiencing, we need to honor our own feelings and not rely on the outside world to dictate how we feel about ourselves. We do this by not giving our power over to others or even to the ups or downs of our days.

Feel what you feel but don't let any of it overpower you.

August 21
Following the Lead

"Being led is not an extraordinary event, reserved for mystics and ascetics; rather, it is the normal order of things."
—Harry McMullan III

Living our lives and including in that efforts of growing spiritually may be a new concept for some. And many of us may have been bogged down in religion in our lives so that in essence the true spiritual connection we sought with God was missing.

But once we begin to seek the connection, and work on it to the best of our ability, there will be times when we will know that we got an answer to prayer, or we were healed of something that needed healing, or even that we are being led to do a particular thing.

As a writer by profession the act of putting words together isn't a spectacular event in my life. So to say that I felt led to write something, which happened to me in a way that I would never have expected, may not make a large impact on others, but it did on me when it happened.

And while it may not have been an extraordinary event, it was a moment of true spiritual connection for me. When a connection like that happens it cannot be denied. And sharing it with others, putting it in words isn't such an easy thing, even for a writer. It's just something that you feel and you know within that it's real.

And just as surely as you know the sun will come up in the morning, you know there is a Higher Power who is there, who guides you, and listens to your requests. It's a knowing that can only be found within, but once it's there it will remain a source of hope and faith for the coming days and years.

We never know what events in our lives will give us this knowing, but I believe that if we are open and willing to receive it, we will get it.

A spiritual connection is ours if we seek it.

❧

August 22
Choosing the Route

"The battle of life is, in most cases, fought uphill; and to win it without a struggle were perhaps to win it without honor. If there were no difficulties there would be no success; if there were nothing to struggle for, there would be nothing to be achieved."
—Samuel Smiles

There's a mountain I like to climb near where I live. One side of the mountain has a trail that for the most part is pretty easy to climb even for those who don't exercise much. The other side is difficult, a lot more so than the easy side.

No matter which side of the mountain is climbed, once you get to the top it's the same. The same view, the same mountain. So if given a choice there is no reason to take the difficult side just for the view, unless you are looking for more challenging climb.

And so it is with life. We all have many challenges, hurdles, mountains even. We don't always have choices about taking different paths to master those challenges, but when given an option to choose the easy side or the difficult side, we can choose to take the easy one, knowing that the view, the victory is the same.

Sometimes we make life more difficult by fighting it. We try to figure out the future or we live in the past. We hold grudges and fail to let go when forgiveness would be easier. We don't do what we know is the right thing and instead choose to move forward in something we know is wrong. We try to make people into who we want them to be instead of letting them be who they are.

Choosing the easier route in anything we face in life, especially the most challenging, will help us reach our goals. We stop fighting what we don't know and go with what we have experienced as means to an end for us. One person's accomplishments may have been reached in a different way than ours, but that doesn't make our way wrong. If it works for us, we ought to do it.

When given a choice, choose the path of least resistance.

∞

August 23
Keeping at Growth

"He who is not everyday conquering some fear has not learned the secret of life." —Ralph Waldo Emerson

Dealing with fears or feelings when new situations trigger them can be a difficult thing. We may have thought that we had worked through certain issues and fears and they no longer existed in us, only to find out that some new situation triggers those same old feelings.

Take for instance the fear of abandonment. Maybe in our lives someone walked out, a person who was important to us turned their backs and left our lives. So we fear that happening again. And maybe we worked through it so we just don't feel it every time we have close personal relationships with others. But then we sense that someone may be about to leave us and those old fears and feelings are as fresh as they were when the tragic event happened.

Feeling them again and experiencing that fear doesn't mean we haven't grown; it's just something that we may have to work on more in our lives. It's a sensitive issue in our lives, one that may take more work than some other issues.

And there probably are a number of old feelings that may be living under the surface in our lives that can be triggered by the smallest event. What we do with those feelings and how we handle them can be new for us even if the feelings are old and maybe not even be based on reality.

We can stop and really think through the situation, realizing that some of what we feel is based on a circumstance or event that has nothing to do with the present. We may need to talk it over with someone. Prayer and meditation work. Not panicking, but rather stopping and using a recovery behavior we know has worked for us will bring us peace quicker than letting the fear take over.

As much as we learn and mature, we still never reach perfection, so we should not expect that from ourselves. Using things we know to help us through the rough spots is the best solution when old issues come flooding back at us.

Sometimes feelings are out of sight, and out of mind, but lurking just below the surface.

 familyhood

August 24
Love is the Answer

"Love is patient, love is kind. It does not envy, it does not boast, it is not proud. It is not rude, it is not self-seeking, it is not easily angered, it keeps no record of wrongs. Love does not delight in evil but rejoices with the truth. It always protects, always trusts, always hopes, always perseveres. Love never fails." —The Bible

It is often written and discussed that people operate out of two things. One of those is love and one is fear. When we are envious, boastful, rude, self-seeking, and angry, among other negative acts we are coming from a place of fear. When we want good for others, when we are honest, hopeful, faithful, kind, and true, we operate out of love.

Whenever we find ourselves in a situation where we feel uneasy and unhappy, we can think about love. We try to react in a loving way rather than out of fear. If someone is irritating to us and we let it get under our skin we will end up reacting and making matters much worse. But if we think of a way to react in love we will most likely find at least some peace in the moment.

Instead of talking bad about another person we can either keep our mouth shut or try to think of something nice to say about them. We all have good things and not so good things that we do. If we focus on their bad stuff that's all we will see, but if we attempt to see them through the eyes of love we may discover something better.

Often if we are loving to another person, especially those who aren't all that loveable, they will start to change. It may be a very gradual change, but if we keep at it they will change. Most likely the ones who seem so unlovable are that way because they don't have self-love.

And maybe that's true for us too. Maybe when we operate out of fear it's because we don't have enough self-esteem. We don't love our self enough to love another. In that case, we need to work at treating our self from a place of love and not fear.

Treat yourself and those around you with love and see your world begin to change.

∽

August 25
Expectations
"Anger always comes from frustrated expectations."
—Elliott Larson

It is difficult to go into any situation having no expectations. When we enter into any relationship, whether it is work related or personal, we want certain things. But our expectations may be far off from those on the other side of the relationship.

What's especially difficult and frustrating is when there is a lack of communication in the situation, when not only are we not getting our needs met as expected, but the other person is not capable of entering into conversation about the relationship.

It isn't fair to become angry when another person does not meet the needs that we expected. We simply need to allow that person to be who they are and do what they do. If we need to move on we do that. If we need to adjust our expectations we can do that as well, but we don't try to demand that they become someone they are not simply because of our expectations.

The best way to enter into any relationship is to not have expectations. Often our expectations can cause a relationship to fail before we even give it a chance. If we want more from someone than they are willing or able to give, we have choices about that situation.

We can try to demand more and if not given our desires we move on. Or we can allow the other person to give what they are able and not demand more. Then we seek to have those needs met from other people.

Perhaps we need to be more forthcoming about our needs in a relationship if we are finding ourselves frustrated or angry with the other person. Maybe if they knew what we wanted they would be more able to meet those needs. And if they are not able to meet our expectations we can stop waiting and hoping for that to happen.

Most importantly relationships require communication — from both parties involved — in order for expectations to be met. Sometimes the other person tells us what they want and we are so busy trying to get our needs met that we don't hear them. They may have told us in the very beginning what they wanted out of our relationship and we still try to force our desires. Listening to the other person is just as important as saying what we want.

To avoid frustrated expectations communication is essential.

∽

August 26
Doing Our Best
"God makes three requests of his children: Do the best you can, where you are, with what you have, now."
—African-American Proverb

Life, with all of its challenges and decisions, really comes down to one simple thing: doing the best we can do with what we have. And our best can change with time if we are learning and growing, it's just that in the very moment where we are, we only have the potential to do *our* best, not what another person can do.

As a beginning guitar player sometimes at home I can work through my music and play pretty well. I may not play it perfectly, but for me I can see progress and be proud. But let me show up for my music lesson and rather than hitting a few bum notes, I'm doing good to hit a few good notes. It's performance anxiety that causes me to function less than I am truly capable. It's my issue of worrying about what someone else thinks about what I'm doing or even about me that causes nervousness to be an issue.

What we must keep in mind as we go through our lives and meet various challenges is that nobody expects us to do anything but what we are capable of doing. If the quote above is true, then even God only expects us to do our best. We don't have to worry about what someone else thinks if we aren't harming them. We really can only do our best so there's no reason to worry about doing anything more.

We all do things that others wish they had the skills for. We don't think less of them for not being able to perform a task well that we can do without much thought or effort. Most of us will never play quarterback as well as Peyton Manning, nor be as good of a musician as Eric Clapton, or even be able to act as well as Reese Witherspoon, but it doesn't stop us from performing our best within our lives. And as great as those three people are at the tasks they perform, I'm sure each and every one of them spent countless hours learning their trade, and still do practice in order to be skilled.

We strive to grow and learn new things, but we don't berate ourselves when we are not able to perform as good or learn as quickly as we would like. We just keep trying.

Doing nothing is the only assurance of not making a mistake.

August 27
Needing Others

"We need others. We need others to love and we need to be loved by them. There is no doubt that without it, we too, like the infant left alone, would cease to grow, cease to develop, choose madness and even death." —Leo Buscaglia

Many people have the idea that it is wrong to need other people. Sometimes this is because they have experienced extreme pain from the loss of a loved one due to death or a breakup of some sort. And some people were taught as children that they should not ever need anyone.

Neediness and needing others is not the same thing. People thrive on love and nurturing. We were created to be in relationship with other people. Some of us need more interaction than others.

Sometimes because we have opened ourselves fully to another only to have lost that person in a devastating way we retreat from all interaction, or we get only so close to those in our lives. We have our guard up. We build walls that may never be penetrated. We constantly watch people come and go in our lives because they cannot cross our boundaries, the ones we have built on fear.

And when we have these walls we lose out on a lot in life. Yes, we may avoid pain, most likely we do avoid a great deal of it, but we also don't allow ourselves to love or be loved and without that we are empty shells. God works through our relationships and interactions with others. When we shut off from people, we close the door on God as well.

Getting and giving love can happen in many ways. Even if we don't have a romantic partnership we can give and receive love from others, and we should do this even if we have a special love relationship. We give and receive from our friends, community, coworkers, neighbors, anyone in our lives who we can share kindness with will offer us opportunities to share love.

If we have a particular need and it is not getting met we can ask for help from someone close to us. Sometimes we may just need a hug or a listening ear. And it's almost guaranteed that a good friend would be flattered that we asked and then in turn feel they could come to us for the same.

To continue to grow emotionally and spiritually we need to love and be loved. We cannot ever expect one person to meet every need so it's important to have a circle of people and love in our lives.

Giving and receiving love is important and something we should all seek; never be ashamed of it.

∽

August 28
Counting Blessings
"Man is fond of counting his troubles, but he does not count his joys. If he counted them up as he ought to, he would see that every lot has enough happiness provided for it."
—Fyodor Dostoevsky

Most of us spend a great deal of time wanting something that we don't have. We want a relationship, or a better one. We wish we had the car our neighbor just got. There's a better job out there, we just know it, if we could only have it. And the list goes on.

And while there's nothing wrong with wanting more out of life, there is the issue of being grateful for what we have. There are those who would think they had won the lottery if they had the lives that we lead. Like those who sleep in cardboard boxes while we grumble about our heating bill being too high. Or the guy down the street who has to catch the bus to work and stand in the cold to wait for it, while we complain because there's a bit of frost to clean off of our windshield.

Then there is the issue of relationships. When we are single we wish to be with someone. And while that's human nature and a normal attitude it is not the worst thing to be alone. It feels lonely and sad, especially around holidays. But if only we can stop and think about those who may be alone because of the recent death of a spouse, or the wife whose husband is cheating and she is dealing with that issue at the moment.

There will always be those who appear to have more than us as well as those who have a lot less. We ought to count our blessings every day rather than bemoan that which we do not have. Life, God, the universe, gives us what we need whether we know it or not. And life is not always fair, just ask a homeless person about it. Sometimes those who have no place to call home have been as fortunate as us, but circumstances caused them to lose what they had. It's true, some end up that way because they refuse to work or made bad choices, it's not our place to judge.

Our job is to be grateful for what we have and to give what we can to others. Whether we give material gifts, or love, a hug, or a listening ear, we have things to offer those in need. And those who need something from us may not be the homeless family; it may be the person who sits on the pew next to us at church, or our coworker, a neighbor, or our best friend.

Being glad for what we have and giving back will bless us more than anything.

✑

August 29
Setting Goals
"The more intensely we feel about an idea or a goal, the more assuredly the idea, buried deep in our subconscious, will direct us along the path to its fulfillment."
—Earl Nightingale

Setting goals is an important part of growth in all areas of our lives. Most of us have things that we want or desire to achieve that may seem too far out of our reach to get. But that should not stop us. Some of what we want is well within our means of achieving; we just fail to reach for it.

Setting a goal is the place to start. And it's especially important to write down our goals. There is some kind of magic that occurs when writing down what we want on a piece of paper. We need to believe that we can achieve our goals as well.

Once I was setting some yearly goals with an instructor of mine. I had one goal that was especially scary; something I wanted to do, but had so much fear about it that I said, "That's what I want to do, but just because I want to do it doesn't mean I will."

The instructor told me I might as well wad the paper up and throw it away if that's how I felt. He was right. I set the goal but was already talking myself out of achieving it. We have to try to reach our goals and it is okay to set them higher than we think we can reach. If we fall short we probably will still get farther along with something than we would have had we not set the goal.

Some people set goals as New Year's resolutions; others take the time whenever they decide there is something they want. It doesn't make a difference when we set the goal, what matters is that we do it and that we believe we can achieve it.

Setting a goal that we know is unachievable is not a good idea, because it sets us up for failure. Deciding to lose 100 pounds in two months and making that a goal is not going to bring it to fruition. Setting a goal of losing about 5-10 pounds a month and 60-100 pounds in a year is more reasonable and much more likely to be achieved.

Write your goals down and believe you can achieve them and great things will happen.

∽

August 30
Failure is Not Trying
"I am not judged by the number of times I fail, but by the number of
times I succeed; and the number of times I succeed is in direct
proportion to the number of times I can fail and keep on trying."
—Tom Hopkins

No matter how hard we have tried to reach goals in our lives, but have fallen short, the only time we truly failed were the times we gave up and let go of our goals. Life is a series of events that we label success and failure, but we all know that the difficulties in life are what teach us and the times in our lives when we felt the most distressed usually turned into the most spiritual growth.

If we feel ashamed or guilty for our past mistakes, or for failing to reach a particular goal, it's time to let go. We let go of the guilt and shame and move forward. We must forgive ourselves for not being perfect because that is not expected of any human on this earth.

To fail is to give up. To fail is to never try. Not reaching a goal just means we need to try harder or set a new goal. It's good to set our goals high, but we may need to set them a bit lower in order to achieve them. They need to be realistic or they are not worth striving for, and only set us up to not reach them thus setting off feelings of being ashamed.

Remember that we never fail if we continue to grow. We may not have reached goal A, but we learned to be more patient along the way. Or goal B eluded us, but along the journey to try to reach it, we learned a new skill or way of coping. Just as people are placed in our lives to help us grow and to meet our needs, so are our plans and goals means of growing and learning even that which we may not have strived for.

Do not feel ashamed for failure; instead let it give you momentum for the next goal.

⤚⃝

August 31
Conflict Produced

"A lot of people are afraid to tell the truth, to say no. That's where toughness comes into play. Toughness is not being a bully. It's having backbone." —Robert Kiyosaki

Sometimes people are so afraid to say no they make plans and promises without any intentions of keeping them. This in effect is worse than just saying no in the beginning. They do this to avoid conflict, but in the end the inability to be honest in itself causes more conflict than the simple no would have in the beginning.

There is absolutely nothing wrong with saying no to a request by another person unless it's in a situation where we are employed and the task is part of our job, or our child asks us for help and we can give it, we ought to not deny that to them. But here we are talking about relationship issues with friends, love interests, partners, and even business associates.

We should not make plans to do something with or for another person if we don't want to keep those plans. And if we are too afraid to say no up front, the worst thing to do is never contact them to break the plans. Just ignoring them and hoping they will go away so we can avoid confrontation does not do anyone any good. We will lose the friend and any respect they had for us.

Sometimes breaking plans is unavoidable. When this happens, we ought to be honest and let those involved know as soon as possible. Our integrity is at stake when we don't do what we say we will do. Breaking plans occasionally because it cannot be helped is one thing, but lying about why we broke the plans or just disappearing without even breaking the engagement is cause for others to avoid us in the future.

And perhaps what we desire is for that person to go away, to not be a part of our life. This needs direct communication as well. Although face-to-face conversations are always best in relationships, there are times when this is not possible. Or sometimes we just are not able to do that, but there are easy ways to contact those we cannot face: phones, instant message, e-mails, and texting to name a few. Any of these ways is better than leaving someone waiting around to hear from us.

Letting someone know about broken plans is the right way to handle the situation.

❧

September 1
Feeling Discontent

"Perhaps our eyes need to be washed by our tears once in a while, so that we can see life with a clearer view again."

—Alex Tan

We all have those times in our lives when we cannot seem to find a way to feel better about things. We may be feeling down because we can't have what we want in a job, relationship, or some other area of our life. And no matter what we do it seems we just feel sad and discontent.

It happens to everyone. We may not think so because some people don't allow others to know their feelings. They keep things bottled up so as to avoid appearing human. But those of us who try to be in touch with our feelings and emotions know that we will go through these times.

Sometimes we can pinpoint the reason we feel blue and at other times we don't really have one particular thing. If we can't have something we want and we keep trying to get it, the solution to that is to just let go. We can turn whatever it is over to our Higher Power and see what happens.

Sometimes we are hurt by other people. We cannot force someone to love us. We can't make people spend time with us or be who we want them to be in our lives. Sometimes when people don't meet our needs we feel rejected. But usually it's not so much that they are rejecting us as much as it is they are trying to take care of their own needs. If this is one of our issues we must learn to differentiate what are our issues and what are theirs. And we need to have multiple sources for getting what we need, including giving to ourselves.

Life is going to have all kinds of struggles. We just have to get through the times in our lives when we've got the blues and keep trudging forward until we walk out of the haze and into the brightness of a new day.

Persevering through the rough times gives you wisdom.

❧

September 2
Finding the Answer

"The truth is that our finest moments are most likely to occur when we are feeling deeply uncomfortable, unhappy, or unfulfilled. For it is only in such moments, propelled by our discomfort, that we are likely to step out of our ruts and start searching for different ways or truer answers." —M. Scott Peck

Experiencing life brings many challenges and often we seek answers, resolution, change, starting, ending and so forth. And many times it is difficult to find these things we seek because of our emotional involvement with them. We push too hard, get frustrated and angry, and whatever solution we seek seems to move farther from us.

Finding peace with a particular issue or even peace in our lives, may mean we have to get so upset that we finally have to throw our hands in the air and say, "I give up." The saying, "Let Go and Let God," has been passed around for a long time and it works.

We cannot orchestrate the universe, not even our own small world. When we think we want something so bad that we think we have to have it and it doesn't happen, there's usually a good reason. When we lose something that we had such as a job or a relationship, most likely its time was up and our lesson was learned from either that situation or it was time to move to the next learning opportunity.

We will all experience numerous times in our lives when we didn't get what we wanted or lost what we had. And we may never know the reason. But we can find peace in our world by letting go and using gratitude in our lives for the things we do have.

We move into action because our situations make us uncomfortable and unhappy. Sometimes we need to be motivated to do something different. The struggle may seem endless in the moment, but when peace comes we can look back occasionally and understand why, and at other times, just be glad we found peace again.

Finding peace after a storm of life hits is worth the challenges presented to you.

∽

September 3
Integrity

"Integrity is telling myself the truth. And honesty is telling the truth to other people." —Spencer Johnson

When we seek to improve our self-esteem and grow in self-love we must be true to ourselves. We must love ourselves fully, without judgment. Honesty with ourselves is where we start the process.

We do not lie to ourselves about who we are. If we do things that we know are wrong we don't justify that, we stop doing it. We don't pretend to be someone or something that we are not if we choose to love who we are.

Trust is an important part of any relationship. To have trust, all parties involved must be honest and true to their word. Integrity means we are who we say we are. We do what we say and say what we mean and life goes a lot more smoothly than when we don't tell the truth.

If someone says they are going to do something time after time, and they never do it, eventually we know that the words are hollow. They probably intend to do what they say, or perhaps they just say what they think others want to hear. Most of the time what anybody wants to know is the truth in a situation even when the truth hurts. Whether or not others are honest does not justify us to be dishonest. It's still our integrity that we are responsible for.

We cannot be honest with anyone else if we cannot be honest with our self. It is not possible to be dishonest in one part of our lives and not have that carry over into other areas. Honesty and dishonesty are either part of us or they are not.

Our integrity is vital to both our self-image and what others in our lives see. We ought to be honest about the smallest things in order to be honest about the big stuff as well.

Honesty starts with me or I cannot be truthful to anybody else.

෴

September 4
Trusting
"We're never so vulnerable than when we trust someone — but paradoxically, if we cannot trust, neither can we find love or joy."
—Walter Anderson

Some of us have trust issues. They may go all the way back to childhood when we had parents who lied to us, who never did what they said, and we never knew what to expect from them. They may still be acting out these same behaviors with us as we have grown into adulthood.

And now that we are all grown up, we deal with even more situations that require trust. Sometimes, for me anyway, it seems that the situations where trust, or rather distrust, becomes an issue happens in phases; as in, over and over in a period of time where it makes me question even the most trustworthy of people. I begin to doubt every word that is spoken by people who interact in my life because others have lied and broken my trust.

But to not trust means we cannot have real relationships. And those of us who work on recovery issues of all sorts want real relationships. We want trust and truth. We desire the best life and love has to offer. We cannot give up on people and live a full life.

It's difficult though to continue to open ourselves up to knowing that we will be hurt again. We will go through the pain of someone walking out on our relationship. We will experience the loss of trust again in our lives and we will hurt from it as long as we continue to have relationships that mean something.

Being vulnerable means we have lives full of intense emotions, both joy and pain. We must learn to handle the disappointments when others are not true to us, when they lie or walk away for no reason, so that we may experience love when it does come. And it will. Sometimes when we least expect it and from places we never dreamed it would appear. But we won't have love or joy if we are not willing to take the risk of trust.

Trust that God will give you what you need when someone is not true to you.

✍

September 5
Keep On Keeping On
"Don't give up before the miracle happens."
Unknown

We have choices about things in life. When defeat, rejection, loss, and other negative events happen we can give up, or we can forge on with hope of a renewed strength for the future.

Even when we lose at love, or think we cannot face that thing again that keeps bringing us pain, or that we just cannot take one more step. Do it anyway. Keep going. Don't give up; because sometimes we may just give up before the miracle.

What if we quit and that thing we so much desired in our life was just around the corner? If we had just struggled one more day, or held on one more moment, or maybe let go just one last time we might have made it. We won't know the answer to those questions if we give up, if we quit before the end.

It's hard. Life lessons are difficult. Pain and loss are not fun and sometimes we just don't care that through all those troubling times we grow spiritually and mature. It's still icky and we don't want to experience any of the down times. And there are times in our lives when it seems those painful events just start to pile on top of one another until we feel buried beneath them so deep we honestly don't know if we can dig out.

But we need to do it anyway. We must move forward, feeling all the painful emotions along the way so we can move past them. Not feeling things and just girding up and moving on won't really make things any better or easier. We'll just get struck with the feelings later on down the road of our journey.

So keep on keeping on, feel what you feel, cry and vent as you need to, but don't give up. What you want may be right around the next turn and if you stop now you will miss out.

Don't give up because you might be inches from that thing you want.

&

September 6
Anger Release
"Anger is a signal, and one worth listening to."
—Harriet Lerner

Human beings get angry. There are justified and unjustified reasons we become angry, but to deny that we are will never solve any issue.

When any negative emotion is within us, it causes us to see that something is not right. We may label a feeling anger that is more correctly defined as hurt or some other issue, but whatever it is we need to allow ourselves the time and energy to feel it and release it.

Feeling our feelings is how we move on. Suppressing our feelings, especially anger, is how we find ourselves in the middle of a big mess emotionally. To deny a feeling does not mean it doesn't exist. To justify it does not determine that we need to hold onto it. Even if we have reason to be angry it's still our feeling and one that is not conducive to love, joy, and peace.

We get angry for a reason. It may have very little to do with the situation at hand, and a lot to do with our baggage and unfelt and unexpressed anger from the past. Sometimes anger is telling us that we need to make a change in a situation or get out of it completely. Anger in itself is not bad. Anger can cause inertia to make big or small changes within and around us.

There are healthy ways to release anger: pound a pillow, punch a bag, run, take a fast walk, meditate, pray, ride a bike, any number of things can help us to feel and release the anger. Holding it in will only add fuel to the next situation where anger exists.

Anger can help you know when something is not right, but you ought to never hang onto it.

∽

September 7
Things Happen for a Reason
"When God closes a door, he opens a window."
—Unknown

One of the most difficult things to understand is how we can desire something so badly and not get it. No matter how many times we pray, no matter that we feel we deserve something, we still don't get it. And we get frustrated with God, maybe people too.

Every once in a while we have an experience where that door just will not open for us, or if it does it gets slammed in our face before we know it, but we realize quickly that it was a good thing that we didn't get "it."

That's when we understand the quote above. And maybe while we realized why we didn't get "it" we also noticed that there was at least one other "it" waiting for us, or suddenly seemingly out of nowhere something better presented itself. A thing we didn't have to beg for; something for which we didn't have to sacrifice quite so much.

These are moments in our lives that bring wisdom. They are the experiences and events that nobody can really teach us, but that we learn through the suffering of not getting and the surprise of receiving something else.

Often we are so busy looking at the closed door that we do not see the open window. When we pray for something we ought to pray that we can have wisdom about it so that perhaps our desire for something we aren't going to get will fade more quickly and our eyes will not be blind to that other thing that's there, just waiting on us to notice it.

If you just look past that closed door you might see an open window.

∽

September 8
Communication Requires Listening
"The value of persistent prayer is not that He will hear us, but that we will finally hear Him." —William McGill

How many times have we thrown up the same prayer and not heard an answer, yet seemingly out of the blue something we prayed for was answered? It's most likely that the answer came when we finally listened. And sometimes the reason we finally listened was because we were at the end of our rope and let go.

Just as communication with people requires both speaking and listening, so it is with our Higher Power. We must stay open for the answer we pray for or we won't see it when it arrives.

As the saying goes, "Be careful what you pray for … you just might get it." It's necessary for us to consider first what we are asking and then to be ready to receive when the answer comes. If we are praying for a situation to get better and the answer is for us to take an action that is frightening for us, we still have our answer and we must proceed.

Sometimes when God says no the yes comes immediately and at other times we may not get a yes for quite some time, if ever. But if we are going to trust God and ask Him for things, we also must trust Him enough to give us the right answer.

God is love so what He does is always in our best interest when we allow Him to run things in our lives. No matter how much we may think we want something and keep hitting a wall, we keep praying that God's will be done and it will. He'll put those people in our lives who can teach us the lesson we need at the moment. And He will use us to teach others.

When you pray be certain you want what you are asking for and listen for the answer.

ନ

September 9
Giving it Away
"The miracle is this — the more we share, the more we have."
—Leonard Nimoy

One of the Twelve Step recovery slogans says that you have to give it away to keep it. Thus by sharing what we have learned, by giving love and compassion, by just being there, we help others.

Holding on to our wisdom and knowledge won't help anyone else. And while we can't learn a lesson for another, we may keep them from having to go through certain things and from falling into pitfalls and traps. After all, Alcoholics Anonymous and other programs using the same formula, have found this approach successful for many years.

Often what we need is a listening ear or a shoulder to cry on. Perhaps just a hug. There are things we cannot do for our self, but we can do it for one another. As much as we do these things for someone else, the favor will be returned to us. It may not be from the person we gave to, but it will come to us from somewhere.

The universe, our Higher Power, gives us what we need when the time comes if we are open to receive it. It's up to us to give what we have to others in need and we can be sure that what we have will not run out if we are helping others.

You have to give it away to keep it.

∽

September 10
Healing First

"The things you want are always possible; it is just that the way to get them is not always apparent. The only real obstacle in your path to a fulfilling life is you, and that can be a considerable obstacle because you carry the baggage of insecurities and past experience."

—Les Brown

The older we get, the more open we are, and the more we experience, the more likely we are to have a lot of baggage to carry from these experiences. Life lessons don't have to turn into burdens that move with us along our journey, but they often do turn into just that.

The way we avoid carrying a heavy load and living in the past is to heal from something before we start anew. Many of us have in our lives gone from a soured relationship with pain and anger and walked right into something else. It's easy to do because beginnings are fun and it helps us to "get over" the last one. But if we didn't feel our emotions from the breakup and heal from the pain then it just turns into baggage.

There is no time limit written in stone on when it's the best time to move on because it varies by circumstance and what we do to heal from pain and loss. We will know when it's right if we are honest and true to ourselves. But to move into anything new with baggage from our past is only going to cause failure in the new relationship.

This is not to say that we are ever over something completely, most likely we're not, if that person meant a lot to us. But we do need to be able to distinguish the actions and behaviors of our new interest from those of the former so we don't project the old onto the new.

Another thing to remember is just because a former relationship failed, it does not mean that we are a failure and that everything in the future will be the same way. We may have chosen the other person for all the wrong reasons, including getting over another person.

We may simply need to choose better and for different reasons than in the past. And we can trust ourselves in that a whole lot better when we aren't burdened down with a load of baggage.

Shed the baggage by healing your heart and then move forward.

∽

September 11
Grow Faith not Fear

"You block your dream when you allow your fear to grow bigger than your faith." —Mary Manin Morrissey

Fear is a natural part of us; it's an essential element, in fact. Fear protects us at times, and it helps us to be cautious, keeps us from moving too fast into situations in our lives.

But fear can also be a block. It may block us from love. It can block our success and even attempts at things. And it can keep us from growth. We must recognize fear and allow ourselves to feel it when we know that it's a healthy emotion at the time. But what we don't want to do is hide behind that fear.

We may have tried and failed. Perhaps in relationships we have been hurt and we are just too scared to face that again. Or maybe we've had a business collapse or failed at a job where we were employed by others. That's water under the bridge, not reason to give up because we fear we might lose or fail again.

There are a few things that can be very helpful when we are afraid to move forward: prayer and talking about our fears with someone else. God will hear us and help us through and give us courage. Our friends, mentors, clergy, therapists, or family members can help us just by listening and by talking through the issues. They can help us determine what valid things to fear are and what is just an imaginary boogeyman under the bed.

Our self-esteem and confidence will grow each time we walk through our fears. We will see that fear is not something we should empower in our lives. It is there. It may be there often, but it does not have control over us. We can be stronger than our fears and come out on the other side with renewed faith and success at that which we attempted.

Fear will only grow as large as you allow it, just as faith will do the same.

✧

September 12
Seeing Clearly

"God let me hit bottom so I'd appreciate what He sent me."
—Anonymous

We often wonder why our prayers seemingly go unanswered. Even while we are taught that God does answer our prayers, when we suffer, and don't get what we ask for it appears that we are not being heard.

Sometimes we realize that even as much as we thought our prayers were not heard, that there was a reason that our prayers did not get answered the way we wanted and in the time frame that we expected. We may discover this in an instant or over time.

I went through a period of time, actually for years, asking for something that I wanted. And in a series of a few months the thing that I prayed for was presented to me and then pulled away time after time. It hurt and I blamed God, until one day I just gave up. If that's the way it was going to be then fine, that must be the way He wanted things to go. And within a matter of hours after having let go out of frustration I was offered the thing I had been wanting.

It was, because of the timing, something that I knew was the answer I had been looking for. And had I not been in the place I was when it came to me, I most likely would have walked right past it because it did not fit the mold I had formed. I believe that because I hit bottom I was able to see this as a gift from God.

It takes what it takes to have faith. It took what it took for me to see clearly the answer when it arrived. We don't understand when we don't get what we want, when God has something better. And as long as we stubbornly seek what we want that doesn't work, we will keep getting it, at least until we can't stand the pain any longer and let God give us what we need instead.

When you hit bottom with pain it's easier to see the answer from God.

∽

September 13
Black and White Thinking
"There is nothing either good or bad, but thinking makes it so."
—William Shakespeare

Situations in life are affected by our personal experiences. What appears one way to one person does not always appear the same to the next, because events in our lives have not been the same.

What we bring to each situation is unique to us because the whole of our lives comes along with that. Our spiritual journeys, our relationships, family of origin issues, these all play into who we are as adults. No two people have the same exact experiences although we all share in some.

This can make relationships difficult. No matter how good we are at communication that too is affected on both sides of a relationship based upon what each brings to the table.

Things are rarely black and white, good or bad. They just are what they are. And there are shades of gray in them as well. We, as humans, fail. We do things we regret and we hurt other people, sometimes based upon what they think about the situation more so than what we did.

We need to listen to what another has to say. We need to really hear what they are saying and not hear it from just our point of view. We need to try our best to discern their communication without letting our experiences or old hurts alter what they said.

Mostly we need to remember that things are not always as we perceive them. And that the situation involves more than our experiences and thoughts. We can give others the right to think and feel as they will based upon where they are on their journey.

There is often no right or wrong, but something in between.

∽

September 14
Clarity and Direction

"Efforts and courage are not enough without purpose and direction." —John F. Kennedy

What do we do when we don't know what to do? When we are uncertain of the path we are supposed to take, the next right thing to do is often difficult to discern.

We must first and foremost be true to who we are. We follow our journey. We honor what our core beliefs are, what we desire. We keep in mind how the course of our life affects our friends, family, partners, etc., but we also must remain true to ourselves.

A husband and father may choose to change careers because in his heart he knows he has to do it to be true to himself. He has a purpose and direction. Things may be more difficult for a while, but it's something he knows will be better in the end for his life.

When we don't know what we want we have a very difficult time determining what efforts and decisions need to be made. When we are seeking a college degree, for instance, there is a plan set out and we know what classes we must take to get our diploma. There are options as to when we take certain classes and we have choices about electives. This is an easier path to follow than our journey of life because it has a written plan.

On our path, we have wide open opportunities and we must determine our purpose and direction, what our final goal is, oftentimes to determine our next move. If we want to get to point C, we must go through A and B. If we have not determined our destination point in some form, then we cannot set sail to get there.

We shouldn't always set our goal too specifically, but we can have a purpose and direction in which to travel. Without that, we are too scattered, and all of the efforts and courage in the world will have us doing little more than spinning in circles.

Determine purpose and direction and then put all you have into it.

September 15
Emotional Stability

"Feelings are much like waves, we can't stop them from coming but we can choose which one to surf." —Jonatan Martensson

We all have good days and bad days and many days that fall in between. Sometimes they are triggered by events, or other times by weather or physical changes, and even skipping a meal or losing sleep can cause us to get out of sync within our own emotional status.

When we have one of those days where nothing seems to go right, or when we are suffering from negative emotions, we need to remember that we will be okay. We can stop and pray or meditate to try to focus on what is right and also to find peace and serenity. Maybe we need to do something different if possible with our day, but often we are at work or handling some other responsibility and we just can't walk away.

Playing into how bad things are won't make them better. Thinking positively and staying calm will help. We can ride the wave of "poor me" or we can jump on our surf board and find some joy or peace in the struggle of the day.

All of us have days filled with internal turmoil and days that are full of joy. We tend to remember those less than fun days more than those that are easy and full of peace and calm. But we have both.

When grieving a loss or some other pain is part of our day we can remember that with time things tend to feel better; we won't feel as raw and vulnerable as time passes. We may feel as if we have been sliced open at times and that we cannot make it through the next moment, but we can and we do.

Remember that life does not follow an even and steady path. There are peaks and valleys and everything that falls between. We can learn to keep our emotions in check whether we are on the high or low end of the spectrum.

We can't always choose what the day will bring, but we can choose how we react to it.

❦

September 16
Foxhole Prayers

"The trouble with our praying is we just do it as a means of last resort." —Will Rogers

We often find ourselves saying foxhole prayers, those that we say because there's nothing left to do. But how much easier our lives would be if we could only remember to pray before we are at a place where we have become desperate.

If we pray, then we have some belief that it's being heard. It's odd that we don't remember to pray up front and instead often save it for last. We will contact our friends, sponsors, family, coworkers, therapists, or anybody who is available to ask advice or to tell about our woes — all the while neglecting to contact God for help.

God can and will still help us when we get in a mess, but we might avoid such predicaments if we would only seek guidance, strength, wisdom, and knowledge from our Higher Power up front.

Prayer can give us peace in the midst of our turmoil. Sometimes it may just be the act of stopping long enough to pray that gets us out of whatever thing we have gotten in the middle of. Certainly God can have a place in that peace, but just to think about God, that He is there with us every moment gives us a sense of peace and calms us.

Before we call on other people over a problem or a situation, we ought to seek out God's assistance. Connect to God first and then see what happens. It's a difficult thing to remember, but one that, if practiced, will prove to be a valuable asset for a good day. And keeping a spiritual connection will help us stay on track so we don't have to end up in a foxhole crying out for help.

God is present always and should not be sought as a last resort.

❦

September 17
Patience Equals Peace

"The key to everything is patience. You get the chicken by hatching the egg, not by smashing it." —Arnold H. Glasgow

The need to be patient seems at times to come about at every turn.

We are either waiting for someone to come or for them to go. We are impatient about time moving too fast or too slow. We get in a rush and find ourselves in a traffic jam with no way to get where we are going fast. We wait on God to answer our prayers and we are impatient.

When we are impatient it is probably about as far from peace as we can go. When we are impatient we become oversensitive and every feeling is exacerbated. We push too hard. We become agitated too easily. We cause some things to spin out of control.

Patient is one of the most difficult things to be when we are in the midst of something that requires it. But given our options there's usually little else to do than be patient. We will get what we need when we need it.

We live in a world where instant gratification has become a reality in some ways but not all. But because we do have some things so quickly and at hand immediately, we have come to expect all things to be this way. The universe does not operate at computer speed. Nature has not changed because of technology.

So it is with relationships and issues with work and anything that isn't immediate. We must "give time, time" as someone once said to me. We seldom have much of a choice in situations but to be patient.

Finding patience in the midst of waiting will bring peace.

∽

September 18
Fair Treatment

"Expecting the world to treat you fairly because you are a good person is a little like expecting the bull not to attack you because you are a vegetarian." —Dennis Wholey

We expect a lot of things in our lives and one of them is that if we do right; if we are kind and loving then we will get all of those things in return. But the reality is that sometimes no matter what we do, we do not receive back what we give.

We do not have control over what anyone else does, whether it's a parent, boss, partner, friend, family member, or some random stranger. If we do try to control an outcome by acting a certain way then we are either being manipulative or playing games.

But just because we do not receive the same treatment as we give in every situation of our lives, we should still be kind and loving and try to do the right thing. While we do this, we also take care of our self; we don't allow abuse or mistreatment of any kind. We do what we need to take care of ourselves. We walk away if we need to.

Nobody, God included, expects us to roll over and play victim. But expecting everyone to be kind and loving when we are is just not reality.

If we know that we have not treated someone fairly or kindly, then we can be at peace no matter how they treat us in return. We only have control over our own actions, behaviors, and thoughts. That's our focus: to continue to be kind and loving.

And remember, just because one person or 10 people treat us badly, we still should not expect the next one to as well.

Continue to be kind and loving even when it appears nobody else is.

❧

September 19
Asking for Help

"The healthy, the strong individual, is the one who asks for help when he needs it; whether he has an abscess on his knee or in his soul."
—Rona Barrett

Whenever we are dealing with something, learning a new thing, or simply just need support it is not only okay to ask for help, it's what we ought to do.

Whether we are experiencing pain over something, need help lifting a heavy item, need advice on how to do something, or maybe just want a listening ear, it is a good thing to reach out to another. Others have gone through what we have, or perhaps just bouncing ideas off of them will help us make a decision or solve a dilemma.

Many of us want to be too strong. We think that we have to do it alone, that asking for help means we can't handle things ourselves, but that's just not true. None of us was equipped for every situation. Just as one is unable to lift a heavy object, another may be in need of help writing a letter. One may be strong in relationships, while the other could have been through breakup after breakup.

God gave us each other to help. All of us were given our own unique gifts and talents and we ought to use what we have been blessed with in support of those who were not given that particular gift. And we should never feel less than for seeking help, rather we ought to realize that it takes a certain amount of strength to admit we cannot do all things alone.

Asking for help shows strength not weakness.

❧

September 20
Knowledge of God's Will

"Sought through prayer and meditation to improve our conscious contact with God, as we understood Him; praying only for knowledge of His will for us and the power to carry that out."
—Step Eleven of Twelve Step programs

When we pray for the knowledge of God's will for us, and the power to carry that out, we ought not to then question why certain things do not happen the way we want. We can't have it both ways. We cannot have our will be done and God's will be done unless they are in line with one another.

Sometimes even when we think that we are in the midst of something that feels so much like it is an answer to prayer, we find that it wasn't the particular answer we were seeking. Perhaps it is a lesson to be learned that we aren't even sure what issue it involves. Maybe it leads to the answer we are seeking, but we just don't see the big picture — yet.

We just have to keep seeking conscious contact and praying for knowledge of His will and the ability to do it. We won't be asked to do anything without also being blessed with the gifts and ability to do that. And if we rely only on our will, we will continue to struggle like a fish out of water.

It's not an easy task to follow God's will, especially if we don't know what that is. But if we pray for knowledge of it we will be more aware. There are times that we may not know what the next right thing is, or why something happened, but we can see what isn't right, and just maybe see that we were very blessed that things did not go the way we wanted.

God does know best and He will not lead us into wrong things. We go there ourselves. He will use experiences to teach us, to help us grow closer to him, and for us to gain wisdom. If something feels wrong, it more than likely is. God things click, they don't cause us a whole lot of problems unless we struggle against them.

We more often than not know what's going on with things in life, although we often act shocked and want to believe that we didn't. Our intuition is good, most likely because God's using that to connect with us. When we follow our intuition, when we go with our gut, we seldom are wrong. And this is not to say that we won't have difficulties, pain, and loss, it just means that we are being led if we would just use the tools we were given to follow that lead.

When you are in God's will you will know it and feel peace.

∽

September 21
Be True to You
"This above all; to thine own self be true."
—William Shakespeare

Being true to who we are is really the only way we can be if we choose to be healthy mentally and spiritually. Although some change is inevitable, and we can modify a lot of our behavior and thinking, we never do this overnight and some of who we are will never be different. Change comes with a lot of prayer, meditation, struggles, pain, and growth — eventually.

We cannot suddenly wake up one day and like the color yellow if we've always hated that color. We don't just make up our mind that we should change our thinking and have it changed instantly. Certainly God is able to make a sudden change in us, but if that happens we'll know it.

It's okay to have standards for whom and what we allow into our lives. If we don't want a certain career then we should not seek that no matter who tells us we should. And by the same token if we aren't attracted to a particular trait or behavior in people we should not expect that we can be in a deep and caring relationship with a person who has that characteristic. We don't have to try to be something that we are not just to mold ourselves into who we think others want us to be, or if we think there's something wrong with us for being the way we are.

Each of us is unique. If we all liked the same exact things we might as well be produced from a cookie cutter. We don't have to like what we don't like and we don't have to try to be attracted to that which we are uninterested.

We may think we are shallow minded for not liking certain things, for not being able to look past something, but trying to go against a core belief within us and pretending that thing doesn't matter just won't get it. We may work on the issue and change eventually, but pretending it isn't there because we aren't proud of it won't make it go away. And in reality there's most likely nothing to be ashamed of. We either like certain things or we don't. That doesn't make it right or wrong.

You cannot be true to yourself if you try to mold into what you think others want you to be.

∽

September 22
Hope Always
"Hope is like a bird that senses dawn and carefully starts to sing while it is still dark." —Unknown

If we knew what the next moment held, or the next hour, tomorrow, or next year, we would most likely live our lives in a different way than we do not knowing. But since it's impossible to know the future, most of us choose to live our lives in a positive hope filled manner.

I'm certain that we have all experienced those moments in our lives when we had given up on something only to have that situation turn around. Maybe we thought we'd never find a job, get our bills caught up, find peace in life, get sober, move on from a bad relationship, or start a new one. There are always going to be disappointments. But like the bird who sings before the sun rises above the horizon, there is hope.

Without hope we might as well just give up. It can be the only thing that keeps us going at times. And we have it because we've experienced those moments when just around the corner we found what we so desperately needed or desired.

Yes, we can crawl in a hole and give up on life when we find things aren't going the way we would like them to. Or we can hold out hope and pray for what we want and need. And while we wait for those things, we can remain active in the world both by giving of ourselves and our talents, and by receiving what others have to give to us.

Either way, life goes on, it goes on with or without our presence so we ought to show up and be accounted for. We will very often get what we totally do not expect and sometimes this feels like a gift and at other times this feels like a slap in the face, but being open to life offers us lots, we just must take the good with the bad, or seemingly bad. Sometimes what we perceive as bad — having something taken away or not getting what we want — is in reality a gift in disguise.

Hope keeps you going in the face of trials, disappointments, or in times where patience is needed.

❦

September 23
Holding Onto Peace
"Find the peace that prevails even when the turbulent waters of the river roar through your life."
—Melody Beattie

It is such an easy task to say we have peace in our lives; that is, until the storm hits. And because life has times or turbulence, just like it has those days where we seem to float down a peaceful stream, we must ensure that we have ways to find peace when we lose it.

A person can't really force peace, but to get it we can slow down, take a deep breath, and think things through. We can go to a place where we know we can find it, such as a mountaintop, a favorite reading or meditation place in our home, on a trip down a country road, anywhere that allows us to find serenity.

We don't find peace stressing about tomorrow, or worrying about yesterday. So staying in the moment is a start. Sometimes what we have to do in order to have peace is wait, and at other times we must take action. We back away, or we move in. Situations call for different solutions.

Peace comes with faith in a Higher Power. It comes with the knowledge that there are rocky times in all of our lives and that we cannot expect perfection within us or around us. We get peace when we understand that feelings are what they are and not something that defines us. We can find peace in love, forgiveness, and grace.

Often we hold onto the past with such a tight grip that there's no room for peace. We cling to hurt and wrongs done to us, which only continue to make us a victim. We need to move away from the grip on turmoil and we do that when we forgive; when we put love first; and sometimes simply by the grace of God.

When we find peace, we ought to try to hold onto it, and when we can't keep it in our grips we remember how we got it so we can go back when we need to, when the turbulent waters roar too loudly in our lives to find it.

Find out what brings you peace and remember it so you can return when it's lost.

◈

September 24
Individuality

"When I was four years old they tried to test my IQ, they showed me this picture of three oranges and a pear. They asked me which one is different and does not belong; they taught me different was wrong."
—Ani Difranco

There are events in our lives like the one above which may form us and affect us the rest of our lives. But we don't have to allow inappropriate lessons to control us in our adult lives. We are each individual and unique and to try to fit ourselves into the mold of another will only stifle us. To know that we are okay just as we are is a very settling and secure thing in our lives.

We are okay as we are, while continuing our spiritual quests and emotional growth. We don't have to do it in any particular way; we do that and our lives in our own unique way. We were created to be different so there's no reason to try to be just like someone else or just the way someone wants us to be.

Sure, we have Twelve Step programs, counselors, sponsors, teachers, pastors, etc., to guide us, but we still have freedom to be who we are and to go about our lives just as uniquely as we were created. To be different in any way from the next person is never to be perceived as wrong or right for that matter, it just is.

We ought not conform to what we think others expect of us, of who we are. We will never be happy trying to fit in with what we think others expect because we'll always be changing to be like who we are with at the moment. We can't be a whole and happy individual if we are not able to be who we are.

Spend a few minutes each day thinking about doing what you want based upon your desires and not what you think others want from you. Being your true self rather than a chameleon is the only way to be truly happy and fit in as well.

You were created to be unique, why would you want to be anything else?

∽

September 25
Fear of Change

"Don't fear change, embrace it." —Anthony J. D'Angelo

Many of us fear change so much that we end up in ruts. Fear of the unknown, of change, is often something that keeps us stuck in our jobs, bad relationships, overweight, uneducated, using drugs, drinking excessively, and on and on.

Change is inevitable so we might as well embrace it when it happens outside our control because that's going to happen quite frequently. And it really is a blessing when it occurs because it always leads to something better eventually.

None of us ever wants the shock of losing a job either by the company downsizing, fazing out our particular position, or simply getting fired. But often people will say after this happens that it was the best thing because they ended up in a better job or one more suited for them or it simply got them out of their rut. Sometimes the familiar, even if we are miserable, seems better than change. Yet we stay in the miserable place because we have too much fear.

We fear change in other ways as well. What if we lose that extra 50 pounds we are carrying and we still don't feel loved, then what? Or if we leave a bad relationship we wonder if we'll just end up alone and lonely. But alone and lonely can be better than bad.

What ifs can keep us stuck in patterns of self-defeating behavior. We rarely know what tomorrow holds and if we do it might have just been a lucky guess. If we know too much what the next day has in store, we may be in a rut because predictable days mean we aren't growing much. The more we grow, the more changes come our way. And we must embrace the changes if we wish to grow.

Often change is out of our control and it can hit us when we least expect it. But we need to learn how to not immediately feel negativity about change and rather look at it for what it is, an opportunity for growth and maybe a new experience. Maybe that change that hits us broadside that we have no control over is exactly what we needed to motivate us to get out of the rut.

Change is going to happen with or without your participation.

∽

September 26
Selective Sharing

"It takes your enemy and your friend, working together, to hurt you:
the one to slander you, and the other to get the news to you."
—Mark Twain

It's the truth that even the best of us will occasionally pass on some news that would better be left unsaid. Sometimes we do it to one up someone, or to turn them against another, and sometimes it's just innocent, a lack of thought perhaps.

We have all experienced a time when someone told us something another had said that cut us to the core. And we can find no reason that our "friend" told us this information. Sometimes it's good to know what's being said about us because we need to protect our reputation as best we can, or maybe we have behavior that needs to be corrected. But usually when someone speaks out against us it's not something that we really need to know. Often we already know the thing about us that they are passing around. Maybe we are loud and obnoxious and they said that. Or perhaps we cheated on a spouse or partner and they spread that around. It does nobody any good to pass around this information.

We have choices within our own control about spreading news about another. We can do it or we can keep it to ourselves. Sometimes it's a judgment call whether or not news needs to be passed along. If in doubt, it's most likely better to be quiet.

What we don't have control over is what others say about us. We may have trusted the wrong person by telling them certain things only to have that news passed along. It's our choice if we confide in that person anymore. And we may decide to be more choosy about who we do tell our secrets and other details to.

What we don't want to do is shut down and close ourselves off from others. We don't let one bad apple spoil the whole bunch.

In Twelve Step programs that's what sponsors are for, to tell our stuff. And sometimes they cannot be trusted so we must deal with that issue and get a new sponsor. If we aren't in a program, we ought to find a trustworthy friend who we not only feel okay about confiding in, but who we also trust that what we tell others stays with them and does not get passed around.

People are not perfect and we cannot expect them to be. We can be careful; and we also should watch ourselves that we aren't one of those who runs and tells.

Find one safe person you can trust; and likewise be that person for another.

∽

September 27
Staying Open

"Love is always open arms. If you close your arms about love you will find that you are left holding only yourself." —Leo F. Buscaglia

Whether it's within friendships or love relationships we can go through rough times where we feel that the best thing to do is shut ourselves off so that we don't suffer any more loss or pain. And while a temporary withdrawal may be okay, a long-term solution to avoid pain is not the best option.

Love is the lifeblood of living. To not love is to not live fully. Pain will come, of course, because nothing stays the same and we will lose in love and life. People will die, or walk away, but we can be content in knowing that what we shared was real while it existed.

If we want to never feel pain and avoid it at all costs, we will also never feel happiness and joy because we won't allow ourselves the openness to allow anyone or anything into our lives that we may later lose. It's a risk, but one that is essential to truly healthy and whole lives.

We don't have to always be completely open to every person who comes into our lives. We may only open up completely once we feel safe, but to shut down is the other end of the spectrum.

When we lose a good friend or romantic partner to death, distance, disagreement, or perhaps the unknown we don't want to lose our opportunity to ever love or be loved again. Sure it hurts, and we need time to heal, but heal we will and life does go on.

We have the resiliency to move forward with life and love even after loss, but we must stay open — both to the love and the pain that could follow. To do otherwise is to die ourselves.

Closing off to love is a kind of death.

September 28
Faith is Action

"Faith is not trying to believe something regardless of the evidence; faith is daring something regardless of the consequences."
—Sherwood Eddy

When there's something we want in our life and we have taken all of the steps necessary to get it we must often wait to see if we will get what we desire or not. We must have faith and let it go. If we have done all we can do to get a certain thing we desire, there is nothing left to do but pray, have faith, and let it happen or not. If it's meant to be it will come to fruition.

Worrying will not make it happen. Getting stressed about an issue never solves it, although stress and worry may move us to action such as prayer, but the stress alone won't fix the problem or get our needs met.

Sometimes we have faith as a last resort, and at other times it's the beginning. Growth requires us to have faith. Believing that there is a Higher Power who cares about us, whom we can trust, gives us courage and faith to move forward, even when we don't get what we want.

We have all not been given the job, relationship, automobile, house, the person, place, or thing we wanted numerous times. Yet we are still able to go to God and ask for help for another thing because we have faith. Sometimes we have to have faith to see why we didn't get what we wanted.

Having faith is an action. It is a letting go and letting God act. Faith means we believe in something bigger than us who knows what is best and we have assurance that everything we need will be provided to us and there are reasons why we often get an answer of no.

You must practice faith to have faith.

❧

September 29
Manufactured Problems

"If I had my life to live over, I would perhaps have more actual troubles but I'd have fewer imaginary ones." —Don Herold

If we were to go back in our lives and count up the number of times we worried about what might happen, we would probably be overwhelmed by the needless minutes and hours we wasted.

It's seldom that our imaginary worries end up becoming real problems. What we think may happen at a job, in a relationship, or with our children, for example, may not happen at all. We may even dread some change or event only to find that it actually has a positive impact on us once we've experienced it.

Sometimes we can even make trouble where there's not any. We perceive or imagine something to be an issue and it's not one. We create a problem by making too much of an issue of something or pushing others too much.

The more easily we move through life the more calm we remain, the less problems we will actually have. When we let fear override peace there's little way to avoid trouble or disharmony. Fear and peace just don't exist together.

Remaining calm in a storm, especially one that's simply a creation of our imagination is the best remedy. And we do this with great effort. We give as much energy to being serene as we do to the worry and fear. We find what works for us to not make imaginary problems for ourselves. Maybe we find prayer works. Others may need to talk to a friend. Someone else may find distracting themselves from worry with exercise or reading a book is helpful. Obsessing about what might happen is clearly not the answer.

There are enough problems in our lives without creating new ones in our minds. Sometimes our imaginary troubles are worse than any problem we will face in reality. And often what we think is going to be a bad thing is a blessing in disguise.

Don't let imaginary problems take time away from handling real issues in life.

∽

September 30
It's An Inside Issue
"Wherever you go, there you are."
—Earnie Larsen

Wouldn't it be great if we could walk away from our troubles? We could leave a job because we don't like our boss, but the next one may be worse. We might get a divorce or leave a relationship because "they" don't do things the way we want. But is our happiness or distress really caused by others or is it something inside of us? Is it our behaviors that get us into the messy relationships and situations?

Most likely it's a combination of things. And we ought to look at what is the common denominator in our life. It is us. We can't always fix a problem if the other person won't do their share, but we can always work on our own issues. Geographical changes rarely fix our problems.

There's an amazing thing that happens when we pray for others. When in a situation with someone that causes us stress and problems the first thing we should do is pray for the other person. Pray for them to have peace, joy, love, whatever good we can think of. If they get those things, don't worry, we aren't going to miss out on the same good stuff.

Next we can pray for ourselves. Prayer can calm many storms, both internal and external, and it can help us keep ourselves out of further arguments and misunderstandings.

Thinking that the world is against us and all of our problems are because of "them" is not a solution. Looking within at the one thing that we are responsible for will help us. Trying to constantly escape our self is not a solution because we are still there.

Look within and solve your own problems because you can't escape yourself.

∞

October 1
Success
"Success is how high you bounce when you hit bottom."
—George Patton

Just ask anyone who has hit a bottom so low they almost died, and they'll most likely tell you they feel a sense of success for having simply survived the ordeal. Most anyone who ends up in a Twelve Step recovery group and is able to turn their lives around will feel an overwhelming sense of success.

People hit bottom in many ways, some to drugs and alcohol; some to sexual prowess; others may be thieves and liars. There are many things that can send our lives spiraling out of control. And each person's supposed bottom is at their own perspective level; they know it when they are there and it may be higher or lower than that of others.

Successful recovery from issues is a lifelong process. It's something that one can never truly give up on because it will always be there to remind us of a place we wish never to return. Maybe we have dreams about the hell we were in, or we are reminded of it by watching a movie, or some other event triggers the thoughts. Perhaps we get tired of the struggle of recovery and think about returning to whatever made us hit bottom, but usually remembering the pain is enough to keep us away.

We won't become perfect once we begin to recover, and nobody said we should. But we will become better people if we truly seek to be. Our success is unlimited and may not have the same value that we once thought it would. Success can be measured in a lot of ways: one person may become highly educated, another may be an awesome sponsor in a Twelve Step program, someone else might write an award winning novel, and yet another may be a success because they are able to continually stay away from whatever brought them to their bottom. Success is a personal thing.

It's often said about drugs that however high a person gets they will go to an equal low. And so it is that once the drug isn't there a person will hit a state of depression, sometimes within hours of using the drug. Life can be the same in that however low our bottom is we can go to the same level on the other end; the end of success.

Success may be measured by just how low the bottom was that you climbed out of.

ॐ

October 2
Doing the Difficult
"The right thing and the hardest thing are always the same."
—Christina Havrilla

The right thing may not always be difficult but in a lot of circumstances doing the right thing is the hardest thing.

Treating another person with kindness and love when they have treated us with the opposite is very hard to do. We gain nothing, however, by treating a mean person in kind. Mean spirited energy aimed at another probably does us more harm than it does our target. And the fact of the matter is our thinking mean thoughts about someone else never reach their ears.

Instead of negative energy we can be positive when we feel angry or hurt to our very core. Staying mad at someone only keeps us in the victim role anyway and is oppressive and depressive.

There may come a time in our lives where we are attracted to someone in a romantic way, yet that person is in a relationship or married, or maybe we are. The right thing and the hardest thing may be to stay away from that person even if we feel drawn to them with our whole being.

Leaving an abusive relationship; getting help for an eating order or addiction; looking for a job even when we keep getting rejected; slowing down and taking care of ourselves when we need to rest or we are sick; and standing up for ourselves on a job when we are being abused or harassed; all of these things and lots of other situations call for doing what's difficult when not doing anything might be easier.

If life was always easy we wouldn't grow and we would certainly never reach out to our Higher Power. In order to have a spiritual life we must turn our attention to God and most of us would never do that if we didn't have problems or need help.

If the right thing is hard to do that's no reason to ignore it.

᪥

October 3
Focus on Good Too

"I always have two lists: things I'm happy about and things I'm not. It's my choice which list I focus on." —Anne Arthur

It's almost a guarantee that on any given day we will have some things to be very happy about and some things that cause us pain or anger or some other emotion we would rather not feel. Often the unpleasant things are where we will focus.

It's important to take care of all aspects of our lives so we don't want to ignore the negative things that happen, or the difficulties we experience, but we have a choice whether we wallow in the troubling things or think about what's good too.

Sometimes we experience times in our lives when we are happy about things and upbeat, and there may be those in our lives who are suffering with severe illness or loss, which may cause us to try to keep our happiness under wraps. We can be respectful of others and still be happy.

When we choose to focus only on the bad it's easy to fall into a depression that may begin gradually and end up taking over our lives. We don't want to ignore the unhappy things if we can do anything about them, but if we can't then we can turn our focus onto what does make us happy.

If we can't find anything to be happy about and all we are doing is complaining and languishing in our unhappiness, it's time to sit down and think about things. Maybe we need to actually make a list with things in our lives that we are happy about in one column and the other stuff in another.

Celebrate and focus on the "this makes me happy" list. On the other list, where we are not happy, we can look at these things and start taking action on getting them out of our lives or changing them if we can.

Having happiness doesn't mean everything in our lives has to be perfect.

October 4
Humanness

"I laugh, I love, I hope, I try, I hurt, I need, I fear, I cry. And I know you do the same things too, so we're really not that different, me and you." —Colin Raye

We feel alone sometimes. Different. Lonesome. Independent. Isolated. Free. Afraid. Terrified. Peaceful.

Whatever we feel is nothing more or less than what others feel. We may not be in the same place on the same day and moment as our partner or best friend, but it's pretty much a guarantee that if we are in grief, they have felt it as well. If we're feeling sad and lonely, they've been there.

As much as we are unique creatures, we are also very much alike in many ways. Some may not choose to admit to anyone else that they feel fear, loneliness, or maybe even joy. There are those who would never say they have failed at anything, just as there are those who are quite successful who would never admit to their stature.

If we are human beings we bleed just like the next person. We cry, we hurt, we have joy, we feel lost, we love, we hate sometimes, we just are who we were made to be. Trying to be something else by not allowing ourselves to be human is a loss for whoever is trying to do that.

Sometimes we can just be free and loose and let life roll, and at other times we may try to have a firm grip of control on its every motion. Both are essential to life and growth, having their own times and places, but in time we see that we cannot control much in this world. We certainly cannot control outcomes, other people, or the universe.

The more we learn how similar we are the quicker we will find peace because we won't have to fight so hard to be something we aren't or to pretend we don't feel like the next person. Keeping it real will keep us grounded. It will help us to feel our feelings so that we may move on. Denial of a feeling never made it go away it just keeps it buried below the surface and holds back our growth.

Once you understand the humanness of others, you will accept yourself more fully.

October 5
Why Ask Why
"I don't always get to know why." —Judith R. Smith

Often we can get so caught up in asking why that we cannot move on. We want to know why our parents treated us the way they did; or why someone stopped dating us; why our spouse had an affair; why we didn't get the job; why we got sick; or any number of why's.

The problem with why is that most of the time whatever happened was out of our control. We may blame ourselves and say we'll do it differently next time, when we don't even know what to change because we don't know the answer to why.

It's difficult. Many of us are way more comfortable with the known than the unknown. Even if we don't like the reason we can attempt to manipulate our thinking to remove the blame if we know that we are at fault. We can use denial; blame someone else, or anything that makes us feel better instead of owning our issues. But when we don't know why we are left to our own vivid imaginations and that can be a troubling place to be.

Sometimes things just happen and the why doesn't even make sense. Our parents may have treated us differently than we would have liked, but even if we knew why it would not change the fact that it happened. It might help us forgive them more, but if the reason wasn't a good one in our opinion, then it could make things more difficult to forgive.

It's not a bad thing in situations to know why if that information is available, we just want to avoid getting stuck in a place where we need to know why when we probably will never know, or getting to the bottom of it would just cause more strife.

All we can do when reasons are unknown is go on what we do know. If we are aware of behaviors that we are not happy with in ourselves, then we work on growth and avoid that behavior in the future. What we don't want to do is change who we are in order to get an outcome we want, especially if that is based upon a particular loss that we are having difficulty getting over. If we are not true to our self no matter what we do we will end up unhappy.

You don't always have to know why.

October 6
Winners
"If you want to be a winner, hang around with winners."
—Christopher D. Furman

No matter if you're 12 years old or 72 years old who you spend your time with has a huge influence on your level of happiness and healthiness.

None of us would encourage or even allow our children to spend time with people who we know are bad for them, so it makes little sense that we would socialize with those who are a bad influence on us. We don't have to continue to be in situations that are unhealthy. If it's a work situation that we can find no resolution for, then we must seek new employment.

The world is full of people. If we find ourselves depressed and troubled by the company we keep, it's our choice and responsibility to not spend time with those people any more. When we spend our time with healthy positive people, we will be more healthy and positive.

Winners are those who have a positive outlook on life, who meet challenges head on, albeit hesitantly at times, who look for good rather than bad, but accept reality. Winners try their best to be free of gossip and judgment, although they know they are human and fall short of perfection, they still try. Winners seek peace over turmoil, and love over fear.

If we want to gossip and find strife there's plenty of it out there, but living that kind of life only brings on more of the same. Just as hanging with winners makes us winners; hanging with losers makes us losers.

You become your environment so make it healthy.

October 7
False Limitations
"Argue for your limitations and surely they will be yours!"
—Marshal Sylver

Even for those who may have been blessed by parents who provided them with an almost perfect life growing up, there are no perfect families and we all have our limitations. Being raised in a nurturing and loving environment is ideal, but even those who experienced that may have difficulties in life when they are met head on by less than ideal conditions outside their family of origin.

Any one of us, from those raised in abusive homes, to those in near perfect conditions, can argue forever that we can't do this or that because of something that we see as limiting. We use excuses like: I just don't have enough talent; I don't have a degree, or the right education; I've never been good at that; I always mess up; last time I tried that I failed; I am no good at relationships; and so on.

When we glorify our limitations we manifest them. What we believe about ourselves will basically be what we do with our lives.

If we can turn around our self-defeating thoughts, we will find ourselves having self-fulfilled prophesies of success, rather than utter failure. "I think I can," may be our new motto. "I think I can do this, maybe not perfectly, but I'm going to give it a shot." Maybe it didn't work last time we tried, or we never tried because we'd already doomed ourselves to failure by saying we could not do it.

We really do not have anything to lose by taking the positive angle on life. We may try and fail, but that's always better than never trying. Life is meant to be lived, not merely tolerated until we die.

Limitations are just excuses to never give all you have to life.

᪥

October 8
Cumulative Growth

"Practice makes permanent." —Bobby Robson

Growth and learning both take time and effort. As adults we get easily frustrated when we don't think we are progressing fast enough whether it's a recovery issue or some other learning opportunity.

Often when we are growing or learning new things we are unable to see the growth. It's gradual and we are not able to see the movement because we are in the midst of the growth. Others often see and recognize it before we do.

It's easy to get discouraged when we practice something over and over and don't feel we are getting anywhere, but if we continue the recovery efforts, or other learning process one day we will be aware of just how far we have come.

It may be good from time to time to look back at where we were. If we were a drunk at our bottom or an addict barely hanging onto life, and now we are clean and sober for a month, year, or more, we can easily see things in our lives that are better and ways that we have matured in our behavior.

If we are learning a new skill, we may need to remember back to the beginning when we knew nothing and see that we have learned a lot, it's just hard to see when we grow tiny bits every day.

What's important is that we continue to practice since this is how we learn. Sometimes growth comes in spurts. We may suddenly see our growth after not noticing it for a long time. We certainly won't grow and learn if we don't continue to try.

Growth and learning are cumulative; a little at a time and soon you reap the benefits.

❧

October 9
Having Support

"The love, the acceptance of other persons makes me into the unique person I am meant to be." —Peter G. van Breemen

Having a support group is an important part of life no matter where we are in our recovery, growth, or maturity.

This support can come from a recovery group, church, family, or friends, and is usually best if it's a mixture of many. We may have friends at church or in a recovery group who have never met our friends that we do other things with. All of the different people in our lives are our support group regardless of what heading of acquaintance they fall under.

When things are going great in our lives we may not feel the need to have people to turn to, but let us suffer a loss, or have a need and we soon discover the importance of friends and family for support. Having many people in our lives to turn to does not mean that each of them know everything about us. Some friends will be closer to us and know our darkest secrets; some may be there simply because they make us laugh; and another may be there because they have had similar grief in their life. The more variety the better when it comes to having people in our lives.

When we feel loved we are better able to love ourselves. When we love ourselves others are drawn to us. As others are drawn to us they become part of our social network of support, and we become theirs as well.

If we don't have this support in our lives we can get it by starting where we are. We add one at a time until eventually — sometimes suddenly — we realize that we are in the middle of something that will not fail us because it is strong and diverse.

Even when we are single and spend a great deal of time alone, we can still feel love and support from those in our lives. We will never truly feel alone when we know that there are people who care.

Having others to lean on when in need makes the down times so much easier.

❧

October 10
Overcoming Weakness

"A man's greatest strength develops at the point where he overcomes his greatest weakness." —Elmer G. Letterman

Everyone has weak spots, things in our lives that must be worked on more than others. Some because of what was done to us, some from things we did to ourselves, and others just something we were born with.

Weakness in any area of life does not always equal bad or wrong. It just means something that we must spend more time nurturing. Often what was once our greatest weakness becomes a strong point for us.

There are many people in the world who have overcome great obstacles to become presidents, CEOs, great parents, champion level athletes, and so forth. Bookstores and movie rental stores are filled with the stories of these people who grew up with nothing and made themselves into something not only good, but sometimes great. And there are those who may have been born with disease or handicap who rather than using that for an excuse turned it around to help others.

Just because we don't have every gift and talent in existence does not limit us from using what we do have. While we nurture what is weak, we also remember to develop and use those things about us that we are strong in.

And while we grow strong in our weaknesses we will remain humble in knowing that we are not perfect just as nobody else is. Overcoming weakness is one way we grow. None of us would grow or mature much if everything was simple, or easy, or given to us.

You grow strong because you have things to overcome.

∽

October 11
Forgiveness is for the Forgiver

"When a deep injury is done us, we never recover until we forgive."
—Alan Paton

Forgiving when we have been wronged personally is one of the most difficult things we have to do. But until we forgive we carry that injury with us as if it was happening over and over. We remain the victim of the abuse as long as we continue to give the other person power by not forgiving them.

We must remember that forgiveness is for us, not the person we forgive. And it does not necessarily mean that we condone what was done. We also must keep in mind that we forgive unconditionally, without expectation that the person will change their behavior in the future. We are not in charge of other people's behavior; therefore forgiving them likely won't cause any changes in their actions.

Often the person we are trying to forgive has not even apologized or asked us to forgive them. And their behavior may not be anything new and it certainly is unlikely to change, but we still need to let go of our anger and resentment; again this is for us not them.

It's also likely that we won't be able to forgive in a moment's time. It takes time, prayer, giving it to God and taking it back over and over. It takes a willingness to let go of our anger and resentment with the knowledge that we have in a way let someone get away with their behavior.

When we forgive someone we can also set a boundary, one that will hopefully keep us from their harm again. If we were unjustly accused of something, or just treated badly in some way, we can protect ourselves from further harm by staying away from that person or situation if possible, but sometimes this is not an option. We can't always cut ties with someone we need to forgive because they may be a parent or a child.

When we forgive we free ourselves from living as the victim. As long as we continue to hold a grudge we keep the wound of hurt open. Freedom for ourselves comes when we forgive.

Forgiveness is essential for peace and freedom.

∽

October 12
Choose Optimism

"The optimist sees the rose and not its thorns; the pessimist stares at the thorns, oblivious of the rose." —Kahlil Gibran

Living in the world we do it's very easy to become jaded. For those who used to be optimistic and then were just beat down to a point where everything turned sour, it's easy to see why they aren't too enthused about life in general.

But there really is a better way. Living the life of an optimist is really much lighter than its opposite. When there are only clouds hanging over us and we portray that in our actions and speech, all we do is continue the gloominess.

Yes, sometimes optimism is a kind of denial, a lie even, I suppose. To say "I'm good" when things are really not going well may be stretching the truth, but if we look at what is right in our life we truly can say that. There are very few times in our lives that every single thing is just as we want it to be. When that does happen it's fantastic and usually lasts a short time until a new issue comes around. But also there is always something positive in life even in our worst of times.

As someone who in the past lived under a cloud of pessimism I can attest to the fact that a positive, optimistic look at things is clearly the better route.

We all know people who only see the thorns in life and those are the folks we hope to not get stuck talking to. Sure, from time to time, we all have it rough and we need to lean on each other for support. We can't always see sun on a cloudy day. What we can do is begin the practice of optimism and it will grow in us and become a part of who we are. People will be attracted to what we have and our lives will become better.

Optimism is not putting on blinders to what's wrong; it's simply facing things from a healthy perspective, one which offers us an opportunity for success. Gloom and doom thinking can become a part of us just like positivity can.

Choose optimism over pessimism and life will be better.

∽

October 13
Practice Routines

"It's not so much quantity as it is quality. In our daily preparation, it's routine stuff. We emphasize fundamentals: we catch the ball and try to throw it straight. You try to find some type of comfort zone where if my practice habits are good, they carry over into the game."

—Randy Ready

Daily preparation and routines are important to team sports, just as they are for individual athletes, musicians, doctors, bankers, ministers, and every other person. We practice the small daily routines in our lives and we are able to handle the big game of life, no matter if our job is on the ball field, in an office, or home.

Certain practices or habits can benefit our emotional and spiritual lives. A daily routine of reading our recovery books or spiritual materials will help us to start our day centered. Meditation and prayer are important elements to each day as well, and help us along our path of recovery and growth.

We can make these daily practices routine in our lives to the point where we miss them when we don't do them. They become a part of our day just as brushing our teeth and eating are.

Having a routine may sound boring to some, but it's easier to do what we need to do when we have time set aside for it each day. Some folks get up earlier in the morning to read, meditate, and pray. Others do these things at night. When doesn't matter so much as doing.

It's often the small things that we do every day that have the most impact in our lives. And the really great and magnificent things that we do are rare because it takes many small steps and hours of daily preparation to reach the heights. We simply aren't made to do great things every day, but we are equipped to do what it takes on a daily basis to produce the end result.

Any sports team that wins a championship will say that it took hours of seemingly mundane practice of the same play over and over to achieve the greatness that was exhibited in the championship game. So it is with us.

You must practice the small things to reach the top.

᪥

October 14
Trust in Self

"Trust in yourself. Your perceptions are often far more accurate than you are willing to believe."
—Claudia Black

Most of us could not count on our fingers the number of times our instincts told us that something was one way, yet we tried to believe and twist it otherwise. We knew that a particular person was not right for us in friendship or romance. We perceived that our next action in some life changing event was wrong, but we did it anyway. We quit something before we were finished. Basically we knew something but doubted our self.

It's important to find that place within us that we can trust. When we really know something and we try to shift reality it will not work. It's important to stay positive in life, but to claim that we can do something impossible does not make it so. To pretend that someone who has always been unloving to us and others is suddenly going to change is not reality.

We know ourselves better than anyone else can know us, but so often we look outside of us to find our answers and make decisions. We can trust our gut instincts; that's our wisdom. It may have failed us in the past, but we have grown to a new level and we can trust our perceptions to be just and true.

Once we determine to trust our instincts we begin to see that we really can believe in our own knowledge and wisdom. Our lives are made easier when we don't try to force something to work which is not meant to work.

Your instincts are there for a reason.

᪥

October 15
Behavior

"True remorse is never just a regret over consequence; it is a regret over motive." —Mignon McLaughlin

There are those who participate in life with behavior that models a bull in a china cabinet. They mow over anyone who gets in their way with poor behavior, both in words and deeds. And often these same people will offer up an apology that is so superficial it leaves those in their wake shaking their heads in disgust.

The ninth step of the Twelve Steps of recovery instructs: "Made direct amends to such people wherever possible, except when to do so would injure them or others." Those who work the steps don't always find forgiveness for the actions they are making amends over. But the amends are made anyway. Twelve Step programs teach us to change our behavior as we learn and grow, so hopefully motives are changed in the future.

It's important to understand that behaviors have consequences and that often a simple, "I'm sorry," does not fix everything so it is important to learn from our mistakes and try to change our behavior in the future so that we don't repeat that which is not kind.

Living our lives as if a simple apology will fix any wrongful act is not the solution. Our desire should be behavior that is kind and loving, and if we do something that needs an apology we offer it.

Apologies should be used when needed, not as a way of life.

October 16
Love Returns

"The more you love, the more love you are given to love with."
—Lucien Price

Just like the lyrics of the song, "looking for love in all the wrong places," oftentimes we do the same. We seek love and we don't find it, because we are not only looking in the wrong places, we also aren't giving love out.

Sometimes we can need to be loved so much that we turn others away. We become needy and emotional and our behavior reeks of that which does not attract, but rather repels. Most people are not attracted to needy people.

When we discover a healthy way of giving love we will find ourselves almost overwhelmed by what we receive in return. We may not immediately find the romantic love we seek, but we also discover that we just don't need it as much as we thought because we are loved, and we have learned self-love as well.

Not only do we feel loved we are able to love others in unselfish ways, in actions that are giving and not self-seeking. And the Universe gives us back the love we gave in larger doses than we meted out.

We each have a need to feel plugged into something. Some of us have lost our parents and may not have any living family. Some may have family that is unable to show love and we need to feel loved. It's important to our well-being to find a place to share our love with others. There are always options. Volunteering, joining a church or recovery group, or any number of places where there are others who need love just as we do.

Once we are able to give love and find its return life becomes more full and joyous and it alters our behavior to stop seeking because we have found.

Love returns to you in greater amounts than you give, but you must give first.

∽

October 17
Recognizing Gifts
"With everything that has happened to you, you can either feel
sorry for yourself or treat what has happened as a gift. Everything is
either an opportunity to grow or an obstacle to keep you from growing.
You get to choose." —Wayne Dyer

We learn from mistakes, pain, and heartache, at least we should learn from these things. In the book, "Quiet Strength," by Tony Dungy, he writes about a son he and his wife, Lauren, adopted who cannot feel physical pain. Someone with this affliction never learns to not eat something right out of the oven, or even not to touch the hot oven again, but for most of us, we learn this lesson early on.

There are those who have suffered severe injuries which cause physical disabilities, yet those people rather than feeling sorry for themselves go on to achieve great things. A person with a missing leg uses a prosthetic leg and runs marathons, or plays wheelchair basketball. Someone born without vision becomes a great musician. The list could go on and on.

And so it is with life issues including those that begin with our family of origin. For positive people who insist on growth rather than blame, the bad things that happened to us as children are just incentive to be better people. It is a gift if we choose for it to be. And if we choose to live in blame we will continue to live under the oppression that was placed up on us in our younger days.

We ought to each take what we are given and use it for good and not lament that which we do not have or which was taken from us too soon. Each day of life is a gift and ought to be treated as such. It is our choice and making the right decision on which side to look at will make or break our lives.

Choosing to learn rather than wallow in pain is always the best option.

∽

October 18
Gratitude

"Develop an attitude of gratitude, and give thanks for everything that happens to you, knowing that every step forward is a step toward achieving something bigger and better than your current situation."
—Brian Tracy

When events in our lives don't go the way we want, an attitude of gratitude will help us to see and accept that things happen for a certain reason. Often we don't know the reason we can't have something that we desire, but we can offer our gratitude for that which we do have.

Sometimes we need to reframe our thinking about situations. Perhaps we really despise our routine day-to-day chores like cleaning house, mowing the yard, going into work, and so forth. But if we stop to think about it, we can find gratitude that we have a job, and a home, and a yard that needs to be tended to.

It's not easy to be grateful when we are having a rough time. It's difficult to have an attitude of gratitude when the one we love walks away to be with another. And if we are in a job we hate, saying thanks every day for that job is probably not the first thing we think of to do. But each of these things is an opportunity for growth and has some reason for happening.

We will find love again. Not being happy at our job is incentive to find a better one. When we are grieving over these types of situations we can be grateful for what we do have. Even a job we hate is offering income to pay the bills until we can find one that suits us better. And if someone walked away from us in love, then it wasn't meant to be and there's not a whole lot that can be done about that.

When we give thanks for what we have we open the door for not only happiness within, but also to be offered something else in the future. It's how the universe works ... maybe because when we offer gratitude it affects our actions, and maybe because He who gives honors us for being thankful.

Giving thanks in trying times offers more hope for the future than wallowing in misery.

❧

October 19
Resolving Misunderstandings
"To effectively communicate, we must realize that we are all different in the way we perceive the world and use this understanding as a guide to our communication with others."
—Anthony Robbins

We have all had the displeasure of having communicated in a way that we found to be quite appropriate, only to have others misinterpret what we said. This is most often either caused by a lack of actually listening, or it's a perception issue because others don't always communicate in the same way we do.

Once there has been miscommunication it takes willingness by all involved to attempt reconciliation or the issue may never be resolved. One cannot simply take all the blame and expect to move on as if it never occurred if feelings were hurt or damage was done.

Miscommunication must be resolved with further communication between two level headed individuals who have stepped away long enough to talk without arguing. And this means talking about the situation completely by repeating what was said and explaining what that meant coming from the one who said it. The person on the other end must be free to communicate how they heard it and what it meant to them. After both sides have established what the conflict is, hopefully it may be resolved by both parties explaining how they feel.

The worst thing we can do is have a misunderstanding and simply walk away from a relationship leaving one or both parties with hurt feelings. Communication is not that difficult if two people are willing to attempt resolution. And it's usually best resolved among only those involved without bringing others into the situation. This causes further conflict and misunderstanding.

The best resolution to misunderstanding is open and honest communication.

❧

October 20
Holding Our Own
"We must not allow other people's limited perceptions to define us." —Virginia Satir

Our self-esteem can be a fragile thing, especially if we are new to recovery, to working on growing and being all that we were made to be. And because of its fragility, it does not take much at times to feel as if all we have worked for is lost and our self-image is suddenly shattered.

But we must always do our best to not let another's issues damage our growth and how we view our self. Their prejudices, emotions, lack of self-worth, and other issues may cause them to put us down in their own sick way of trying to make themselves feel better or look better in the eyes of others. Another person may even be jealous of who we are and feel less-than so that they resort to gossip and put-downs in order to try to damage us in some way.

Usually when a person has a low self-image they are not comfortable around someone who has a high self-image. When we find ourselves thrown off course by the irrational reaction of another, we know that it's time to stop and do a bit of introspection to reassure ourselves that what another thinks is not necessarily what or who we are. Our opinion of our self, in other words, should not be rocked by the reaction someone else has to us if it appears that it's irrational.

We can't change what someone says about us behind our backs, or what opinion they may hold about us, we are only responsible for our self. No amount of arguing and trying to convince another that we're okay will change their mind, we just have to believe it about our self.

Knowing that another's reaction is biased by their issues is of great value to our self-image.

∽

October 21
Persistence
"In the confrontation between the stream and the rock, the stream always wins — not through strength, but through persistence."
—Buddha

Most of us only get what we get because we keep trying. Sure, on occasion something drops in our laps like a dream job or relationship that we desire, but this is more uncommon than not. Usually we try and fail with things over and over until we get it right.

And upon getting frustrated we will sometimes say we are finished, we give up, we will not try again, but we usually don't follow through with that, rather we do once again put ourselves out there and try. Otherwise we fail to fully live.

Persistence gets us somewhere. It gives us a chance to succeed by attempting and by not giving up when we don't find immediate success. Persistence increases our odds by giving us one more shot at something.

It's very unlikely that a cure for a particular illness was found in the first attempt, it took altering the formula until it worked. When the Wright brothers tried to build and fly the first plane it took many failed attempts before they got it right, but they kept persevering until they did.

Sometimes it takes years to find success at a given task, but we are certain to never achieve if we do not keep attempting. Giving up, quitting, will get us nowhere in life. Persistence will bring us what we want eventually.

If you want something be persistent and see if you don't get results.

∽

October 22
Words Can Hurt

"Gossip needn't be false to be evil — there's a lot of truth that
shouldn't be passed around." —Frank A. Clark

Talking about our friends and enemies is a pretty common thing to do. We don't always mean to be evil and hurtful when we pass things around amongst our acquaintances, but we still do it.

Most of us feel a tinge of guilt when we find ourselves in the middle of a situation with friends where things have been passed around amongst those involved and those who have no part in the incident. We hear something, we repeat it, and then it gets passed around. By the time it gets back to the person who is being talked about it is a hurtful thing.

It's like the secret game we used to do in elementary school where someone would whisper something into the ear of another and then go around the whole classroom repeating it to the next person in the row. Once it got to the last person and they repeated it out loud it never came out the way it started.

So it is with gossip. And even if gossip were repeated exactly as the incidents happened, it still becomes hurtful to those involved.

Even the truth does not need to be passed around by us if it's not our issue to talk about.

It is a difficult thing to keep secrets or not to repeat things that we know about another. However each time we do it we hurt ourselves and the person we talk about. It's just hurtful, negative energy that we don't really need to be putting out there.

Spend more time showing kindness than you do gossiping.

∽

October 23
Giving Life a Chance

"Life is like a trumpet — if you don't put anything into it, you don't get anything out of it." —William Christopher Handy

I often hear people comment that they don't have this or that in life. Sometimes someone will say I wish I had time to work out. Or I wish I could play the piano, or I wish I had money for a trip.

All of these things are possible. We get out of life what we put in. If something is important to us we make time for it. If we don't have money for a trip, we could always get a second job and earn some extra cash for a trip later. If we want to play piano, we take lessons and practice, not many people just sit down at a piano and play perfectly without years of practice and training.

And what about folks who claim they don't have friends and don't have anything to do. For those people it's a matter of getting involved in something. Plug into a church or some other organization where people frequently meet. Don't just show up at church or a meeting, become involved. Give a bit of yourself and it will return many times over to you.

Sitting back in life and waiting for something to happen is not likely going to be successful. What will work is putting something into life and giving to others of our time, a listening ear, a hug, or whatever the need is that is a healthy thing for us to do.

You get much more than you give, but you get nothing if you don't give something.

∽

October 24
Slowing Down

"Slow down and enjoy life. It's not only the scenery you miss by going too fast — you also miss the sense of where you are going and why." —Eddie Cantor

Most of us are so busy moving from one task to the next that we might as well be sleepwalking because that would match our awareness of our surroundings. We finish one thing so we can do the next, but we don't much think about what we are doing.

When we rush through things we probably don't perform tasks as well as we would if we put our full concentration and attention on the task at hand. Rushing makes us more apt to make mistakes, too.

And if that's not enough the pace with which we operate is stress producing and bad for our health. Most likely when we are rushing around from task to task we don't eat right. We may eat the wrong foods and eat on the run; and we may either skip meals or overeat. It's unlikely that when we are so busy we take time to not only prepare healthy meals, but to actually sit down and eat them at a healthy pace.

The old saying that life is a journey not a destination fits here. The journey is what's important. All of the relationships along the way; the opportunities to learn and grow; the chance to dance in the rain or soak up the sun; the smell of fresh cut grass; giggling with a friend; and many more things cannot be experienced fully in a rush.

Life is short; moving at a slower pace enables you to live it more fully.

᪣

October 25
Cynicism
"Better to be occasionally cheated than perpetually suspicious."
—B.C. Forbes

Many of us have become jaded over time by the treatment we have received from other people. Lies, manipulation, cheating, unfairness, and other things can cause us to become cynical about relationships.

We continue to punish ourselves if we let the past dictate today and tomorrow. It hurts when people treat us wrong, but we don't have to let that hurt continue. We can move on from the person who we have lost faith in.

When we continue to carry these issues as a chip on our shoulder, we miss out on lots of opportunities to meet and love other people. We will get hurt again because people are human, just as we've been hurt, we have hurt others. From time to time we'll put ourselves out there and find ourselves getting kicked in the face. But hopefully we will also find love and friendship in other relationships.

We must choose to frame things in a positive way. We aren't going to get very far if we constantly lament about how bad someone treated us. By being suspicious we close ourselves off. Instead we can say, "I was hurt by that person, but that does not mean that everyone is out to get me."

The truth of the matter is that most people are not intentionally trying to cheat us, or hurt us, or cause us any kind of pain or harm. Maybe we just need to toughen up and realize if someone is an unkind person we really don't want them in our lives anyway.

Living a suspicious life only keeps you from finding good.

∽

October 26
Hope Rather Than Doom

"No matter how dark things seem to be or actually are, raise your sights and see the possibilities — always see them, for they're always there." —Norman Vincent Peale

Without hope we die. It may be a slow drawn out death, but to not have hope is moving more toward dying than living.

There's always at least a small amount of hope available in every situation if we only believe. If we have a life threatening disease and we give up hope we are bound to die more quickly than if we believe we can be healed and fight for life. The same holds true in other things less tragic in life.

What we believe will happen often does. We may say over and over that we cannot do something and that will come true for us. Living in the shadows of gloom and doom do nothing but bring us down. Sometimes even in the midst of pain and grief when we don't have the energy to get out of bed we have to pull ourselves up. Go for a walk, go to the gym. Moving our bodies will brighten our outlook on life and bring us more opportunities to find hope.

We never know when that thing that we have wanted to happen that never has is going to come to us. Usually when we throw up our hands and give up, turning it over to God, we soon find what we have been trying to get falls into our lap.

Sickness and death happen, but until we actually take our last breath there is some hope. And on a much simpler level when what we want seems always out of reach if we keep the hope we will someday find ourselves getting that which we wanted.

Possibilities exist if you believe they do.

∽

October 27
Changing Feelings

"We have the power to direct our minds to replace the feelings of being upset, depressed, and fearful with the feeling of inner peace."
—Gerald G. Jampolsky

It may be more difficult at some times than others to find inner peace, but it is available to us. Some of us find it watching a sunset, others taking a long walk, reading a book, meditating, playing, or praying. There are many ways to find inner peace.

We don't find inner peace by feeling sorry for ourselves. We won't get it by blaming others for our pain. And we won't feel peace if we don't try to move forward.

We can face fear with courage and love. When we are upset or depressed we can reach out to others for a listening ear or support. Whatever works for us and is a healthy thing is what we need to try.

To have peace in the midst of a storm is difficult, but possible. God can help us with that. Our past experiences where we got through tough times prove that we are resilient and able to weather what comes our way. And to find peace in the middle of the storm is an even bigger gift, one that is available to us all.

We have to direct our minds to peace and away from misery. We don't run from our feelings, it's good to feel them, but we also move forward. And we are able to move forward by feeling the feelings as they come; we just don't get stuck there.

When we feel down or in fear, we must find the power within to find peace however it comes to us. We can change our thinking to be more positive, less blameful, and thus more powerful.

You have more power in your life than you know.

∽

October 28
Finding Our Strength

"Seeking strength from others prevents us from finding our own strength." —Georgette Vickstrom

Our growth, maturity, strength, and accomplishments are things that happen to us when we do for ourselves. We may learn from others' mistakes, but to truly learn and grow it's our own attempts, struggles, setbacks, mistakes, and successes that teach us.

And just as we learn and grow because of these things, we also become stronger when we have experienced something than when we have heard about it or read about it. We don't know how a broken heart feels until we have one. We won't understand grieving the loss of someone we love until we experience it for our self. We won't know the joy of an accomplishment until we have put the many hours of labor and struggle into it and come out victorious.

To seek to live our lives through others is to limit ourselves immensely. We can always learn from friends and family, and we can lean on each other for support, but real strength and growth comes from experience. Trying to seek these things from others would be like an athlete sitting in the stands watching track practice week after week and then expecting to step in and win the 100 meter dash with no training.

We can gain some wisdom and knowledge if we pay attention to life around us, but the real meat of learning comes with the sweat and struggles, disappointments and joys, setbacks and steps forward, until one day we "get it."

You have to wear out your running shoes if you want to be the champ.

∾

October 29
Patience
"Patience is the ability to idle your motor when you feel like
stripping your gears."
—Barbara Johnson

There are times when patience is an easy thing. And at other times it is one of the most difficult situations to be in, waiting for an answer or a particular thing, or for a situation to change.

When we pray to God for something we can trust that it will happen, but it is always first and foremost in God's time, not ours. We may want it now, but all of the things necessary for that to happen may not be lined out yet.

What if we prayed for our dream job and it was going to be ours, but at the time we prayed for it the job wasn't in existence yet, or was filled by someone who needed it more than we did. But what if we knew that in a month, or five years that job was going to be ours and in perfect timing? It would be easier to wait. The waiting is hard for us because we don't know how long it will take. And sometimes the answer is no, so we wait in vain.

There's a verse in the Bible about having faith the size of a mustard seed. And that particular seed is tiny, yet it yields a massive plant. Our patience takes that kind of faith. It takes knowing that we are where we are supposed to be in the moment and that we won't miss out on that which is to be ours if we remain alert and ready when the time comes.

We really don't have much choice in matters. We do what we need on our end to be available for what we have prayed for. If it's a job, for instance, we have our resume updated and send it to every position that we think sounds like a good one for us. We don't just sit and pray and do nothing, we take action. And after we take that action, then we wait. Waiting is the action of patience.

You will get what you need when the time is right.

୶

October 30
Self-Control

"No one can drive us crazy unless we give them the keys."
—Doug Horton

How many times a day do we blame another person for something that caused us to get agitated? Probably a lot. People say and do things that we find irritating. They may try to control our lives, or maybe they just ignore us.

But it is up to us not to give other people our power. We don't let another decide our mood for the day, or let them drive us crazy. We can avoid such people for the most part, but of course, there are times when those who are irritating to us are in our lives in such a way as to all but be stuck there, such as a boss or family member.

We then have to find and practice whatever way works to deal with that person. Blame and bad mouthing won't make the situation go away. It's unfortunately our job to handle this kind of situation, as with most things in our lives.

When we allow others to control our day we give them way too much power over us. When we set a boundary in our lives and someone else does not honor that boundary we need to tell them. If they cross it and continue to do so, it is still our responsibility to deal with it. If someone is bothering us and we continue to allow that to happen then we are getting something out of the interaction. We may need to do some introspection to find out why we continue to allow abuse and see what we gain from it.

Learning to set limits with others is often difficult, especially those who have stalker type personalities where no does not mean no to them.

Owning your power puts you in the driver's seat where you get to decide your mood.

୶

October 31
Let Go of Rejection

"I really wish I was less of a thinking man and more of a fool not afraid of rejection."
—Billy Joel

If we stopped trying when we were rejected we would all have finished living a long time ago. Rejection begins early in life, earlier for some than others, but it happens.

We may not remember the first big rejection but it could have happened on a playground when we didn't get picked until last. Or we liked a particular boy or girl and they would have nothing to do with us, but instead chose another. None of this kind of rejection ends as we get older; it just happens on a more adult level.

We choose how to deal with it. We can reject the rejection and move on and try again, or we can let it get to us, take it personally, not learn from it, and get depressed. It's always our choice. And sometimes it may seem as if there is consistent rejection in our lives. We may never know why. And if we do, if it's because of a particular behavior, we have the power to fix that and try over.

Searching for a job, finding romantic love, making new friends, all these things offer us numerous chances for rejection as well as for success. It may seem that the other guy always has all the luck, gets all the girls, has the best job, etc., but sometimes we just have to wait longer to get what we want. We eventually do get what we seek or discover that's not what we really needed anyway, so that's probably why we didn't get it.

Rejection isn't always about us. And sometimes when it is about us it's not necessarily negative. We may just not be what someone else is looking for in a partner, friend, or employee. That in itself doesn't make us bad or wrong, it just is what it is.

Let rejection roll off your back and move on, you'll find what you are looking for somewhere else.

∽

November 1
Judging Success
"Success is not in what you have, but who you are."
—Bo Bennett

At times in our lives we've all probably questioned whether or not we are a success. We often judge this on our education level and job; our status in the community; if we have children and if so how they are doing in the world; if we have a great home and vehicle; and other things that the world values as success.

Some of us struggle to get most all of those things that if we had them others would deem us a success. But rather than look at our lives in this way, we ought to rather look at who we are. The most brilliant surgeon from the best school in the world who has top notch skills and saves lots of lives would be called a success. But does this same surgeon have a good home life. Is there a marriage or no time for that? If there are children do they know they are loved and cared for, or do they just know there's plenty of money?

The most successful person is the well-rounded one. Someone who may or may not have the best education, but does the best with what they do have. And they give to others in the community of their time and energy. They also provide not only financially for their family they also provide love and compassion, and most of all attention.

We can't all be in the top one percent of the wealthiest people, but we can all be good to those we care about. We can be kind to ourselves by not judging success or failure on dollar amounts or recognition. Sometimes those who are the greatest givers to society go unnoticed.

Be the best you and you'll find all the success in the world.

ལྕ

November 2
Waiting it Out

"Patience and delay achieve more than force and rage."
—La Fontaine

Pushing and forcing an outcome is usually a bad idea. When we force our will upon a situation before the time is right for it to work out, we do little but cause more delay and we may even close the door on that thing we are trying to get.

Sometimes waiting is the answer. We do our part, but we don't push, and we wait. We may have to sit on our hands at times to stop ourselves from sending an e-mail, or dialing the phone, but in the long run we will find patience and waiting are often the best actions.

Forcing a situation would mirror trying to rake the leaves on a gusty day or trying to put an elephant in a paper cup, it's just going to bust and fail. We cannot force a thing before its time and the harder we push the farther away it will get. This is not an excuse to sit back and never do anything, it's a solution for some instances, those that need time and space to move forward.

Sometimes we need to step back and get a bit of clarity about an issue before proceeding. Delay does not always mean we will be denied something. But pushing and forcing something will usually cause it to go away or end. And if not that, it may cause even more friction and possible delay.

Patience is difficult, but its rewards great.

ལྕ

November 3
Withholding Judgment
"Judge not, lest you be judged."
—The Bible

We have many opportunities every day to judge other people. We judge looks, behaviors, wealth, poverty, single, married, gay or straight, but in so doing we only waste time and energy.

When we judge others we are often acting out of a place of fear rather than love. If we find fault with the behavior of another person, we can avoid contact with them, but it is not our place to judge if they are "good" or "bad."

Each of us is a unique creature with years of experiences that are ours and ours alone. To judge the actions of another based upon the little bit of knowledge that we have about them and what they have lived through is not fair. Like the saying goes, "never criticize a man until you walk a mile in his shoes," you just never know where someone else has been and what experiences caused their actions so to stand in judgment is worthless.

Usually when we judge another we are either trying to make ourselves feel better or putting ourselves down. We feel better than or less than when we look at another and decide that they are or are not doing what we think they need to do.

Anytime we are judging another person we don't have time to love them. Judging others brings about negative thoughts and keeps us apart. It interferes with close relationships and causes disharmony.

We ought to let a person be who they are without our judgment. We are not superior or inferior to others. Our judgment does not correct another person's poor behavior, rather when we feel judgmental we would better serve them by saying a prayer for them.

When confronted with a situation where we feel we are standing in judgment it helps to stop and repeat the phrase to ourselves, "judge not lest you be judged." That will usually stop our negative thoughts about another.

It's easier to judge than to love sometimes, but love has greater rewards.

෴

November 4
Feel Your Joy
"Remember, happiness doesn't depend upon who you are or what you have; it depends solely upon what you think."
—Dale Carnegie

Feeling joy is a good thing and one that we should allow ourselves to experience at every opportunity.

There are those who try to steal our joy. They are the negative people of the world, those who see the glass as half empty and are unhappy in their own skin so they prefer us to be that way in ours.

We don't have to allow the negativity from others to infuse our lives. There is more than enough pain to go around, but joy stolen does not have to happen. If we are excited about an accomplishment, if we feel joyful about a situation, or if we just feel the joy of being alive, it's ours to experience.

Feeling joyful because we are blessed in some way is our way of thanking God and the universe for our blessing. To find negativity in every situation is reserved for those who want to be unhappy.

Feel what you feel, good or bad, and your life will be fuller.

November 5
Abandonment

"I have a great fear of abandonment. That somebody or people that I really care for will leave, so I've always sort of held people at a really good arms length. You embrace them, but only to a certain degree."
—Sandra Bullock

The fear of losing love can keep us from finding it since we may put up walls and hold others at arms length. We may attempt over and over again to find that special love relationship and find that it never works. Perhaps we set failure in motion because we fear love's loss and find fault with another whether there is reason to or not.

When we fear abandonment it makes it difficult, if not impossible to truly become close to another. We find intimacy difficult because we just assume that the other person is going to walk away so we only show them part of who we are while keeping the rest hidden.

The truth of the matter is, often those we love do leave. We grow apart, one person may be untrustworthy, and people die. This is part of living life. And I mean living. Otherwise, to never open up to another, to never risk love and loss is simply existing in this world. Existing and living fully are totally opposite ways of experiencing life on earth.

We can face these fears, slowly if we need to. We don't have to throw ourselves out there totally for every person who comes along, but we can try to trust one person at a time or more if we feel safe. It's scary, but if we always expect the worst we will get it.

Being abandoned is never a good feeling, but it is no cause to stop living life. We will find people who love us for who we are, who are trustworthy, and who won't leave us until it is their time to go for whatever reason that is. We cannot hold onto anyone anyway. We only have the moment.

Trust a little more with each relationship and find that there are some worth the risk.

∽

November 6
Taking Action

"If you don't go after what you want, you'll never have it. If you don't ask, the answer is always no. If you don't step forward, you're always in the same place."
—Nora Roberts

It all sounds so simple when we think about it, but we tend to make life more difficult by over thinking and worrying about what could be.

We never get anywhere if we are always stuck at a crossroads unable to move left or right or forward. We must make choices and take risks at least daily, but usually many times each day. Every situation offers us the opportunity to sit silently in fear or to move forward. We may face real risks or imaginary ones, but we only fail when we don't act.

We can choose our battles wisely. We don't have to go skydiving or take a dangerous whitewater rafting expedition to say we've faced fear. Some of us fear a job change, ending or beginning a relationship, or some other simpler decision.

Indecision can become a block in our lives. We may need to ask questions, research our next move, but stating that we don't have knowledge of what to do is not an excuse that will get us far in life.

Most of what we fear is the unknown. Sometimes this unknown can be scarier than being stuck in a bad situation, but we must face it if we wish to move forward in our lives. In order to get where we want to be we will likely face many challenges and must make a lot of decisions. Occasionally we'll make the wrong one, but that's not reason enough to give up.

Taking action is what gets you to the next place.

∽

November 7
Opportunity

"You've got a lot of choices. If getting out of bed in the morning is a chore and you're not smiling on a regular basis, try another choice."
—Steven D. Woodhull

Life is full of choices. If we are unhappy in any situation we have opportunities to get out of it. Sometimes that takes more work than at other times. And we may have to face many fears to make things different, but life is too short to stay miserable in a situation.

If we are in a job that we dread going to every day, we owe it to ourselves to find a new job. It's very unlikely that we have no other options. It may seem that we don't have a way out at times, but usually if we look closely there are other opportunities for us.

When we make a decision that turns out to not be a good thing for us, it's never too late to turn it around. Maybe we made a bad choice in a relationship; this does not mean we have to stay in it. Hopefully we learned something from it and we will decide to move on. At other times we may have chosen not to act when given an opportunity, and while that situation may never come around again, we will be more open the next time.

Regardless of where we find ourselves in life it's never a good idea to stay in a miserable situation. Life is short and the world is large. Living life in a place that keeps us unhappy is not living at all.

"You've made your bed, now lie in it," is not a real option for those who know they have choices. But if we choose to stay in that bed we can; that's an option too.

There are vast opportunities so staying in a bad situation is one you should avoid.

᪥

November 8
Jealousy
"The jealous are troublesome to others, but a torment to
themselves." —William Penn

When the green-eyed monster of jealousy rears its ugly head it's never a good thing for anyone involved, but usually the one who suffers from it is worse off in the end.

Jealousy has its source in low self-esteem because when we are sure of ourselves we don't have fears of inadequacy and abandonment, so therefore we have more trust. When we are confident in ourselves we are not consumed by jealousy which can tear any relationship apart.

Often when a person feels jealous it's because they fear loss and abandonment and think that their life can't go on without a particular person. Becoming dependant on another is not in our best interest anyway, and fearing that we cannot survive without someone is a sure setup for jealousy even when there is nothing to warrant it.

Sometimes people will do things that give us reason not to trust. These things should not be ignored or shrugged off as our jealousy issues, but rather something we need to face and deal with. In extreme cases people have issues of jealousy so severe that they don't even want happiness for those whom they claim to love. They see it as some kind of threat when a friend or family member spends time with someone else. Again, this is an issue of low self-esteem that can only be dealt with by the person who is jealous.

Awareness is the first step to rid ourselves of the ugly jealousy traits, but it takes more than that. We must look deep inside and work hard to overcome our issues so that we don't push everyone away who crosses our path.

When you feel jealous stop before reacting to see how it's going to affect others.

∾

November 9
Lying Hurts
"A liar will not be believed, even when he speaks the truth."
—Aesop

Lying has its consequences in the fact that eventually nobody believes one who lies. We may believe that little white lies are not a big deal, but when someone tells us lies it eats into our trust for them.

If we've had someone in our life who lied to us continually such as a parent or a partner, this will effect future relationships and cause us to have trust issues. We will have problems believing people who may have never told us a lie, but we have been damaged by another because of their dishonesty.

This will hurt us in the long run if we do not deal with it and stop assuming that all people lie like those who may have hurt us in the past with their mistruths. Usually the pathological liar types will show themselves early on in relationships with us. Others may be a bit more sly and not let others see who they are right away.

Lies perpetrate more lies so it's easy for someone to spin themselves into the web of deceit quickly. We can trust others until we are given real reasons not to trust, rather than live under the false assumption that they are just like the last one who lied to us.

Learn to trust each person as an individual, not based upon what others did to you.

∾

November 10
Self-Improvement Opportunities
"There is only one corner of the universe you can be certain of improving and that's your own self."
—Aldous Huxley

Many times in our lives we are either the object of scorn, or the one who stands in judgment of another. We find fault with another or find ourselves in the line of fire from someone who wishes to put us down.

The reality of life is that other than caring for our children, we only have ourselves to work on. We are responsible for our own side of the street and how we live our lives. We can improve upon where we are no matter how good of a person we are. But one thing is for certain, we cannot do this for another, and they cannot do this for us.

We have many opportunities for growth and change in our lives. Every day presents us with those opportunities, sometimes in big ways and at other times with simple, less conspicuous ways.

When we focus on another person's issues we only cheat ourselves and most likely damage our relationship with them. We can set boundaries if another is bothering us in some way, but to try to change that person is not our job. Our responsibility lies within.

We have plenty of work to do when we set out to improve our lives. Often others will try to do our work for us, usually in a way that is not welcome and not likely to help. They choose to tell us how we ought to do something. The only thing this does to our benefit is show us how not to treat those we care about.

Taking every opportunity for growth within is a challenge that we can accept when we are on a recovery and growth path. Staying out of another's growth opportunity gives them the chance to do their own growing as well.

Stay on your side of the street, there's plenty of work there.

November 11
Doing Things Differently
"To reach a goal you have never before attained, you must do things you have never before done." —Richard G. Scott

There are times in our lives when the desire to grow and move forward is a powerful force that cannot be snuffed out without doing it. We may not see that in order to reach a new goal or destination that we may have to look outside the box and do things in a way that we have never before done them.

If insanity is doing the same thing over and over and expecting different results, then we certainly know that we don't want to follow that route so we must try things a different way. Most likely we will need to seek help in some way to do this. We may seek information from books, the Internet, or people, but if we don't know how to proceed out of our routine it's a good idea to seek such help.

Sometimes we get stuck in the rut that says "my way is the best way and it's familiar so I will keep doing it." Getting out of that mindset and trying something new and different can be a scary area to pursue, but well worth the rewards if we do it and reach the goal we seek.

We won't get very far in life if we hide behind fear and "I can't" thinking. What we will get is a safe existence for the most part, probably full of regret and envy of others who have forged ahead and found new experiences in their lives. Many times what we do in life is a risk of sorts; changing jobs, beginning or ending a love relationship, having or adopting a child, all these things require us to think and do something different than we did yesterday.

Do something different and see where it leads.

∽

November 12
Making Amends

"Classic remorse, as all the moralists are agreed, is a most undesirable sentiment. If you have behaved badly, repent, make what amends you can and address yourself to the task of behaving better next time. On no account brood over your wrongdoing. Rolling in the muck is not the best way of getting clean."

—Aldous Huxley

Sometimes forgiving ourselves can be more difficult than doing so for another. We make amends and then we struggle with what we did to another person and we can't seem to let go of it.

When we do wrong we must make amends. Doing so is apologizing and then not continuing the behavior. If we just say "I'm sorry" and do it again the apology is worthless. But to continue to beat ourselves up over what we did won't get us anywhere either. We can transfer our brooding energy into learning new ways to behave so that we won't need to make amends again for the same thing.

Most of us never intend to hurt another person, but sometimes we do. It's okay to be less than perfect since nobody is and we all will make mistakes from time to time where we need to make amends and forgive ourselves. It's a process just like everything else in life. We may even make mistakes in performing the amends, and that's just okay too.

We don't have to beat ourselves up all the time. We are good enough and right where we are supposed to be. The lesson is there to be learned in the moment so we need to get it.

Forgive yourself as fast as you wish to be forgiven.

November 13
Thoughts and Actions

"We can act ourselves into right thinking easier than we can think ourselves into right acting." —Anonymous

It's very easy to get ourselves into a tizzy over things when we think rather than act. Sure it is good to think things through, but sometimes we can get stuck thinking about a problem or issue until we feel crazy and upset. We lose sight of the issue because we have spun ourselves into a worrisome mode.

We can act our way through something by taking the actions that we know are right and treading easily with those we aren't so sure of. We don't have to tackle a whole issue when it can be taken in small steps. Usually things aren't handled in one big action anyway.

Maybe we're stuck in a job we don't like. It's highly unlikely that we'll just call someone up and after talking a few minutes step into our dream job. Most likely there will be a search for the right job, then an application with resume. Next we'll set up an interview, then actually make the appointment. Following that will be more phone calls or interviews and maybe we'll get the job or perhaps we'll start the process over again with another potential employer. None of that will be done with one swift action.

We can't just sit at home and think about the job we want, we can't even simply pray about it. We have to take the action to actually find the job, apply for it, and follow through all the steps to try to get it.

Everything we do requires action. Praying is an action too it just needs to be followed by some legwork as well. Sometimes we judge where we are against others or even where we wish we were. We can't get from here to there without doing what it takes to succeed in our dreams no matter how much we think about it.

Taking action is the way to get where you want to be.

November 14
Fun is Good

"Are we having fun yet?"
—Carol Burnett

If we cannot answer yes to the question above we probably are filled with stress and tension, aren't getting good sleep, have aches and pains, and may be quite grumpy or even depressed. Life was not meant to be all work and no play. And when we neglect to have fun we pay for it in the end.

We are busy and stretch our time to get all we can out of life, but often we neglect to play. Children know how to enjoy life. Sure, they don't have all the responsibilities that we adults have, but they can be good examples for us.

We need to find things that we enjoy doing; things that make us laugh like children. We can do simple things like play in a water sprinkler; go to an amusement park or ride the go-carts; go to the zoo and make silly animal noises; anything that gives us a giggle and relieves some of the daily stresses of life.

If we know any children to do these things with it will help because they are usually uninhibited and know how to have fun and be silly. Somewhere in the growing up process many of us lose the ability to let go and have fun.

When we incorporate play into our stressful lives we sleep better and are more effective in the things we do when we get back to them. We may be in a line of work that doesn't allow us to laugh much so we have to make the best of the time we do have to be childlike.

Give yourself permission to act like a child sometimes and you'll find that life is more fulfilling.

∽

November 15
Playing it Safe

"If you're never scared or embarrassed or hurt, it means you never take any chances." —Julia Soul

Rarely, if ever, will we find a person who has never had any fear or hurt or found themselves in an embarrassing situation. We all have fears and anxiety about things that are not in our comfort zones. And we all make mistakes that cause us to feel embarrassed.

We can go through life always playing it safe, never taking a risk, or venturing out to do things we have never tried before. If we do this we will avoid embarrassing situations for the most part. Of course, we won't get to have as much fun and we won't grow much as people. We probably will become bored if we aren't already.

The opportunities we have in life very often contain things which we fear and we may fail when we first attempt them and feel like fools, but in living full lives we must, as Eleanor Roosevelt said, "do the thing you think you cannot do."

We don't have to start with every challenge or fear, but we need to start with something. We can do one thing that we fear. If we're afraid of water we can take swimming lessons. Maybe we're afraid of heights so we start with a height we can manage and go up a little more. If we're afraid to go to school we can start with one class and see how that goes and then take more in the future after we see that we can manage it.

It's up to us if we want to live or exist. Letting fear stop us, playing it safe is the easy way, but not the most rewarding. We can and will conquer those things that hold us back when we truly give it a shot.

Hiding behind a fear will only keep you hidden.

✦

November 16
Physical Health

"To keep the body in good health is a duty ... otherwise we shall not be able to keep our mind strong and clear." —Buddha

Taking care of our physical health is just as important as our spirituality and emotional state. Without our body we are nothing on this earth, so to ignore our physical health is to neglect ourselves completely.

When we push ourselves to keep going when we are really too tired and need to rest, we do a disservice to ourselves. To trudge on and not miss work or some other obligation while we feel the need to rest can in turn cause us to miss much more than if we'd rested when we needed to. We push to exhaustion and illness at times because we don't want to miss out or feel that things cannot go on without us.

When we are tired we need to rest. When we are sleepy we should sleep. If we need a break from a routine of work or volunteerism we should take it. Pushing through is not always a good thing. We may have been programmed to believe that we always have to do things no matter how bad we feel; that's not good advice and we can let go of that now.

When we continue to do when we are sick or in need of rest will often cause us to become physically ill. Our immune systems cannot function properly when we are not rested. So we ought to consider that when moving forward through illness we may miss out on more than if we would just stop and take care of ourselves when we need to.

Missing out on one day to rest could save you from losing days or weeks to illness.

∽

November 17
Good and Bad Judgment
"Good judgment comes from experience, and often experience comes from bad judgment."
—Rita Mae Brown

Our lives do not always follow a path that is smooth and easy. Some of us went down the road of drug abuse or alcoholism and had lots of experiences from bad judgment that taught us. If we had not made the decisions we made that caused us pain and loss we might not have learned the lessons that we did.

Our experiences can help others, and we never want to see someone else go down that same road, but because we have we cannot judge when they do and we find ourselves more able to understand why.

I often find myself beginning to judge another for some action or behavior. More often than not the situation is very similar to one I was in when I was the age of the one I am standing in judgment of. It causes me to pause and reflect upon my own life and how readily able I find myself to judge someone else.

My path took me to the depths of despair, but the lessons learned many years ago have stayed with me; they usually do when we truly find ourselves that far down.

I was reminded of this when a famous athlete from my home state, who at the time of this event was in the NFL making millions of dollars, was busted for cocaine possession. It was shocking and many people were interviewed or posted online their reaction to it. Words such as stupid, loser, thug and others were thrown around and I wondered how many of those who were casting judgment had ever done anything they regretted when they were 25 years old.

We often make mistakes in our lives and our memories are short lived about them sometimes. We can be grateful for our lessons learned and realize that when others make mistakes that it's time for them to learn something too. We can give others the same right to make a mistake as we had.

Bad judgment teaches you lessons, but you are not to judge others for theirs.

∽

November 18
Freedom

"There is only one success: to be able to spend your life in your own way." —Christopher Morley

Many of us find ourselves living a life free from those things which used to bind us once we begin down the trail of recovery. Whether it's freedom from an addiction, an abusive relationship, family of origin issues, or any other thing that binds us and keeps us from joy, we can be free of it.

When we find ourselves in that place, having broken free, it's usually where we discover just how much we have been under the control of people, places or things. Sometimes when we are in the middle of an issue we don't see it. But when we are free we can begin to live the life we want, not one controlled by anyone else or anything else.

Of course there are rules and laws in the world, but within the parameters of these we really are free, at least if we live in a country that gives us liberty. It's easy to come out of an oppressive situation and not realize the freedom so it is important to know that it's there.

We truly can spend our time the way we choose and that's a wonderful success story in and of itself. It's something that those in recovery groups can share with newcomers as part of the rewards of recovery.

Breaking free from oppression gives you the ultimate freedom.

November 19
Patience in Progress

"Patience is also a form of action." —Auguste Rodin

When we are on a journey through recovery, or simple acts of life for that matter, it is difficult to be patient with our progress. We made a decision to change a behavior, to grow in or emotional health, perhaps we are mending financial errors or a relationship, and it does not happen overnight.

One way to remember to be patient with progress is to realize that whatever we are trying to move away from, or grow through, or recover from did not get the way it is overnight. The damage we did to our lives with drug addiction, overeating, alcoholism, anger issues, and on and on, did not just suddenly happen. And so it goes with turning our lives around. It is a process and it takes time.

If we are in debt because we didn't work or spent all our money on drugs, it would take the lottery to get us caught up in one fell swoop.

It's the same when we hit bottom in addiction, it's going to take a lot of small steps to get out of that hole; baby steps or crawling, and time.

We want what we want when we want it. That's just how most of us are, but it takes patience and persistence to get where we want to be. We can take the small actions as they come to us and in the long run all of those will get us to where we are going. Most of the time we really don't know our destination, we may think we do, but during the process things change, we change and our destination may not even turn out to be as we thought it would.

As we move through our lives and recovery we can know that each and every step has value, even when it's two steps forward and one back, we are making progress. Patience with this may be hard most of the time, but it is a valuable tool.

Patience helps us deal with the time it takes to get where we need to be.

∽

November 20
Self-Care in Relationships
"Never allow someone to be your priority while allowing yourself to be their option." —Unknown

Many of us will, from time to time, find ourselves in a place where we don't do what we want or need to do because we are doing for another. We may do this out of kindness, but sometimes we do it from a needy place because we think that if we don't we won't have that person in our lives anymore.

It's certainly okay from time to time to put ourselves last instead of first, but it's not good to do it the whole time we are in a relationship, whether it's a friendship, romantic, work, volunteer, or any other kind of relationship.

People who put themselves first all the time in relationships are not that fun to be with. We've all known the type who always talks about themselves and never lets anyone else discuss anything. Or those who don't have any manners such as saying thank you when you do something for them, as if they simply expected it.

Our lives should never be put on hold for another, especially when they don't appreciate or even notice. Relationships are give and take, ideally 50-50, but sometimes that doesn't happen every moment. But we need to take care of who we are and not have ourselves used or abused by another. We ought to also be mindful of how we treat others and not do that to someone else.

If we find ourselves feeling a bit on the used and unappreciated side of the relationship, we can talk it over with the other person. If that doesn't make things any better then it is time to walk away and take care of ourselves.

Don't put them first when they put you last, you're only hurting yourself.

≪

November 21
Life Is Difficult

"Conquering any difficulty always gives one a secret joy, for it means pushing back a boundary-line and adding to one's liberty."
–Henri Frederic Amiel

We all face times in our lives that are more difficult than others. Sometimes we have to say no when we know they would rather have us say yes. But to be true to ourselves we know that we have to do the right thing.

There are times when the truth hurts another person. Perhaps we have to end a relationship because we don't have the feelings necessary for the other person to move forward. They may insist that we not end it, but we know it's what has to be done, no matter if it hurts, and know that ending a no-win situation now is better than later.

There are other times when we deal with sickness and death of friends and family. We may prefer to do anything but visit a loved one in the hospital or attend a funeral, but again, we know that it's the right thing to do so we face our difficulty and do it.

When we find ourselves in difficult situations we have options on how we can handle them. Facing our difficulties head on rather than hiding away and living in dishonesty is the best thing. It takes a lot out of us, and the situation may get worse before it gets better, but we do it anyway.

We grow from each and every difficulty we face and conquer. We find that we feel better doing the right thing, than we do when we face issues in a way that is dishonest to us and others.

Eventually if we hurt someone in the process of being honest, they will see that we did what we did because it was right for us and them in the long run. Often telling a lie may seem like a solution, and it may bring temporary relief in the situation, but in the end the truth wins out anyway, so it's better to be honest and up front in the moment.

Doing a difficult thing the right way will bring growth and peace.

≪

November 22
Be Your Best You
"Do not wish to be anything but what you are, and try to be that perfectly." —St. Francis De Sales

At times in our lives we may find that others try to shatter our self-image. It may be that we don't do things the way they think we should, or they offer criticism for other reasons, perhaps because they feel inadequate compared to us.

But we really don't need to let what others think about us have an affect on who we think we are. We cannot let others' insecurities cause us harm by making us think we are inadequate. We are good enough, what we do is sufficient.

Just because we do things in a different way from another does not mean we are not okay. We all have areas there we need to grow, but we are still okay as we are in the moment.

There are also things we all have to be proud of and we ought to remember those things. Graduating from college; buying our first home or fifth home; raising healthy and happy children; landing a good job or simply doing a good job at the one we have; being an active member of society who gives time and/or money to those in need; the list could go on and on.

Make your own list. Put on it the things you've done that you are proud of. Don't forget things that took a lot of strength, perhaps you left an abusive relationship or stood up to a bully in your life. If there's not much on the list of things you've done that you feel good about, it might help to ask those close to you what they see. Often others will see the good in us when our minds are clouded by our failures.

Whenever you feel down it's a good time to check your accomplishments list.

∽

November 23
Reining in Anger
"If you kick a stone in anger, you'll hurt your own foot."
—Korean Proverb

So many times when someone angers us, we spin ourselves into a place that may feel out of control. Some of us throw things, others kick and scream, and sometimes we are so mad we want to hurt the other person. Hopefully we don't proceed in an effort to hurt another because we've been hurt since that solves nothing.

It helps to remember that having anger does not take away what the other person did to hurt us. Nothing really makes what they did go away, although an apology from them and forgiveness by us will help a lot.

If at all possible we can ease the situation when we treat those who anger us with love, kindness, and compassion. Yes, this is a tall order and perhaps one of the most difficult things we can do, but it does diffuse the situation and can restore us to peace.

Holding onto the anger by letting it fester and by telling everyone we can how angry we are won't do much to make it go away. We probably will just get worked up over and over as we tell it to anyone who will listen.

Anger is not a bad thing. It is a signal that something is wrong and often helps us to move on from a situation that is not healthy for us. It's how we handle the anger that is good or bad.

When we find ourselves feeling crazy with anger we can count to 10; walk away from the situation and return after we've calmed down; or take a few minutes to pray even if the prayer is simply "help." Or we can kick and scream and yell and gossip. It's our choice really.

How you handle your anger says a lot about where you are in life.

∽

November 24
Understanding Our Power

"Things turn out best for the people who make the best out of the way things turn out." —Art Linkletter

Fighting what is can be a very frustrating thing to do. When we want something to be one way and it goes another way, acceptance is the best solution.

And so it goes when we have difficulty with other people. We may want a romantic relationship with someone who only wants to be our friend. Or it's possible to work with someone who we cannot seem to get along with no matter what we do. We only have the power to change ourselves, or to accept the situation. What we cannot do is make the other person change or behave in the way that would make us happy.

Prayer is power because if we have faith we believe that God can make the changes or put us in a different place. Letting go helps since we really have no other option. Insisting that things are bad and will never get better won't solve anything. It's best to think in a positive vein, to believe that we have the power to change a situation by moving forward in our lives, and not attempting to force someone else to be a certain way.

Making lemonade when life hands us lemons is how we deal with those things that are out of our power and control. Understanding what we have power over and what we don't is how we are able to make lemonade.

Do what you need to do to make your life better without expecting someone else to do it.

∾

November 25
Punishing Others

"Everyone makes a greater effort to hurt other people than to help himself." —Alexis Carrel

There are occasions in our lives where we have all either punished someone or been punished by someone. We punish one another for simply being who we are, or for being honest. We often hurt other people to punish them for hurting us, even when the infliction of pain was not intentional, more likely it was inevitable since none of us are perfect.

We punish others for being human. We see someone make a mistake, or ignore us in some way or simply not do something the way we think they should. But rather than love them in their humanness, we punish them. We talk behind their backs, we cut off communication with them hoping we'll "show them," or we in some other way chastise them either directly or indirectly.

When we are in relationships with others there will from time to time be conflict, sometimes relationships end because they just are not meant to be. But to move forward in such a way as to hurt someone because they left us does nobody any good. Talking badly about someone to "get them back" because they hurt us will not heal; it will just cause further pain and expend wasted energy.

A better way to deal with the pain is to look inside to see if we may have caused anything to go wrong with the relationship. If we find some defect of character that is causing us to have a lot of problems in relationships, then we need to work on that. If we look at ourselves honestly and don't find a problem, then we can just move on and know that if it was meant to be it would have been.

We ought to also monitor our behavior towards others to ensure that we do not seek to punish when we feel wronged. Instead of hurting someone to get back at them, we can operate out of a place of love and think of healing rather than hurt.

Punishing someone else really just hurts you in the end.

∾

November 26
Self-Discipline

"Mental toughness is many things and rather difficult to explain. Its qualities are sacrifice and self-denial. Also, most importantly, it is combined with a perfectly disciplined will that refuses to give in. It's a state of mind — you could call it character in action."

—Vince Lombardi

We often think of addiction and recovery as all or nothing situations, that is, an alcoholic no longer drinks, or a bulimic never again purges, and a drug addict stays completely clean from drugs.

And while this is true about those things, we each have things in our lives that we do that aren't healthy. We may smoke cigarettes; or eat too many sweets or chips; or maybe while we aren't really an alcoholic we have a drink every night just as a habit; or we stare at the television too much.

All of those things and others, while nothing to send us to treatment or Alcoholics Anonymous, can keep us from being as healthy as we wish. We can practice self-discipline and grow stronger in the meantime.

By going on a diet when we are only 10 pounds overweight, we can save ourselves from having to really struggle on a diet later when we get to be 40 pounds overweight. Even if we only have a few pounds to lose we can be healthier and rid ourselves of poor eating habits by changing our eating routines and getting more exercise.

There are those who smoke cigarettes who know they should quit but believe that they have given up everything else so they don't want to stop. Many recovering alcoholics and drug addicts will say this. But nicotine is a drug that is harmful to our bodies, as are other ingredients in cigarettes.

I don't like to be addicted to anything, to let anything control me. Whether it's a drug or alcohol, potato chips or chocolate, a television show or real life drama, I want freedom from addiction. And while to a heroin addict or to someone with an eating disorder these may seem like small issues, they do offer us a chance to practice self-discipline which makes us stronger in who we are. We can practice the big things in small ways and in doing so we learn about ourselves and become healthier all at the same time.

If there's anything in your life that feels like it's an unhealthy habit, determine a plan for giving it up. Pick the day to begin and set an ending goal. While you are beating your habit fill its space with healthy options. For instance, someone who needs to lose weight and does not currently exercise may discover some form or recreation that will not only help them lose weight, but may be something that they will continue after the dieting stops.

If anything controls you, you don't have control over your own life.

୶

November 27
Learning by Doing
"As one goes through life one learns that if you don't paddle your own canoe, you don't move."
—Katharine Hepburn

No matter how spoiled and coddled a person is in their childhood, or some even as adults, real life experiences both with successes and failures, are what propel us through life, growth and recovery.

We may lament every time we perform at a level less than we expect of ourselves, but for every supposed failure we learn and grow. We don't gain wisdom or strength through other people's lives and experiences. We learn and grow when we attempt and fail and even when we do something with success because we did it.

Just as an athlete cannot become a professional or set a world record simply by watching how someone else did it, neither can we live our lives and make it on our journey with only observation as a tool. We learn what we can from others, sometimes we may avoid certain failures when we see another experience them. But as a rule our growth is ours from doing rather than seeing.

We may feel as if we paddle upstream at times. And perhaps we want others to do for us, but in the long run we gain much more wisdom, strength, and growth through our own actions. Even when the going gets tough, we can rest assured that we will come out on the other side of it with the experience that taught us something.

Even when the current is rough, you must paddle if you want to get through it.

୶

November 28
Shades of Gray
"Things are not always as they seem ...." —Phaedrus

We can get ourselves into some mighty big messes when we think things are one way, but find out they aren't as we thought. Often this is because of communication errors.

We also bring into each situation our individual experiences, so how we react may not be the way someone else might react which can cause conflicts when dealing with others.

Things are not usually black or white; they contain many various degrees of gray. When someone says something, we hear what we hear whether that's how they meant it or not. We may feel lied to while the other person insists they told the truth. Usually if we can keep the lines of communication open and discuss the incident we can figure out that it was more of a misunderstanding than a lie.

Sometimes we don't understand what's happening in our lives. We may see hardship as a punishment, but that's not how life works. Yes, we suffer consequences for things we do, but God doesn't punish us. Life lessons teach us if we use them as such. Often when we are in the midst of an issue whether it's on the job, at home, in a love relationship, or any other situation, we don't see and understand things clearly. That's why people say hindsight is 20-20 because our vision becomes clear once we get past an event.

We many never make up with those we've hurt or those who have hurt us, usually because either or both involved will not take the time to fully communicate about the issues. There are two sides to every story. If we could only remember that when we find ourselves in a spot that we don't understand our lives would be much easier.

Remember that whenever conflict hits, things are not always as they seem.

෴

November 29
Living Fully
"Bloom where you're planted."
—Unknown

Getting frustrated with our present circumstances is a common occurrence for many of us. But just because we aren't exactly where we want to be we do not have to be stuck there forever.

Many will say we are right where we are supposed to be no matter what's happening. There are lessons to be learned, wisdom to gain, and faith to be built and usually we don't get those things without some displeasure and often pain.

It's easy for us to get stuck thinking that because we are not where we want to be at the moment we will never get there. That's always a possibility, especially if we live our lives believing we can't get anywhere. But it's unlikely that where we are in life today will be the same in the future. When the lesson is learned we will probably find ourselves in a new situation.

The thing we must do is continue to live our lives fully wherever we are. If we are unhappy we work on the issues that are causing us to feel that way. Perhaps we are simply bored because we've gotten stuck telling ourselves we can't do more than we are now. Our current situation is not always because of our own doing, but getting out of it, making necessary changes, is something we can do if we want to move on.

Just as a flower blossoms even if planted in an odd spot, we can live our lives fully wherever we are. To constantly bemoan our position is not how we bloom. We do it by living up to our full potential no matter where we are.

It's up to you whether you wither or bloom.

November 30
Honesty

"I hope I shall follow firmness of virtue enough to maintain that I consider the most enviable of all titles — the character of an honest man." —George Washington

Being honest is not always easy, but it is much simpler than trying to keep up with lies. When we tell the truth we don't have to remember what we said.

Once we have lied to someone we cannot expect that person to believe us in the future. Maybe we told a "little white lie," but it still puts the mistrust in between us and the person we said it to. Usually when a person has been lied to it matters not how great the lie, what matters is there is now distrust and it's nearly impossible to overcome.

One of the most difficult things to deal with is when we are lied to and the one who told the lie continually tells us they didn't lie; that we just misunderstood. This is even harder to get past when they tell us numerous lies and say they weren't dishonest. We cannot believe anything they say.

Those who have a difficult time trusting will find it next to impossible to believe someone once they've caught them in a lie. And this is a hard spot to be in for those who have trust issues because they probably think people lie even when they don't.

Sometimes it may seem easier to lie, and maybe in the moment it is, but in the long run lying is just not the answer because we tend to start believing even our own lies.

We must be honest in small ways if we hope to be honest with the really important stuff. This does not mean that we have to tell someone they do indeed look fat in a certain outfit if asked, we can instead find something complimentary to say about some other aspect of how they look. We can use some common sense about answering questions of that nature. But when it comes to lying because we find the truth uncomfortable, the truth's still going to be there, why add a lie to it and make it worse?

Telling the truth keeps you from having to add more lies to cover lies.

∽

December 1
Pleasing Others
"It's none of my business what you think of me."
—Unknown

Some of us worry about what others think and try to please them with our actions.

We can't please everybody, no matter what we do. There will always be those who think we should do things a certain way even when we have been successful in the way we did them.

A lot of us still try to please our parents. Even as adults we may still use what they think as a barometer of how we should carry on our lives. Some of us do this knowing that they are dysfunctional and probably won't ever "approve" of what we do but we try to please them anyway. It's quite futile to think we can get anywhere this way.

Often those who begin Twelve Step programs or go to treatment find family members, spouses, and others less than thrilled. This is usually attributed to fear of change. Those left behind know that life as they knew it won't be the same anymore, even though the person is going to have a better life. If we are taking care of ourselves in a healthy way, we must forge on and try not to worry about what they think.

What matters most is what we think of ourselves. Are we working on being better people? Do we try to do the right thing even when it's difficult? Are we free of addictions and other things that are not healthy for us? If we feel good about where we are today and where we may be in the future, that's a positive that we can hang our hat on. The rest, what they think, well, it's really not our business.

If you believe in yourself you're already a winner.

∽

December 2
Recharging Your Energy

"When you are in the valley, keep your goal firmly in view and you will get the renewed energy to continue the climb."
—Denis Waitley

It is important to know yourself and how you find renewed energy. Knowing where we get our energy and how to recharge ourselves can go a long way in leading a happy life.

We all have various energy sources, along with things that zap our supply. Sometimes there are people we spend time with who will pull us down. They may be into a lot of drama or they latch onto us in some way and suck the life out of us. There are those who are negative about everything and being around them pulls our energy away from us as well.

If we know people like that it's best for us to stay away from them. However, this cannot always be done if we work with or for a person like this. But we can avoid getting our energy zapped by them by being more aware of it. If we can avoid these situations we do, and when we can't we go in with knowledge of what they do which helps us to fend off their influence.

Some find renewed energy from attending meetings, others by reading meditation books or other motivational material. Some may find that taking a brisk walk or working out at the gym is rejuvenating. Taking time to be alone and to regroup our thoughts can work, as does talking things over with a friend. Sometimes we can get the energy boost we need simply by getting a good night's sleep.

Whatever we know works to recharge our batteries is where we start. If we have no idea it's time to start finding out. Turning off the things that drain us is highly important. And also keep in mind that it's easier to recharge if there's some juice left in our battery, once it's dead we have a lot farther to go to get back our power.

Find what recharges your energy supply and do it as much as you need.

❧

December 3
Live Each Moment

"To live each moment to the full, because the moment never comes again." —Shabnam Paryani

"Live each moment" was the message a friend of mine wanted passed along at his memorial service. A man with a fighting spirit, who truly did live each moment, ended a fight with cancer that lasted nine years.

Many times we live our lives waiting on a particular thing to happen so we can do something. We think once we get married we'll be happy. Or once we get to a certain pay level life will be good. Whatever our thinking, if it's not focusing on our happiness at the moment, it's probably futile.

Time flies quickly. We seem to blink and our children are grown and out of the house. When we are 20 years old we think people who are 50 are old, and then before we know it, we're 50 ourselves.

A person who has looked death in the face numerous times, such as my friend who had cancer for nine years, gets a new outlook on life. They don't worry about missing an hour of sleep to spend time with a friend or family member. They don't work non stop in order to make another buck, because they value their time more than riches.

None of us knows when our day will come to pass on from this life. Some of us will go quickly and others will spend their last days with a terminal illness. But we all have this moment. Every second we are alive is living. And we should not discount the moments of our lives just because we don't have everything we think it takes to make us happy.

Stop each day and ask yourself where you would be at that moment if you knew your life would end soon.

∽

December 4
Living an Independent Life
"I would rather sit on a pumpkin, and have it all to myself, than to be crowded on a velvet cushion."
—Henry David Thoreau

Those of us who live our lives independently are often misunderstood as being snobby or thinking that we are better than others. We do for ourselves and don't expect others to do for us.

Maybe we are independent because we didn't have someone to care for us when we needed to be nurtured, so we learned to fend for ourselves. There are those who are independent by default, because they were so dependent in the past that nobody will help them anymore and they had to learn to do for themselves.

We ought to be cautious about being too independent, to do it alone even when we need help is not a wise thing to do. Asking for help does not make us weak and dependent; it just means that we have wisdom.

Doing something that we are not equipped to do when we could have asked for help is not independence.

Those who are highly independent need to be certain to have plenty of people in their lives anyway. Just because we are independent we don't need to forgo giving and receiving love. And independence does not mean that we don't rely on God.

There's a full spectrum of needs out there. It's not healthy to be too needy, and it's unhealthy to be so independent we cut off all relationships. Balance is the answer, as it is in so many aspects of life.

Live as independently as you can and you will feel strong and vital.

∽

December 5
Burning Bridges

"We should think seriously before we slam doors, before we burn bridges, before we saw off the limb on which we find ourselves sitting." —Richard L. Evans

It's easy to find ourselves in a place where we want to burn our bridges. We get angry with someone or upset about a situation and we never want to be faced with it or that person again.

However sometimes once some time has passed on a situation and our emotions have calmed we find that it wasn't quite as bad as we thought and we regret having shut the door on it or the person.

Once the door has been slammed in an angry manner and resentments have flared on both sides, it can be close to impossible to heal the situation. So taking some time to let ourselves heal and cool may help us avoid burning bridges that keep us separate from others.

Once we've spoken something in anger, once we have slammed the door on a relationship, no matter if it's business or personal, it is unlikely to ever be healed and returned to a healthy place. It's not impossible, but it is much more difficult to resume a relationship if it's ended in such an abrupt manner.

When we are in a situation that needs healing, it is often necessary to take a break. We can take a time out and let ourselves figure out what to do in a calm way rather than in the midst of our anger. Others may not understand that we need time; that we require a break, but it is imperative that we do this if we feel we need it.

Making a decision to change any kind of relationship requires careful consideration. If we leave in haste, whether a job, marriage, friendship, or any other situation, we will more than likely burn a bridge and never be able to resolve the conflict. This finality may not be what we intend, but it may be the result.

A decision made in anger and haste will often not bring the desired result in the long run.

❧

December 6
Grieving Losses

"All I know from my own experience is that the more loss we feel the more grateful we should be for whatever it was we had to lose. It means that we had something worth grieving for. The ones I'm sorry for are the ones that go through life not knowing what grief is."
—Frank O'Connor

When we are in the midst of grief from a loss whether it's caused by death or some other separation, it is difficult to find gratitude, but we can be glad that we were blessed with the person in our life, blessed enough that we do grieve.

And the way we grieve may not be the same for each loss, and it probably differs from how someone else might grieve in the same situation. There are not set in stone ways to do it. There is no right or wrong.

Grieving may hit us with mild or severe depression. We may experience anger. We may have a lot or a little emotion surrounding it. We may even think at times that we aren't doing it right. Most likely we are feeling just what we need to feel and handling things the best we can. We certainly do not need to add more stress to the process by questioning if we are doing it right.

But what we do need to do is feel our feelings. It is normal and healthy to grieve and to deny it to surface now will only mean that it comes back later. If we are sad and need to cry, it's okay to do that. Maybe we feel a lot of anger. If that's the case then we find a healthy outlet for that, maybe a trip to the gym, or by taking it out on a punching bag, whatever works.

Living life comes with good and bad times. To love means also to lose for most of us. We lose friends, family, partners, and pets, but to deny ourselves that love is not to truly live.

Grieve in whatever way you need to; there is no rulebook.

❧

December 7
Healing with Laughter
"We don't laugh because we're happy — we're happy because we laugh." —William James

Laughter is a healing force. It's not wrong to laugh in the face of grief or tragedy. It is always helpful and healthy to find something to laugh about, even if we laugh through our tears.

If we are in a rough spot in life we can find something that makes us laugh if we look long and hard enough. Some of us might have just the thing handy. Maybe a favorite movie that we have watched over and over that brings laughter. There may be people in our lives who are good for a laugh.

Most of us know of something that brings humor in our lives. So when we feel down, or even when we are just stressed and overworked, it's time to pull out that thing that makes us laugh so hard it brings tears.

If we don't know what makes us laugh we need to find out. Sometimes laughter can come in unexpected times when we are distraught. It may seem inappropriate to laugh. We may have preconceived notions that if a particular thing happens in our life we aren't supposed to laugh about anything. This is just not true. As long as we don't laugh at someone in a hurtful way, laughter is something we need and should seek.

Once after one of my cats died I told a friend about it. He said, "I don't care, I hate cats." And he didn't until he saw how sad I was and then he offered comfort. After this same friend passed away I shared with others this exchange about the dead cat and we all got a good laugh out of it, and this was in the midst of early grieving our loss of him.

So while what he said to me was certainly not funny when he said it, in his passing it is now a source of laughter for me. We just never know where we will get it, but we need to find laughter.

To laugh is healing and necessary for happiness in a world that is often filled with pain.

❧

December 8
This Too Shall Pass
"Don't worry about a thing, 'Cause every little thing gonna be all right." —Bob Marley

There are times in our lives that it feels like when it rains it pours. We may have a succession of difficult things to deal with and as soon as one situation is resolved, or healed, another one pops up.

And while we probably don't feel like we handle it well, we probably aren't the best judge of that when we are in the midst of all of the trauma and turmoil.

One thing that helps is to let go and let God. Yes, this is so much easier said than done, but one thing that may be helpful is when we get something catchy like the song above stuck in our head. Every time we start to feel the panic of what's to come, the unknown, we can call the song to mind and it really will ease the tension.

Things do work out. Maybe they don't go the way we want, and perhaps we have to go through a lot of discomfort and loss to get through the rough patches. Life is change. Nothing stays the same, whether it is when we are feeling on top of the world, or feel like hiding under a rock. Change happens.

And because of change we can know that this too shall pass. Everything is going to be alright. Whenever we are in the middle of what seems to be never ending stress, we can rest assured that one day this will turn around.

Let go and let God. Sing a catchy song. Listen to music. Scream into a pillow. Meditate and pray. Rest. Work out. Go for a walk on a sunny day. All of these things are options to help us through the rough patches.

Never give up, even when the going gets rough, because everything will come around and it'll be alright.

∽

December 9
Keeping Our Perspective
"Most of us miss out on life's big prizes. The Pulitzer. The Nobel. Oscars. Tonys. Emmys. But we're all eligible for life's small pleasures. A pat on the back. A kiss behind the ear. A four-pound bass. A full moon. An empty parking space. A crackling fire. A great meal. A glorious sunset. Hot soup. Cold beer." —Unknown

What is important in life? This question is usually best answered after we have suffered a real loss and not when things are going great.

We can get so wrapped up in the daily activities of life that while important in the moment, are not truly the most important things in life. What matters is love of family and friends. Giving to others. Finding peace in our lives. Having long-term relationships. Nurturing those around us who need it, especially children, whether they are ours or belong to another.

What doesn't matter is getting stuck in traffic for 10 minutes. Losing a dollar in a vending machine. Having to pick up a piece of trash someone threw down. And all the other things that are nuisances to us, but just really don't matter much in the grand scheme of things.

When we do let the little things get to us in a big way, that's a signal that we are off track and need some rest and relaxation and time to regroup. We may need to sit down and make two lists. One list of what really matters and one list of the things we worry about and get upset about that really do not matter.

If we have good friends with mutual love and respect we are blessed. If the neighbor won't mow his grass is it really a big deal? What will matter five years from now is what we need to focus on. Make that list and see what unimportant things can be taken from worry.

Remember that those you love and care for are important, other stuff not so much.

❧

December 10
Time Management

"Avoiding the phrase 'I don't have time...,' will soon help you to realize that you do have the time needed for just about anything you choose to accomplish in life." —Bo Bennett

We've probably all heard and used the excuse of not having time. Maybe we think of it as valid, and perhaps it is at times, but we have the power to manage our time. We can do the things we want to do if we truly have a desire.

Sometimes we use not having time as an excuse not to move forward. We may use it as a reason to not take a risk, a step that would offer us a chance to succeed in a new way, but also one that might allow us to fail.

Every person has the same amount of hours and minutes in a day. We have to decide how to spend that time. Most of us are employed so a certain amount of hours are dictated by our job. It's what we do with our free time that makes the difference.

There are those who say they don't have time to exercise, using that as an excuse for obesity. But these same people may be found in front of a television several hours a day. They choose to spend time there rather than walking or working out at a gym.

Some of us claim we're too old to do things. We say that it's too late to further our education or to pursue the profession we truly desire. It's not too late, we're not too old, and we do have time. We decide how to spend a great portion of each day. It is true that some people have more obligations on their time with children or caring for aging parents, but we still have choices.

How we spend the time we have is up to us. We can continue to use the excuse, "I don't have time," and never do anything. Or we can learn to take some time out of each day to follow a dream.

Time is an obstacle that you can use as an excuse, but you're the one who loses out on your dream.

∽

December 11
Knowing Others
"What we see depends mainly on what we look for."
—John Lubbock

When it comes down to it, there are very few people who we really know. We may know someone for a lifetime and not know that they have something so painful held inside that they never tell it to anyone. We may judge a person for not acting the way we think they should, when the reality is, we don't even know how they should act with something that is so painful that they don't tell anyone, sometimes even a spouse or best friend.

There are those of us who are open books, who may have had bad things happen to us or maybe we've done bad things. We are able to talk about and work through the issues. Still others struggle daily with something so severe to them that they have kept it a secret and it's too painful to let it out.

When we start to judge another for their actions we can stop and remind ourselves that we do not know what is truly going on with them because we have not walked in their shoes and they may have more pain than we can imagine.

What we can do is show people love, whether they show it to us or not. We don't stand for abuse, but we also don't expect others to act the way we do. If we are aware of a change in someone and we are worried about them, we can talk it over with that person and offer our assistance to get them help.

All of us struggle. That's something that is important to remember. While some are bright and sunny to everyone they see, their pain could be worse than the grumbler who complains about everything. We can't judge a book by its cover.

Showing love and compassion for those who seem at odds with us or life may be just what they need to finally open up. We shouldn't force this on anyone, but just make ourselves available to let them know we care.

Treat the troubled with love and pray that they will get the healing and care they need.

᪥

December 12
Staying Calm

"The most important skill in staying calm is not to lose sleep over small issues. The second most important skill is to be able to view all issues as small issues."
—Paul Wilson

The stresses of life can at times seem overwhelming, yet when we get wound up and worried about what's to come or what has happened we really don't make things any better.

Peace and serenity can be ours with much practice, patience, letting go, and letting God. We do not have to sweat the small stuff. By keeping in mind that which we do have the power to change and that which we do not will help us keep things in perspective.

Frustration is an easy thing to come by, but when we learn to let go of that which really just does not matter and those things we can't do anything about anyway, we will find ourselves more in a place of peace and calm than anxious.

The ebbs and flows of life promise that whatever is going on will eventually change whether we're on the upside of things or feeling rather down. As much as we resist change it is part of life and healing too.

The people in our lives can cause frustration for us as well. We cannot and should not control others so it's best not to even mull over in our minds how they could better live their lives.

It's impossible to stay calm in the midst of attempting to control the world around us. Serenity starts from within and spreads across our lives if we can give it a chance, just as much as frustration can send us into a tailspin.

Start from within to find calm and serenity will fill your life.

᪥

December 13
Acceptance
"Acceptance of one's life has nothing to do with resignation; it does not mean running away from the struggle. On the contrary, it means accepting it as it comes, with all the handicaps of heredity, of suffering, of psychological complexes and injustices."
—Dr. Paul Tournier

Acceptance does not mean we like where we are, where we've been, or what has happened to us. It means that rather than living in denial we accept that we are in a certain place or have had certain experiences and we learn from that so that we may grow and move on.

If our finances are not where we need or want them to be, we can't fix them by sticking our head in the sand. We must accept our situation as being what it is and look for ways to correct it.

If we have an addiction, admitting it/accepting it is the first step in breaking it. When we have let ourselves go physically we must accept our present situation if we are to lose weight, get fit, eat right, or stop abusing our bodies with various addictions.

If we are experiencing a breakup or divorce when the other person is leaving us, it does no good to make excuses and pretend that they'll be back and that it's really not over. Acceptance will allow us to heal.

Denial and acceptance are opposites. One hides from a situation or problem and the other meets it head on. Having denial won't wish away our problems, situations or issues. Acceptance of what is allows us to make the changes in behavior that will lead to healing.

While denial can numb us to life's issues, it will only give us a temporary respite from our pain. Denial can represent fear while acceptance offers hope.

If we don't like our present lot in life, we must first accept that we are right where we are no matter what our situation. Then with a clear head we can begin to work at turning our lives around and getting ourselves to a place where we want to be.

Running away or hiding from our problems will never change them; acceptance is the beginning to healing.

✍

December 14
Getting Started and Finishing
"It is a matter first of beginning — and then following through."
—Richard L. Evans

For some getting started is the hardest thing. And for others the most difficult thing is the follow through; finishing what was started.

We all have our struggles. And we all have points in our journeys where we really have a hard time just doing what we set out to do, even if it's just beginning.

It's easy to find excuses to wait before we start and then we find we never get started because there's an abundance of reasons to wait.

For instance, it would be difficult to begin a diet around the holiday season starting in November with Thanksgiving and going to New Year's Day. That's understandable. However, if we began a diet in the summer, by the time we got to the holiday season our new eating habits, our new way of life would have become familiar and easy. So we can be wise about when we begin things.

Getting started for some is the hard part. There will always be reasons not to do something and if we spend our time thinking of those things and making up new ones we won't even find out if we can finish. Excuses include: fear of failure, laziness, the inability to give up something else to fit in the new thing, lack of initiative, not believing that we can do it, and maybe having others tell us we won't be able to do what we set out to do.

Our self-esteem depends upon our believing in ourselves. If we never try we never succeed. Our self-image is not dependent upon us winning a huge prize or becoming millionaires. It is based upon who we are and how we see ourselves. Our battles are often not even known or seen by anyone else. These things that we want to do, but can't seem to start or finish, they are individual to each of us, and we are the only ones who can do them.

Take that first step today by setting all the excuses aside and then see if you can finish.

∽

December 15
Multiplying Good
"What we focus on, we empower and enlarge. Good multiplies when focused upon. Negativity multiplies when focused upon. The choice is ours: Which do we want more of?"
—Julia Cameron

We all know people who are always experiencing the "poor me" syndrome. They will go on about how tired they are; how bad their lives are; and numerous other things. Even when we reply in a positive way they still come back with "but" and start on another tangent about how bad things are in their life.

We certainly go through times in our lives that are more difficult than others. Often when one thing goes wrong for us, another may soon follow, and sometimes they just continue for a while. But if we dwell on the negativity we'll get more of it.

I believe that we ought to be grateful in the midst of our losses. I had a series of things happen to me once. I lost a young pet to disease; then soon after that a friend passed away; a storm caused me to lose things that needed to be replaced at a time when money was already tight; and then I busted the storm door on my house by accident.

It seemed that everything was going against me. However, the storm did not hurt me or my home and pets. Even though I was unhappy at my job I did still have it in a time when many people were losing theirs due to a failing economy. I had good health even though I was watching friends die or suffer with cancer. There is always a positive within negative things that happen.

I choose to focus on the positive and turn away from the negative in life. I don't bury my head in the sand, but I do believe in the wonder of gratitude and I practice it.

We all have things that go wrong in life, whether they happen in close succession or with long spaces in between, they are tough to deal with. We can better handle all of what life throws at us if we look for what is good in life instead of living the "poor me" lifestyle.

Try to multiply good rather than burying yourself in how bad you think things are.

⌀

December 16
Repeating Mistakes
"Insanity is repeating the same mistakes and expecting different results." —Frank Herbert

It may be time for some of us to free ourselves from the spin cycle of our mistakes. Some people just don't seem to learn lessons even when they are presented over and over. We have no problem with some things, but when it comes to certain aspects of our lives we just don't learn.

Some people seem to repeat mistakes in relationships. They have affairs with people who are married and then wonder why the relationship didn't work, and then they do it again with someone else who is unavailable. Or they start another relationship within days of a heartbreak ending with someone without taking the time to heal and see their issues so that they don't repeat the mistakes made.

Life is tough enough without putting ourselves in situations that resemble hot stoves. We touch a hot stove and recoil and most likely it will be a long time, if ever, before we make that mistake again. But with some issues we just never do what we need to stop the pain.

We cannot expect to walk into a fire and not get burned. Repeating mistakes is the same thing as walking into a fire. If we've been there before we should not go back ... if we've ended a bad relationship or left a situation that was harmful to us, it's never going to work to go back.

These repeat mistakes cause harm to our self-esteem and may push us to continue taking wrong paths because we just don't care enough about ourselves to do any better. Before we go after that relationship we think we need, or that living situation that looks better than where we are, we need to remember that whatever thing we are going after is not as important as who we are and how we see ourselves.

Repeating mistakes digs into our self-image until all we can do is seek out things that we really know aren't healthy because we're coming out of a damaged psyche. Healing from one thing and learning from mistakes without having to repeat them are good ways to build our self-esteem which also better enables us to stay on a healthy path.

Repeating mistakes chisels away at self-image and causes you to keep doing the same thing.

∽

December 17
Sense of Self

"Part of having a strong sense of self is to be accountable for one's actions. No matter how much we explore motives or lack of motives, we are what we do." —Janet Geringer Woititz

Excuses and blame are often what we use to explain away our indiscretions. However, when we know who we are and choose our actions well we most often do the right thing and when we don't we are able to say so.

It's really not possible to live our lives making decisions and taking action out of a place of good judgment if we haven't first learned who we are, how we operate, and why we do things we do. When we have learned these things about ourselves, and only then, are we able to control our behaviors and stop the patterns of failures.

It sounds simpler than it is. Most of us who are recovering from various things need at least a little help. Often it takes many hours in therapy to learn these things about ourselves. When we know what makes us tick we can better control things that are ours to control and not try to control those things we can't.

In addition, we are able to set boundaries with others when we know what our boundaries are. We know when to say no and when to say yes. We know which behaviors from others we cannot tolerate and are able to say so when they occur. We are accountable for ourselves and we don't place blame on anyone or anything unless there really is a reason.

Getting to really know ourselves can be painful at times. There may be things that happened to us in our childhood that spun us into some negative behaviors as adults. But to continue to blame adult behaviors on childhood events is not how we learn better behavior. We can work through our issues and come out stronger on the other side.

None of us is perfect, and nobody reaches that status, but growth comes with work and life runs more smoothly.

Get to know what makes you tick and you'll find ways to do things differently that have been problems in your life.

December 18
True Friends

"A true friend never gets in your way unless you happen to be going down." —Robert Edwards

Often people will say that trust is the most important thing about friendship. We trust that when we divulge our deepest darkest secrets that the friend won't divulge it to the world. We hope that our friends will always be there for us when we're down, and that they can and will celebrate our victories too.

And if we truly want someone who we can trust and who is a true friend, we will hope that when we are about to make a big mistake they will let us know. Sometimes we aren't able to see what we are doing because of emotions. And maybe our friend has some wisdom because they have followed a similar path that led to destruction or have witnessed it at some point.

It may sting to be told the truth. And we may feel it's none of their business what we do, but in the long run we will be grateful for a friend who is honest enough to risk our friendship by telling us what we don't want to hear.

If someone tries to dissuade us from doing something healthy and good because they are jealous, we'll know the difference. It's a true friend who will let us know when we are on a path that is destructive. If we stop and think about the fact that by telling us what we don't want to hear they know that we may be angry and that they can lose our friendship, we will eventually see that it's done from a place of love and not anything else.

A true friend will be there in good and bad times. A true friend will only get in our way when they know they have to stop us if they can from making a huge mistake. A true friend will allow us time to be angry when we don't like what they told us. A true friend will risk our friendship when they feel it is necessary to keep us from falling.

If you have a friend who can be honest with you, keep that friend close.

❧

December 19
Difficult Times

"The pessimist sees difficulty in every opportunity. The optimist sees opportunity in every difficulty." —Winston Churchill

Times of difficulty may challenge our inner core. They may cause us to lose faith in God and everything else we believe in. When difficulties continue, when we can see no end in sight, it is very easy to fall into not only a pessimistic viewpoint of the world, but also we can find ourselves falling into depression.

Trying times can be dealt with even when it seems there is no solution. The first thing we can do is take things one at a time. We can take each moment and each day at a time and not put the whole world and all of our issues on our shoulders at once.

If we continue to seek something and we can't quite grasp it, perhaps a job or relationship, we may need to really think about things and see if we are causing our own failures.

If, for instance, we have been seeking employment for an extended period of time, but we cannot seem to get hired, even when we are qualified and get interviews, there is something going on that is in our control. Is it something we are not being truthful about on our resume that is picked up on in the interview? Or maybe we push too hard and say what we think the interviewer wants us to say, whether it's what we really believe?

If we continue to run into walls, in whatever we are attempting and failing at, we may need to seek advice from a trusted friend. We can keep spinning our wheels and insisting the problem lies outside of us, or we can look within and see if we are causing our own stumbling blocks in life.

Some difficulties are things that are not in our control. If the economy is bad there's little we can do about the cost of necessities, but we can control our spending on things that we just do not need.

When faced with hard times, it is important to reach out for help from those we trust. We don't have to face everything alone, and often others can see things that we just cannot see when we are in the midst of difficulty. Asking for help is not a sign of weakness. Whining about how bad things are is not asking for help.

When we seek help from someone it's important to be completely honest and not withhold certain information. If we truly want help we can't expect someone to be there if we cannot be honest.

Difficult times happen to everyone, it's your choice how you deal with it.

∽

December 20
Procrastination
"If you want to make an easy job seem mighty hard, just keep putting off doing it." —Olin Miller

Procrastination is one of the most difficult things to understand and stop because it often becomes a habit. Usually when we need to change a bad habit we have to replace it with a good habit.

We don't procrastinate about things we love to do, of course, so it is those things we don't want to do that we put off. The delay in doing is usually worse for us than the actual doing of the duty. And once we do that thing we dread, the thing we procrastinate over, we feel better. So why not just do it rather than put it off?

According to Harold Taylor, "procrastination is the intentional and habitual postponement of an important task that should be done now." If it's intentional we may have to do some soul searching to figure out why certain tasks always get pushed back on our agenda.

It seems that the easier life becomes with all of the gadgets and tools we have, the more readily we find places to occupy our time and things that help us procrastinate. Checking e-mail or surfing the Web can be a problem if we find ourselves spending hours at a time online when we intended to and needed to do something more urgent and necessary.

When we identify those things that we procrastinate over, we should begin to create a good habit by doing those things first. Once we get them out of the way the rest of our day is a breeze and we don't have to worry about and dread that task.

For some people making a to-do list helps get all tasks done rather than always leaving the dreaded ones undone. On the to-do list there might also need to be a reminder not to get distracted by whatever it is that pulls us away from our tasks. For some that is surfing the Internet, for others it's standing around the proverbial water cooler for a chat about the latest football game or upcoming election. We can start to set limits on ourselves for those activities which help us procrastinate and use that time to finish the project we avoid.

When you stop procrastinating you will actually have more time to have fun.

❦

December 21
Personal Wisdom

"It is easier to be wise for others than for ourselves."
—Francois De La Rochefoucauld

Having the answers and wisdom for others does not always correlate to having wisdom for our own lives.

I'm a proponent of asking for help when we need it. It's a sign of strength to be able to admit when we need help and to seek it from whatever source we find is best at the time. Therapists, friends, ministers, priests, sponsors, and family members may each hold that certain piece of wisdom that we need in any given moment to find our way.

But as much as I believe in asking for help, I also know that most of us have a lot of our own wisdom, we just choose not to follow it because something else takes precedence over it: urges, emotions, neediness, etc. We may seek short-term pleasure when we know that what we are about to do is not right for us, but we do it anyway.

It's often so easy to tell a loved one exactly what it best for them to do, and often very difficult to follow that same logic in our own lives. But usually once we reach a certain point in our lives we have plenty of knowledge and wisdom.

Every experience including every painful event, as well those things which brought us happiness, have taught us something and we have gleaned at least a bit of wisdom. Of course, some lessons are much more difficult to get than others so we have to be taught over a few times, but we do eventually get most things.

If we could rely on our personal wisdom and trust ourselves as much as we want to give advice and have others trust us, we would find our lives flowing a lot more smoothly. Sometimes we may need to stop what we are doing and view what we are about to do as if we were watching a friend. Then we can follow the advice we would give that friend. Most of the time we know what is the right thing.

Use your wisdom for yourself as often as you share it with others.

❦

December 22
Good Energy

"Our mental and emotional diets determine our overall energy levels, health and well-being more than we realize. Every thought and feeling, no matter how big or small, impacts our inner energy reserves." —Doc Childre

Who we spend time with, how we use our time, and what we think about are what affects a great portion of our lives. If we control others or let them control us we suffer. When we spend time with people who have negative outlooks or gossip constantly, we'll walk away from each encounter feeling down and icky.

We can spend time on positive things: reading uplifting books, helping others, meditating, praying, or exercising. In doing these things we will not only have more energy, but we'll feel better mentally and physically.

Stress and negativity bring us down and zap our energy. Just recall when you've spent time with someone whose life is full of drama, or someone who talks bad about everyone they can think of. How do you feel when you walk away from that? Then think about times when you've been around someone who is full of joy, or think of a time when you did volunteer work. You most likely walked away from those interactions with a smile on your face and a song in your heart.

We can choose who we spend time with in our free moments. And in those times when we are close to negativity because of work or some other obligation, we can choose how much of that to take on us and with us.

When given a choice to involve our time in negative or positive thoughts and energy, choosing the positive will go a long way in keeping us healthy mentally, physically, and emotionally.

Take the high road when given a choice and you will find life easier and lighter.

ॐ

December 23
Being True to Yourself

"You can be pleased with nothing when you are not pleased with yourself." —Mary Wortley Montagu

Being true to our self may be one of the most difficult things we do. There seems to be so many demands on us from family, work, volunteerism, church, and all of the many relationships we have.

With all of the things and people we have in our lives there are many and various pulls; things that one person may want that contrasts what someone else wants us to be or do, and most importantly demands that go against our core values.

Being true to self means that sometimes we have to say what others don't want to hear. It means we have to stop people pleasing. We cannot be true to our self and always give others what they want. Sometimes being true to our self means that we can no longer be in relationships that cause us too much strain against who we are and what we believe.

If we simply do something or stay in a relationship to please the other person it's doomed in the long run anyway. It will also erode our self-image if we continually go against what we need to do and give in to the demands of others.

Being true to our self is one way we get to know who we are. We clearly can't define who we are when we are constantly answering to others despite what we want to do and what is right. If others cannot understand our values and insist that we live theirs, we don't have to mold our self into who they want us to be.

If we look at ourselves honestly and find that we have some defects of character, we can overcome those. This is not to advocate being who we are when that's not a good thing. Instead it's about loving our self and doing the things we know to be right. It's also about having the ability to say no when that is needed. It is about following our own path and not that of someone else, or one that is chosen for us by some other person.

Follow what you know is right for you and own your mistakes as well as your successes.

෯

December 24
Rescue Yourself
"Stop waiting to be rescued. Rescue yourself."
—Bobbi Kahler

Waiting to be rescued can become a habit for many. Some people have no idea how to take care of self so they always know that there's a safety net to pick up the pieces (the bills, the depression, neediness, etc.).

There are those who believe that eventually the perfect person will come along and rescue them from the mess of a life they have woven. But the reality is there is not someone out there just waiting to rescue us.

These people tend to go from one relationship to another for fear of being alone. They are so desperate to be with another they latch on to someone, often before they finish with the one before. Carrying baggage from one relationship into another without taking time to heal is never a good idea.

Instead of dreaming of prince charming or princess compassion, we need to learn first to take care of ourselves. Thinking that having the perfect someone in our lives will suddenly make us live happily ever after is a pipe dream.

At times in our lives we must take risks, it is part of how we move forward and grow. However, we need to be there for ourselves if we fail. It's always okay to garner support from friends and family, but if we continue to do things that are not healthy we cannot expect people to be there forever to listen to us yet again.

Loved ones are not there to rescue us. They are there to love us and support us and to help us grow and learn. When we learn to live our lives in a healthy way, when we love ourselves enough, we won't get in positions requiring rescues.

Learn to love yourself and you will not need to be rescued.

December 25
Feeling Anger
"It's okay for me to be angry today. It's growful, if I use it for good." —Unknown

Feeling anger, just like every other emotion, is how we move through and past it. We can no more push anger down and hide it and then expect to be okay than we can just snap out of depression.

Anger can be a catalyst for change. When we feel anger it is a signal that things are not as they need to be for us. Sometimes we can do something about the cause of our anger, and at other times we can simply walk away from the cause of it.

When we do nothing about our anger it can be turned inward and thus affect our lives in a negative way. It affects our behaviors and carries from the thing that caused us anger to the person or situation that did not cause it. How we deal with anger is important.

When we are angry with another person the best thing we can do is be direct and tell them why we are angry. What we don't want to do is curse at them or call them names. Most people will allow us to be angry, but they will not listen to us when we treat them with disrespect.

If someone does us wrong, the conflict will be resolved much easier the sooner we deal with it. Usually if we let things build up it will make us angrier and when we are direct about our anger sooner things are easier to resolve.

When we encounter anger and it's an issue that we have no resolution for, we must find an outlet for that anger through exercise or some way that doesn't hurt others. There is not always resolution for conflict, especially if the other person has power over us at work or in some other situation.

Taking care of ourselves includes feeling and releasing our anger. It's okay to be angry, it's just wise to use it in a way that helps us and not hurts us.

Anger may not be the most wonderful feeling, but it needs to be felt and dealt with for healthy well-being.

⌒

December 26
Enabling Others

"A person who is acting out self destructively has no reason to change if they do not ever suffer major consequences for their behavior. If they are rescued from consequences, they are enabled to continue practicing their addiction."

—Robert Burney

Enabling is often referred to as behaviors that rescue and allow alcoholics and addicts to continue their behavior without suffering the consequences. But beyond that it also relates to rescuing those who are involved in other self-destructive behaviors such as: gambling, eating disorders, the inability to keep a job, relationship addictions or having affairs, and anything else that is destructive to a person.

I've had experience as a full-fledged enabler of an alcoholic having lived with one for several years. It seemed at the time the best route was to let this person drink and just pick up the pieces as they fell. I took care of things to avoid problems and even called every day to ensure they would not be late for work. But with time my self-esteem was crushed and I suffered from depression and had to leave. Enabling did not save the relationship. It just delayed the loss of the relationship a few years.

We really don't do anybody any favors when we enable an addiction or any unhealthy behavior. If we allow a bigot or male chauvinist to constantly trash talk whoever they have issues against, we are enabling. Someone who is a bigot is probably not going to change just because we tell them not to say things around us, but at least our side of the street is clean on the issue.

We are not in charge of other people's lives. It is not always our place to voice our concerns over another's behavior. However, it is our issue when we are in the presence of someone, or in a relationship with someone, who is carrying out actions for which we don't approve. To say nothing is enabling. Whether or not they heed our warning is their issue, but it's also in our best interest to walk away if the behavior does not change. We ought to not hang around for the rescue when their world comes crashing down. If we do then we are just as much a part of the wrongdoing as they are.

Enabling hurts you when you do it, as well as the one you think you are helping.

∽

December 27
Getting Off the Roller-Coaster Ride

"Happiness is not a matter of intensity but of balance, order, rhythm and harmony." —Thomas Merton

Most of us say we want to have peace in our lives. We want peace and joy, but we don't act like it. Instead we live our lives as if we are on a roller-coaster vacillating between the highs and lows and feeling as if something is wrong when we do find that we are in a place of peace.

When we are in the midst of feeling a lot of joy we know that it won't last forever so when change comes, and it always does, we don't need to be distraught and get depressed. Just like when we are down and out about something we must remember that this too shall pass and something will come along to bring us joy.

When we get off the roller-coaster ride that many of us have spent a great portion of our lives on, we may not find peace to be a place of comfort. We may think something is wrong with us because we just don't feel too much of anything. However, not to worry, because more than likely if we're active and living a full life but not having all the highs and lows that we have grown accustomed to we probably have found peace.

When life if full of intensity and stress it's usually full of anger and pain. Living a life on the edge may be fun at times, the highs are great, but the lows are not so much fun. A more level-headed lifestyle can bring just as much happiness without falling into the depths of despair when we fall off the high.

Balance, peace, and harmony may not feel very exciting, but they are the best places to be.

∽

December 28
No Excuses

"There's right and there's wrong. You got to do one or the other.
You do the one, and you're living. You do the other, and you may be
walking around but you're dead as a beaver hat."
—Marion "John" Wayne

We have many opportunities in life to do the right thing or to do
what we know is wrong. When we choose to do something that we
know we should not do there are usually ways we can justify our
actions.

Excuses and blame are easy to think of such as: I didn't mean to; it
just happened; it was her fault; I was just living in the moment; it was
the alcohol; I didn't plan it this way; and so on. And while there are
times that we do things that we know we shouldn't there is always the
opportunity to stop moving forward with our mistake.

Just because we don't see consequences of bad behavior today, it
doesn't mean there won't be any or that when there are consequences
we will know about them. Any time we are involved in behavior that
could harm another person we need to step back and stop what we are
doing.

Life offers us many temptations. We may feel justified in doing
wrong because we are lonely, depressed, poor, or otherwise
downtrodden. But doing wrong has no real excuses, at least not the
kinds that absolve us of guilt.

Walking down the path of wrong will never bring us long-term
fulfillment or happiness. It probably will cause us harm and hurt others
too. It is our decision to do right or wrong, but excuses to justify do
little if anything to right a wrong.

You can decide at any moment to stop a wrongdoing in process.

December 29
Being Alive

"Every day you're alive is a special occasion."
—Unknown

It certainly does not feel like every day we live is special. We have
problems and sickness, bills and heartache. And sometimes it seems as
if there's just no hope.

But when we have the occasion to watch someone fight for life, to face illness with the hope of beating it, that person who fights to the very last moment, we can at least get a glimpse of how important each day is. It was my privilege to watch someone do just that — fight to the very last moment — the will to live so strong. A person who was so full of life and suffered from pain and the agony of cancer treatments, but still found joy in the days she had left and lived just two days past her 57th birthday.

I think it's especially difficult during the holiday season to feel like every day is special. There are those who live for the holidays from Thanksgiving until the New Year's Eve celebrations and the football games on New Year's Day. And others who would just as soon the month of December be just like every other month of the year because not everybody enjoys the constant social gatherings. And there are those too who are left out and feel isolated and depressed because they don't have a party to go to every night.

Those of us who struggle with the holidays can juxtapose our feelings with those who love the holidays. Perhaps their enthusiasm will rub off on us a bit. We can also compare how we feel about life in general to someone who is fighting for their life. We can perhaps glean a little insight into what drives them. Maybe there we can find more hope and joy in our own lives.

Being alive is a gift. It is one we can cherish or despise. Our life is ours to do with what we will despite the bad things that may come our way. Watching someone fight for life can renew our spirits to live fully each day.

Watch someone who is happy to be alive; it can help you find happiness.

∽

December 30
Magnify Blessings
"What a different world this would be if people would magnify their blessings the way they do their troubles."
—Unknown

If we could only trumpet our blessings the same way we whine and moan about what's wrong in our lives what a difference it could make in the world.

Often blessings come in ways that we do not think about. A perfectly timed call from a friend; praise for something we've done; an unexpected chance to spend time with someone we love; avoiding a wreck as we rush around from one place to another in our vehicles.

We are blessings to the world when we buy gifts or provide for the needs of the underprivileged; when we forego a meal out or some other luxury to help another; at those times when we say "I love you" just because we do, even though sometimes it's hard to say; and when we forgive the person who seems the most unforgivable.

Life offers us many ways to give and receive. Both are important and necessary for our well-being.

Sometimes people think that they have to be the best at something to be a blessing; that they have to do a great thing. But many times blessings come in imperfect packages.

During a memorial service for a woman who played the guitar and wrote songs, a 12-year-old boy whom she had inspired and taught a few guitar tricks to, got up in front of the whole church and played one of her songs while he also sang the lyrics. No, it was not perfectly done, in all honesty it wasn't really all that great, but all who knew her were blessed that her song had been performed.

For those who knew what it took for this boy to do what he did, there was even a bigger blessing; a lesson in putting others first even if we have fear or heavy grief. He showed a love that many of us aspire to, but never reach because we are too busy trying to one up the other guy by doing something bigger and better when all we really have to do is that thing we are led to do without fanfare.

Blessings surround you and they are within you. You must be open to receive and give them or you miss out.

⮜

December 31
Goals for the New Year
"Be always at war with your vices, at peace with your neighbors, and let each new year find you a better man."
—Benjamin Franklin

The end of the year is often a time of reflection for many of us. We may look back on the previous twelve months with regret over having not achieved the goals we set at this time last year.

If we tried our best to do what we set out to do at the end of the year, but somehow fell short, we don't need to berate ourselves; we simply need to continue our efforts since giving up surely won't get us anywhere.

Whether we call them New Year's resolutions or goals, the things we set out to do in the coming year are important to us and worthy of every effort we can put forth. It helps to write down what we hope to achieve since somewhere along the way we often forget what it was we set out to do, and because there's something almost magical about writing things down that helps the process of achievement.

One goal we can set that will help with everything in our lives is to operate out of love at all times. It's much more difficult than it seems. When we operate out of love it means we don't gossip, or judge, or treat people unkindly, even if sometimes people probably deserve to be treated that way. It also means we are completely honest with others. We don't enable bad behavior or coddle adults who may need tough love. It also requires us to love our self.

If we set that one goal — to do everything from a place of love — and hold true to it as much as possible, our lives will transform. Often we do things from a sense of fear. Love and fear are opposites and fear can lead us to poor decisions and actions. Love can never lead us wrong. Love, not lust or control, but real love will always guide us to right action.

Just remember that whatever bad habit we wish to do away with and all of our goals for the coming year can be achieved if we truly want them to happen. If we have tried before and didn't succeed, then some would say we just didn't try hard enough.

Make it your goal to live the next year from a place of love and see your life change for the better.

Topic Index

Abandonment
Nov. 5, Nov. 8

Acceptance
Jan. 21, Mar. 25, Apr. 13, May 15, June 17, July 13, July 22, Aug. 4, Oct. 9, Nov. 24, Dec. 13

Action
Sept. 28, Sept. 30, Oct. 2, Oct. 3, Oct. 7, Oct. 8, Oct. 15, Oct. 23, Oct. 25, Nov. 2, Nov. 6, Nov. 7, Nov. 11, Nov. 13, Nov. 19, Nov. 24, Nov. 27, Dec. 31

Addictions
Mar. 29, May 20, Oct. 1, Nov. 18, Nov. 26

Amends
Nov. 12

Anger
May 7, May 18, May 26, June 11, July 5, July 18, Aug. 25, Sept. 6, Nov. 23, Dec. 5, Dec. 25

Answers
Feb. 29, Sept. 2, Sept. 8, Sept. 12, Sept. 16, Sept. 20, Oct. 5

Anxiety
June 3, June 23, June 30, July 15, July 23, July 31, Aug. 6, Aug. 26, Dec. 8, Dec. 12

Asking for Help
Sept. 19, Dec. 19, Dec. 21

Attitude
Aug. 12, Sept. 15, Sept 18 Sept. 30, Oct. 12, Oct. 17, Oct. 25, Oct. 26, Dec. 3, Dec. 15

Balance
Feb. 4, Mar. 10, Mar. 14, Mar. 15, Mar. 17, Mar. 19, Apr. 2, Apr. 25, Apr. 28, May 9, May 10, May 24, May 29, June 15, June 29, July 7, July 28, July 31, Aug. 13, Aug. 18, Aug. 20, Oct. 24, Dec. 27

Beginnings
Mar. 3, Mar. 27, Mar. 31, May 3, May 21, May 31, June 8, June 24, July 30, Aug. 1

Blame
Jan. 27, Apr. 12, June 7, Sept. 30, Oct. 17, Dec. 17, Dec. 28

Blessings
Dec. 30

Boundaries

July 3, Sept. 26, Oct. 25, Oct. 30, Nov. 10, Nov. 21, Dec. 17

Breaking Down Walls
Jan. 22, May 2, July 18, July 25, Aug. 27, Nov. 11

Challenges
Mar. 6, Mar. 7, Mar. 8, Mar. 18, Mar. 20, Mar. 23, Mar. 27, Mar. 28, Apr. 1, Apr. 4, Apr. 8, Apr. 11, Apr. 12, Apr. 14, Apr. 18, May 3, May 4, May 21, May 30, June 3, June 5, June 13, Jun 17, June 23, June 24, July 14, July 23, July 30, Aug. 5, Aug. 8, Aug. 22, Sept. 5, Oct. 10, Nov. 6, Nov. 15, Nov. 27, Dec. 19

Change
Feb. 27, Jan. 13, Jan. 14, Jan. 31, Feb. 12, Mar. 2, Mar. 3, Mar. 8, Mar. 9, Mar. 16, Mar. 17, Mar. 31, Apr. 16, May 27, May 30, June 7, June 8, Aug. 20, Sept. 25, Oct. 8, Dec. 8, Dec. 12

Character Defects
Apr. 2, May 2, June 22, July 28, Aug. 24, Nov. 25

Choices
June 5, June 7, June 8, June 12, June 24, July 4, July 8, Aug. 3, Aug. 12, Aug. 17, Aug. 19, Aug. 22, Sept. 15, Sept. 21, Oct. 6, Nov. 7, Nov. 11, Nov. 23, Dec. 10, Dec. 28

Commitment
Feb. 23, Feb. 26, May 10, May 11, July 7, Aug. 31

CommunicationApr. 21, May 8, May 20, May 31, June 1, June 2, July 1, Aug. 31, Sept. 8, Sept. 13, Oct. 19, Nov. 28

Compromise
July 7, Aug. 16, Nov. 20

Consequences
Dec. 26, Dec. 28

Courage
Apr. 8, Apr. 11, May 4, May 21, May 30, June 3, June 18, July 23, Aug. 4

Denial
Aug. 4, Dec. 13

Detaching
Jan. 14, Jan. 20, Feb. 7, Feb. 13, Apr. 23, May 15, May 18, July 6, July 27, Sept. 27

Direction
Sept. 14

Directness
Feb. 3, Feb. 5, Apr. 20, Apr. 21, May 14, July 1, Aug. 31, Nov. 21

Discontent
Sept. 1, Sept. 17, Oct. 5

Dishonesty

Jan. 30, June 1, June 22, July 29, Sept. 3, Sept. 4, Nov. 9, Nov. 30

Doing Right
Aug. 19, Sept. 18, Oct. 2, Oct. 15, Nov. 21, Dec. 1, Dec. 21, Dec. 23, Dec. 28

Dreams
Apr. 8, May 5, Aug. 1

Emotions
Sept. 15, Dec. 22, Dec. 27

Enabling
Dec. 26

Energy
Dec. 2, Dec. 22

Exercise
Mar. 11, June 28

Expectations
Jan. 4, Feb. 23, Mar. 28, Apr. 1, Apr. 10, June 23, June 26, Aug. 25, Oct. 23, Dec. 1

Failure
Aug. 30, Oct. 7, Nov. 27, Dec. 19

Faith
June 13, Aug. 6, Aug. 21, Sept. 7, Sept. 11, Sept. 12, Sept. 20, Sept. 28

Fear
Jan. 8, Mar. 7, Mar. 9, Mar. 18, Mar. 27, Apr. 8, May 30, June 13, June 18, June 23, June 30, Aug. 23, Sept. 11, Sept. 25, Sept. 29, Nov. 6, Nov. 15

Feelings
Jan. 1, Jan. 6, Jan. 9, Jan. 12, Jan. 15, Jan. 20, Feb. 7, Feb. 18, Feb. 22, Feb. 27, May 18, May 20, June 11, June 20, June 25, July 1, July 5, July 13, July 16, Aug. 2, Aug. 20, Aug. 23, Sept. 5, Oct. 4, Dec. 25

Finishing
Dec. 14

Focus
Aug. 14

Forgiveness
Feb. 6, Feb. 21, May 7, May 26, June 27, July 13, July 19, Oct. 11, Nov. 12, Nov. 23

Freedom
Jan. 9, Feb. 1, Mar. 9, Mar. 29, June 18, July 23, Nov. 18

Fun
Aug. 18, Nov. 14

Getting Needs Met
Aug. 27, Sept. 1, Sept. 7, Oct. 16, Oct. 23

Gifts
Jan. 29, Mar. 6, Apr. 10, May 21, July 20, Oct. 17
Giving Back
Jan. 12, Jan. 23, March 1, Mar. 18, Mar. 28, Apr. 5, Apr. 7, May 19,
May 25, June 9, July 20, July 26, Aug. 3, Aug. 11, Aug. 15, Aug. 28,
Sept. 9, Oct. 23, Dec. 30
Goals
Jan. 26, Mar. 3, Apr. 8, May 5, May 23, Aug. 14, Aug. 22, Aug. 29,
Aug. 30, Dec. 31
Gossip
Oct. 22, Dec. 22
Gratitude
Jan. 28, Apr. 9, May 25, Aug. 15, Aug. 28, Oct. 18
Grief
Jan. 20, July 13, July 16, Dec. 6
Growth
Jan. 1, Jan. 3, Jan. 6, Jan. 10, Jan. 11, Jan. 13, Jan. 16, Feb. 8, Feb. 11,
Feb. 14, Feb. 20, Feb. 21, Feb. 27, Mar. 2, Mar. 3, Mar. 9, Mar. 16,
Mar. 21, Mar. 26, Mar. 31, Apr. 4, Apr. 11, Apr. 16, May 6, May 27,
May 30, June 5, June 24, July 12, July 18, July 30, Aug. 1, Aug. 10,
Aug. 23, Oct. 8, Oct. 10, Oct. 20, Oct. 28, Nov. 21, Nov. 29, Dec. 10
Guilt
Apr. 3
Habits
June 28, July 31, Oct. 13, Nov. 26, Dec. 20
Handicaps
Aug. 5, Oct. 10, Oct. 17
Happiness
Oct. 3, Nov. 29, Dec. 29
Healing
Jan. 2, Jan. 27, Feb. 22, Mar. 4, Mar. 5, Mar. 13, Mar. 25, Apr. 10,
May 7, May 16, May 20, July 13, July 16, July 30, Sept. 10, Dec. 7,
Dec. 13
Hitting Bottom
Oct. 1
Honesty
Jan. 9, Jan. 15, Jan. 30, Feb. 3, Feb. 5, Feb. 17, Apr. 6, May 14, May
20, May 22, June 1, June 20, June 22, July 1, July 9, July 29, Sept. 3,
Sept. 4, Nov. 21, Nov. 30
Hope
Apr. 26, June 10, July 8, Aug. 21, Sept. 22, Oct. 26, Dec. 29
Humanness

Negativity
Feb. 28, May 22, July 8, July 26, Oct. 22, Nov. 4, Dec. 15, Dec. 22
Optimism
Oct. 12, Dec. 3, Dec. 15
Pain
Jan. 2, Jan. 6, Jan. 20, Feb. 5, Feb. 22, Feb. 24, Mar. 13, June 5, June 17, June 25, July 12, July 13, July 16, July 18, Sept. 5, Sept. 15, Nov. 25, Dec. 7
Patience
Jan. 2, Jan. 7, Feb. 25, Mar. 19, Mar. 20, Mar. 24, Apr. 1, Apr. 11, Sept. 17, Oct. 29, Nov. 2, Nov. 10
Peace
Feb. 29, Mar. 30, Apr. 27, June 11, June 12, Sept. 2, Sept. 17, Sept. 20, Sept. 23, Oct. 27, Dec. 12, Dec. 27
Perspective
Feb. 10, Feb. 17, Mar. 10, Mar. 22, Mar. 23, Apr. 14, Apr. 28, May 22, June 6, Sept. 13, Oct. 7, Oct. 14, Nov. 22, Nov. 28, Dec. 1, Dec. 9
Perfection
Feb. 2, Feb. 23, Mar. 25, Apr. 6, Apr. 13, May 12, June 26
Persistence
Feb. 26, Apr. 16, Apr. 18, May 23, Aug. 26, Oct. 8, Oct. 21, Nov. 19
Pessimism
Oct. 12, Oct. 26
Powerlessness
July 22, Nov. 24
Prayer
Apr. 7, Sept. 8, Sept. 12, Sept. 16, Sept. 20
Priorities
May 29, Aug. 13, Oct. 24, Nov. 20, Dec. 3
Procrastination
July 31, Dec. 20
Punishment
Nov. 25
Purpose
Sept. 14
Reactions
Apr. 24, May 8, May 26, Aug. 17, Sept. 15
Recovery Tools
Jan. 4, Jan. 8, Jan. 18, Feb. 6, Feb. 16, Mar. 14, Mar. 16, Mar. 26, Mar. 29, Apr. 9, Apr. 23, Apr. 27, Apr. 30, May 26, May 27, June 15, Oct. 13, Oct. 15, Nov. 18, Dec. 17
Rejection

July 6, Oct. 31
Relationships
Feb. 5, Feb. 19, March 1, Mar. 19, Mar. 21, Apr. 6, Apr. 15, Apr. 23, Apr. 25, May 2, May 13, May 15, May 18, May 31, June 1, June 2, June 4, June 16, June 25, July 2, July 3, July 7, July 9, July 19, July 22, July 27, Aug. 2, Aug. 10, Aug. 11, Aug. 25, Aug. 31, Sept. 10, Sept. 13, Sept. 27, Sept. 30, Oct. 5, Oct. 9, Nov. 8, Nov. 20, Nov. 21, Nov. 25, Dec. 5, Dec. 16, Dec. 18
Resentment
Feb. 6, Feb. 28, May 7, June 11, July 8,
Routines
Oct. 13
Ruts
Sept. 25, Nov. 11
Secrets
Jan. 9
Self-Discipline
Jan. 16, Jan. 17, Jan. 19, Feb. 1, Feb. 10, Feb. 15, Feb. 18, Feb. 23, Mar. 3, Mar. 14, Apr. 2, Apr. 28, May 11, June 28, Nov. 26
Self-Esteem
Jan. 1, Jan. 3, Jan. 13, Jan. 16, Feb. 8, Feb. 9, Feb. 14, Feb. 20, Mar. 10, Mar. 22, Apr. 2, Apr. 3, May 4, May 17, May 22, June 2, June 5, June 27, July 21, Oct. 20, Dec. 14, Dec. 16
Self-honesty
July 29, Sept. 21, Oct. 4
Self-image
Aug. 7, Sept. 3, Sept. 24, Oct. 20, Nov. 22, Dec. 1, Dec. 16, Dec. 17
Self-love
Apr. 13, Apr. 22, Apr. 29, May 13, May 19, June 27, July 2, July 17, July 29, July 30, Aug. 6, Aug. 24, Sept. 3, Oct. 16, Dec. 23, Dec. 24
Self-observation
July 28, Aug. 17
Self-respect
Aug. 19, Sept. 18, Sept. 21, Oct. 30
Sensitivity
Jan. 29
Serenity
Jan. 21, Mar. 24, Apr. 22, Apr. 27, Apr. 28, May 15, June 12, June 21, Dec. 12
Shame
Apr. 3
Spirituality

Mar. 12, Apr. 10, Apr. 17, Aug. 21, Oct. 2
Starting
Dec. 14
Strength
Jan. 8, Jan. 31, Feb. 1, Feb. 22, Apr. 11, Oct. 28
Struggles
Mar. 20, Mar. 23, Apr. 13, Apr. 15, June 16, June 17, June 19, June 27, July 12, July 23, Aug. 8, Dec. 8
Success
June 9, Aug. 1, Aug. 30, Oct. 1, Oct. 7, Nov. 1, Nov. 27, Dec. 19
Taking Care of Self
Jan. 4, Jan. 5, Jan. 10, Jan. 11, Jan. 15, Jan. 22, Jan. 31, Feb. 1, Feb. 2, Feb. 4, Feb. 19, Feb. 29, Mar. 8, Mar. 14, Mar. 17, Mar. 29, Apr. 12, Apr. 25, May 1, May 9, May 18, May 24, May 26, June 15, June 16, June 21, June 28, July 3, July 9, July 10, July 11, July 16, July 27, July 28, Aug. 9, Aug. 13, Aug. 18, Sept. 18, Sept. 19, Sept. 23, Sept. 27, Oct. 6, Oct. 9, Oct. 11, Oct. 24, Oct. 28, Nov. 7, Nov. 10, Nov. 16, Nov. 20, Nov. 29, Dec. 2, Dec. 7, Dec. 8, Dec. 17, Dec. 23, Dec. 24
Timing
Mar. 2, Apr. 1, Apr. 10, May 6, May 16, Sept. 7, Nov. 2
Trust
Jan. 24, Jan. 25, Feb. 24, Mar. 4, Sept. 4, Sept. 26, Nov. 9
Vulnerability
June 20, July 25, Aug. 9
Waiting
June 16, July 9, Sept. 7, Sept. 17, Oct. 29, Nov. 2
Wanting
June 16, Aug. 14, Aug. 28, Sept. 7, Sept. 17
Wisdom
Jan. 6, Jan. 19, Jan. 25, Feb. 25, June 5, Sept. 20, Oct. 14, Dec. 18, Dec. 21
Worry
May 28, June 23, July 15, Sept. 29